TEACHING TIPS

TEACHING TIPS

EIGHTH EDITION

A *Guidebook for the Beginning College Teacher*

WILBERT J. McKEACHIE
University of Michigan

D.C. HEATH AND COMPANY
Lexington, Massachusetts / Toronto

Acquisition Editor: James Miller

Production Editor: Rosemary Rodensky

Designer: Laura Fredericks

Published simultaneously in Canada.

Printed in the United States of America.

International Standard Book Number: 0-669-06752-0

Library of Congress Catalog Card Number: 85-60982

3 4 5 6 7 8 9 0

To my earliest teachers in the classroom and out,
my parents,
Bert and Edith McKeachie

Preface

Teaching Tips was written to answer the questions posed by new college teachers, to place them at ease in their jobs, and to get them started effectively in the classroom.

This edition follows the general plan of earlier editions. Because the book is oriented toward the beginning teacher who faces a number of immediate practical problems, chapters begin with "tips," but these are usually followed by a discussion of research and theory. This edition represents the greatest amount of revision of any I have done. The entire book has been reorganized. The organization moves from those issues and techniques most relevant to beginning teachers to methods and issues likely to be of more concern after one has gotten beyond the difficult immediate problems of the beginning teacher.

In addition to updating the research findings relevant to teaching, I have added substantially to the theory underlying the tips, drawing extensively from the rapidly developing fields of cognitive and instructional psychology. This is most evident in Chapter 7, Lecturing, and in Chapter 13, Reading, but pops up as well in other chapters.

I am pleased that so many copies of previous editions of this guide have been used outside the United States. My increasing interactions with colleagues in other countries who are concerned about improving teaching make me aware of the cultural bias of much of what I say. I trust that *Teaching Tips* will nevertheless have value for everyone concerned about student learning.

The first edition of this book was prepared in collaboration with Gregory Kimble. His wit and wisdom are still evident at many points in this eighth edition. Thanks are also due to Edward Bordin, who revised his section on counseling for this edition and to Claude Mathis and James Stice who reviewed the manuscript. Maria Huntley's word processing and Ginny McKeachie's reference checking earned my gratitude in great measure.

WILBERT J. McKEACHIE

Table of Contents

PART I
Getting Started

CHAPTER 1 / *Introduction*

The first few months and years of teaching are all-important. Experiences during this period can blight a promising teaching career or can start one on a path of continued growth and development.

Most of us go into our first classes as teachers with a good deal of fear and trembling. We don't want to appear to be fools; so we have prepared well, but we dread the embarrassment of not being able to answer students' questions. We want to be liked and respected by our students; yet we know that we have to achieve liking and respect in a new role which carries expectations, such as evaluation, that make our relationship with students edgy and uneasy. We want to get through the first class with éclat, but we don't know how much material we can cover in a class period.

In most cases anxiety passes as one finds that students do respond positively, that one does have some expertise in the subject, and that class periods can be exciting. But for some teachers the first days are not happy experiences. Classes get off on the wrong foot. Sullen hostility sets in. The teacher asserts authority and the students resist. The teacher knows that things are not going well but doesn't know what to do about it.

One likely response of the teacher is retreat—retreat to reading lectures with as little eye contact with students as possible—retreat to threats of low grades as a motivating device—retreat to research and other aspects of the professorial role.

What makes the difference in these first few days?

The new teacher who has techniques for breaking the ice, for encouraging class participation, and for getting the course organized is more likely to get off to a good start. Once one finds that teaching can be fun, one enjoys devoting time to it, and if one devotes that time, one will develop into a competent teacher. Anyone bright enough to complete a graduate degree is bright enough to learn the skills and concepts needed for effective teaching.

What can I do to help you get off to a good start? Simply pass on ideas that have been helpful to me. Some of them won't fit your course or your style, but some may stimulate you to develop your own adaptations.

This is not a textbook in the Educational Psychology of College Teaching. It is merely a compilation of useful (occasionally mechanical) tricks of the trade which I, as a teacher, have found helpful in running classes. What is contained in this discussion will not make you a Great Teacher. It may be that Great Teachers are born and not made, but anyone with ability enough to get a job as a college teacher can be a *good* teacher.

The techniques of teaching that one uses will undoubtedly reflect one's philosophy of teaching. Thus, it might be a good idea for me to state my views here and now. These are some of the considerations that have guided me in making the recommendations in this book:*

1. Education should be guided by a democratic philosophy. This has nothing to do with political-social doctrine, but is simply a statement of my belief that education is a cooperative enterprise that works best when the student is allowed to contribute to it—when teachers listen and respond.

2. Students are adults. I feel strongly on this point. One of the severest criticisms that can be leveled against American higher education is that it perpetuates adolescence for another four years. It seems clear that adult behavior is *learned*. If no opportunity to practice adult behavior is allowed, such behavior will not be learned.

3. Instructors can occasionally be wrong. If they are wrong too often, they should not be teaching. If they are never wrong, they belong in heaven, not a college classroom.

4. There are many important goals of college and university teaching. Not the least of these is that of increasing the student's motivation and ability to *continue* learning after leaving college.

5. Most student learning occurs outside the classroom. This is a both humbling and reassuring thought for the beginning teacher. It

---

* These are based on a list originally developed by Gregory Kimble, who collaborated with me on the first edition of this book.

means that the students' education will neither succeed nor fail simply because of what you do or don't do in the classroom. At the same time it reminds one to direct attention to stimulating and guiding student learning outside class even more than to preparing to give a dazzling classroom performance.

The College or University Culture

A course cannot be divorced from the total college or university culture.

First of all, the university makes certain requirements of instructors. In most colleges you must submit grades for the students' work. You probably must give a final course examination. A classroom is assigned for the class, and the class meets in this assigned place. Smoking in the classroom is ordinarily prohibited. The class meets at certain regularly scheduled periods. It is not implied that these regulations are harmful, but they do provide boundaries within which instructors have to work.

There are, in addition, areas not covered by the formal rules of the college in which instructors must tread lightly. For example, there may be certain limitations upon the instructor's social relationships with the students. In many college cultures unmarried instructors who become intimately involved with their students are overstepping the bounds of propriety. In some colleges it would be deemed improper for instructors to convene classes in bars or off campus. Certain limits upon class discussion of religion, sex, or politics may exist. Instructors must learn not only to operate within the fences of college regulations, but also to skirt the pitfalls of the college mores.

But instructors who consider only college mores in plans for their courses are ignoring a far more important limitation upon teaching, for the college or university culture has not only placed limitations upon instructors, but has also pretty much hobbled the students. Most important are the students' needs for success. To stay in college they must show evidence of achievement. With admission to law, medical, and other graduate and professional schools difficult, they must present evidence of outstanding achievement in college courses to gain admission to these schools.

Average college students have already been rewarded year after year for superior achievement in elementary and high school classrooms. In many colleges they have had experience in their previous classes with instructors who, in a more or less fatherly way, gave information and rewarded those students who could best give it back. Not only has the role of the teacher been similar in these classes, but teaching procedures were probably much the same. Depending upon the college or university, the method used may have been lecture, question and answer, discussion, or something else. The sort of tests, frequency of tests, and methods of grading also have conformed closely to certain college norms. As a result instructors who attempt to revolutionize teaching with new methods or techniques may find that they are only frustrating the needs and expectations their students have developed in the culture of this college. Therefore, each reader will need to adapt my suggestions to the college culture of which he or she is a part.

Research vs. Teaching?

One aspect of the local culture critical for new teachers is the definition of the proper role of a faculty member. In many universities, for example, formal definitions of the criteria for promotion give research and teaching equal weight, but it is not uncommon to find that research is "more equal." This may come about not because of any attempt to hide the truth but because many faculty members serving on promotions committees honestly believe that you cannot be an effective teacher unless you are doing research.

While research on the relationship of research to teaching is difficult to conduct, there is evidence that research and teaching are not necessarily in conflict. Many faculty members are excellent researchers and excellent teachers as well. Some excellent researchers are poor teachers; some excellent teachers do not publish research. The point here is not that you should choose one emphasis at the expense of the other. Rather, find out what the local norms are, and if you feel a conflict, choose the balance that suits your own talents and interests with an informed awareness of the likelihood of support for that self-definition. While time is not infinitely elastic, most faculty members find that a 50 to 60 hour work week is enjoyable because they enjoy both teaching and research. There is never enough time to do everything one would like to do in either teaching or research, but most faculty members find that each provides a useful break from the other. A combination is often more satisfying than single-minded, undeviating focus on either.

Whatever your choice, it is likely that teaching will be a part of your role. Teaching skillfully may be less time consuming than teaching badly.

Teaching well is more fun than teaching poorly. Thus, some investment of time and attention to developing skill in teaching is likely to have substantial pay-off in self-satisfaction and effectiveness in your career.

Research in Teaching

Some of you will disagree with me, at least at certain points. This is your perfect right since my ideas are only partly based on objective evidence. But I believe that my ideas as well as your ideas should be experimentally tested. I hope that this book will not be accepted as infallible, but as the background for research that will give us a better foundation for our teaching practice.

What I have tried to set down here is a set of hints that have seemed to me to be useful. I hope that you can use some of them too and that they add to the enjoyment and learning of your students. If they contribute to your joy in teaching, my purpose will have been fulfilled.

CHAPTER 2

Countdown for Course Preparation

For teachers, courses do not start on the first day of classes. Rather, a course begins well before they meet their students.

*Time: Three Months Before the First Class**

Write Objectives

The first step in preparing for a course is the working out of course objectives, because the choice of text, the selection of the type and order of assignments, the choice of teaching techniques, and all the decisions involved in course planning should derive from your objectives. At this point your list of goals or objectives should be taken only as a rough reminder to be revised as you develop other aspects of the course plan, and to be further revised in interaction with students.

Some of you have heard of behavioral objectives and may wish to phrase your objectives in behavioral terms. If so, do so. But don't omit important objectives simply because you can't think of good ways to convert them to behavioral language. The purpose of phrasing objectives behaviorally is to encourage you to be specific, but usually the behavior specified in a behavioral objective is an indicator of a more general objective you want to achieve. Don't get trapped into thinking that the behavior you list is all you should aim for—and don't become so obsessed with writing objectives that you neglect other parts of planning. The purpose of working out objectives is to facilitate planning, not inhibit it. The clearer you can become about what you're trying to do, the better. Behavioral objectives may help, but there is no evidence that they are better for student learning than other statements of objectives—in

---

* The idea of three months, two months, and so on, I have borrowed from P. G. Zimbardo and J. W. Newton, *Instructor's resource book to accompany Psychology and life* (Glenview, IL: Scott, Foresman, 1975).

8

fact, there is little evidence that teachers who develop behavioral objectives are more effective than those who don't develop *any* list of objectives.* Nonetheless behavioral objectives have the great advantage of pointing clearly to what you can look for as evidence that the objective has been achieved. Your students see your methods of assessing or testing achievement of the objectives as the most important operational definition of your goals; hence goals and testing are inseparable teaching tasks.

It seems logical that course planning should start with thinking about goals or objectives. So begin by thinking about your objectives. What should they be? The answer obviously depends upon the course and discipline, but it is important to note that the objectives involve educating students; the objective of a course is not to cover a certain set of topics, but rather to facilitate student learning. Ordinarily we are not concerned simply with the learning of a set of facts, but rather with learning that can be applied and used in situations outside the course examinations. In fact, *in most courses we are concerned about helping our students in a lifelong learning process; that is, we want to develop interest in further learning and provide a base of concepts and skills that will facilitate further learning and thinking.*

Your personal values inevitably enter into your choice of goals. Although many of us were taught to be strictly objective, I have come through the years to believe that this is impossible. Our teaching is always influenced by our values and students have a fairer chance to evaluate our biases or to accept our model if we are explicit about them. Hiding behind the cloak of objectivity simply prevents honest discussion of vital issues.

In thinking about your goals, remember that each course contributes to other general goals of a university education that transcend specific subject matter, such as being willing to explore ideas contrary to one's own beliefs and knowing when information or data are relevant to an issue and how to find relevant information.

---

* Duchastel and Merrill (1973) have reviewed empirical studies of the effects of behavioral objectives. Amidst the plethora of nonsignificant results are some studies indicating that sharing behavioral objectives with students may help focus their attention or assist them organizing material. So if you've worked out objectives, let your students know what they are, and if possible give them a chance to help revise them. (This study and others mentioned in the text, as well as supplementary works, are found in the *References* at the back of the book. In addition, some chapters are followed by brief lists of supplementary reading from the *References* that are specifically applicable to those chapters.)

In addition to this general perspective you need to keep in mind characteristics of the setting in which you teach. What is the role of this course in your department? Are other instructors depending upon this course to provide specific kinds of background knowledge or skill? What are your students like? What are their current concerns? Self-discovery? Social action? Getting a job?

A committee of college and university examiners developed two books to assist faculty members in thinking about their objectives. The two books, entitled *Taxonomy of Educational Objectives, Handbook I: Cognitive Domain* (Bloom, 1956) and *Handbook II: Affective Domain* (Krathwohl et al., 1964) will help point your objective writing in the right direction. The classic guide for writing objectives is R. F. Mager's little book, *Preparing Instructional Objectives* (1962).

Draft a Syllabus for the Course

When we think about teaching we usually think about what goes on in the classroom. But since most student learning occurs outside the classroom, planning how to help students learn outside classroom meetings is one of the most important tasks of the teacher. A syllabus typically contains such a plan of assigned readings and activities scheduled in dates correlated with lecture topics.

The syllabus will force you to begin thinking about the practicalities of what you must give up in order to fit within the constraints of time, place, students, available resources, and your own limitations.

As you begin to block out activities in relation to the college calendar, you will begin to note when you will want films, guest lecturers, field work, or other things that require scheduling ahead.

Order Textbooks or Other Resources Students May Need

Should you use a text? The revolution in teaching media has not been the advent of television, teaching machines, or computers, but rather the readier availability of a variety of printed materials. With paperback books, reprint series, and a Xerox* machine in the library, young instructors are immediately beguiled by the thought that they can do a

---

* Check the new copyright law before making multiple copies.

much better job of compiling a set of required readings than any previous author or editor.

There is much to be said for such a procedure. It provides flexibility, a variety of points of view, and an opportunity to maintain maximum interest. Moreover, since no single text covers every topic equally well, the use of a variety of sources enables the teacher to provide more uniformly excellent materials ranging from theoretical papers and research reports to case studies.

The "cons" of not using a textbook are apparent. Without a text the task of integration may be so overwhelming that great pressure is placed on instructors to provide integration. This may limit your freedom to use the class period for problem solving, applications, or other purposes. With a well-chosen textbook, you may rely upon the students to obtain the basic content and structure of the subject matter through reading and thus be freer to vary procedures in the classroom. Moreover, the managerial task of determining appropriate readings and arranging to have them available for students is not to be taken lightly. One is torn between potential student complaints about the cost of buying several sources and complaints from the librarian about the cost of multiple copies along with student complaints about their inability to get a reading assignment in the library.

A final consideration is the extent to which you want to use required vs. free reading, as in my use of a "reading log" (see Chapter 10). I use a text as a base to provide structure and then require students to write a log on readings they choose. To assign diverse required readings and additional free reading seems to me to require too much integration even for well-prepared, bright students.

Choosing a text or reading materials. In choosing reading materials the most important thing is that they fit your objectives. One of the most annoying and confusing of practices to students is instructor disagreement with the textbook. It is doubtful that any book will satisfy you completely, but if you use a text, choose one that is as much in line with your view as possible.

Your library facilities will probably help you decide whether you choose a book that omits materials you would like to cover or a book that contains extra material you consider unimportant. Generally speaking I have found that students prefer to have additional material presented in lecture or by supplementary reading assignments. They dislike reading material the instructor later says isn't important, and, surprisingly enough, they also dislike omitting material in the textbook. (Somehow they feel that they're missing something.) This student need for continuity and closure will influence your outline of assignments. Students prefer going through a book as it was written. If the author also wrote the book in a systematic way, building one concept on another, there may be good pedagogical reasons for following the author's order. Since I know of no text that completely suits many teachers, however, I can only recommend that you keep the skipping around to a minimum.

There is no substitute for detailed review of the competing texts for the course you are teaching. As texts multiply, it becomes increasingly tempting to throw up your hands in frustration over the time required for a conscientious review and to choose the book primarily on the basis of appearance, the personality of the book sales representative, or the inclusion of your name as author of one of the studies cited. Yet research on teaching suggests that the major influence on what students learn is not the teaching method but the textbook. Moreover, some of the superficially most attractive textbooks today are "managed books," written in the offices of the publisher rather than by persons who know the field. Managed books vary a great deal in the degree to which scholars are involved. The most egregious cases of plagiarism and errors in content are now disappearing, but one cannot adopt a textbook on the basis of the sales representative's description any more than physicians should prescribe drugs on the advice of the drug company's detail men.

Time: Two Months Before the First Class ═══════════

Work Out a Tentative Set
of Assignments for the Students

The next point at which course objectives influence preparation for the course is in terms of the kind, length, and content of assignments. Two instructors who have chosen the same textbooks will probably stress different materials. Since no one but the person teaching from his or her own text is probably well satisfied with the relative weightings of materials in available texts, it will almost always be necessary to assign chapters on some topics which, from your point of view, are incomplete and to assign others that treat a topic more extensively than you would desire. For the former situation, additional readings or lectures may partially solve the problem. For the latter, no very satisfactory solution is available.

To summarize the argument so far in this section, the following schedule suggests the way in which a course may be planned in a preliminary way.

1. Decide what you want the students to gain from the course.

2. Choose one or more texts or other sources that make the point you want made.

3. Plan the course for the whole semester or year in such a way as to allot appropriate amounts of time to various topics.

It is on this third point that elaboration appears to be necessary. In making plans for the term you need to consult (in addition to textbooks and your conscience) the college catalogue or bulletin in order to anticipate some or all of the following circumstances:

1. For a given term you are allowed a certain number of class periods (about 40–45 for a 3-hour course in a typical semester). Your wisdom must, therefore, be compressed into a period of somewhat less than two clock days. You will want to decide ahead of time approximately the number of sessions to be allotted to each of the topics you want to cover.

2. My estimate of 40–45 days includes:
   a. one day for orientation (which I recommend).
   b. one day for a final summing up (which the students will probably insist on).
   c. one or more class periods devoted to examinations.
   This, of course, reduces the students' time at your disposal to 35–40 hours.

3. Students (unlike the faculty) get holidays. One must consider them in planning a course in order, insofar as is possible, to avoid:
   a. tests or important class sessions just before or just after holidays or major college events, such as homecoming.
   b. having closely related materials presented partly before and partly after a recess.

Midterm or other preliminary grades may be due at specified times. Such estimates of student achievement should be based upon at least one, and preferably more, examinations or other evidence of achievement.

From what I have said in the preceding paragraphs it is evident by now that the easy accomplishment of course objectives may be frustrated in two ways: by lack of satisfactory text material and by the college schedule.

Decide What Should Be in the Course Outline or Syllabus

Compromising as little as possible with course objectives, if you have followed recommendations to this point you now have a rough course outline completed. You have decided what you want to cover in your course and how to distribute available time. You may even make a schedule of where in the course you expect to be at any given date. My suggestion now is that you make such a schedule and have it mimeographed for distribution to the class. But present it as a basis for discussion and possible revision on the basis of their suggestions. Only after getting their ideas should the final copy be distributed.

How complete, detailed, and precise should your schedule be? My answer is "not very," for three reasons:

1. Like most of us, you are apt to change your mind about the details you will cover before you come to a specific topic. There is little point in committing yourself in print to a course of action you will later regard as ill advised.

2. Inevitably, circumstances arise that make it advisable to deviate slightly from the schedule.

3. The students themselves are important variables in determining the pace and structure of the course. Some classes gallop along at a fine pace; others are slow to move. Some classes develop great interest in one topic; others in another. Your schedule should be sufficiently flexible to take advantage of the students' own awareness of how they can best learn.

But if an instructor is really student centered, isn't preparation of a course outline a cue that the course is really instructor centered and that student needs are really not going to be considered? Not necessarily so. Research by Richard Mann and his associates at the University of Michigan (1970) suggests that students see the teacher who takes a nondirective, student-centered role as not interested in the class.

Your course outline should at least contain the assignments for the semester. One very satisfactory way to prepare such an outline is to provide the students with a topic outline of the course. Under the various topic headings, you can schedule assignments and the dates when they are due. This method has the special advantage of relieving the instructor of the task of making assignments every few days and of repeating the assignment two or three times for the benefit of students who have been absent when the assignment was first announced.

As you lay out your schedule consider alternate ways students might achieve the goals of a particular day or week of class. You will seldom have perfect attendance at every class. Why not build in periodic alternatives to your lecture or class discussion? Students who have options and a sense of personal control are likely to be more highly motivated for learning.

Other items that may be appropriate to include in such an outline are the dates when examinations, quizzes, or laboratory exercises are scheduled, announcements of films to be shown in connection with various topics, and the particular libraries in which collateral reading materials have been placed on reserve if the library facilities in your university are decentralized. Including the call numbers of the books required for library use will save a good deal of student time.

Finally, you may include any special rules of classroom behavior you may want to emphasize, such as a statement to the effect that the assignments for the course are to be completed by the dates indicated in the course outline. In fact it is generally helpful to list the responsibilities of the student and those of the instructor. All of these considerations, of course, help set the stage for the course—they structure the situation, help the students discover at the outset what their responsibilities are going to be, and give them the security of seeing where they are going.

Choose Appropriate Teaching Methods

A third and final point at which your preparation for a course is determined by your objectives is in the type of instruction you will use. For some goals and for some materials, an orthodox lecture presentation is as good as or better than any other. For others, discussion may be preferable. For the accomplishment of still other ends the "buzz session" or "role playing" techniques described later in the book may be useful.

Probably most successful teachers vary their methods to suit their objectives. Thus you may wish one day to present some new material in a lecture. You may then follow this with a class discussion on implications of this material or with a laboratory or field exercise. Since your choice in the matter is determined as much by your own personality as by your course objectives, I shall not dwell on it here. From the description of these techniques in later sections of the book, you may be able to decide which techniques are suited to your philosophy of teaching, your abilities, the class you are teaching, and the particular goals you are emphasizing at a particular time.

Generally speaking, it will be wise to find out how the course has been taught in the past and to avoid *major* modifications unless there is some departmental unhappiness with the course.

Check Resources Needing Advance Work

Order films, make arrangements for field work, guest lecturers, slides, demonstrations, or other resources needing advance work.

Begin Preparing Lectures
(If You Plan to Lecture)

(See Chapter 7.)

Time: Two Weeks Before the First Class

Preparation and planning are not done when you've firmed up the syllabus. Now look back over the syllabus to see what resources are required. Presumably your check with a colleague has turned up any gross problems—such as assuming an unlimited budget for films. But visit the classroom you've been assigned. Will the seating be conducive to discussion? Can it be darkened for films? If the room is unsuitable, ask for another. Don't assume that assignments are unchangeable. You probably can't change the time schedule the first time you are assigned it, since a certain time may already be in print with student schedules built around it. But with a term's head start you may be able to shift time of day, length of class period, etc. What are the library policies relevant to putting on reserve any books you may want to reserve? Can you assume unlimited xeroxing of exams and course materials to give to students? What do you do if you want to show a film? Go on a field trip?

Time: One Week Before the First Class ══════════

At this point you're ready to prepare for the first class. For ideas about what to do and how to handle this meeting, read the next chapter.

SUPPLEMENTARY READING

A good brief source on how to define objectives is Chapter 3 in S. C. Ericksen, *Motivation for learning* (Ann Arbor: University of Michigan Press, 1974).

A broader perspective is provided in Kenneth Eble's book *The Aims of College Teaching* (San Francisco: Jossey-Bass, 1983). I particularly like Chapter 2, "Character—The foundation of style."

The relationship between teaching styles and goals is thoughtfully discussed in relation to the limitations of disciplinary perspectives in the book by Paul L. Dressel and Dora Marcus, *On teaching and learning in college* (San Francisco, Jossey-Bass, 1982).

Chapter 2 of the book by Barbara Fuhrmann and Anthony Grasha, *A practical handbook for college teachers* (Boston: Little, Brown, 1983) is titled "The Role of Personal Values in Teaching" and is well worth reading.

CHAPTER 3 / Meeting a Class for the First Time

The first class meeting, like any other situation in which you are meeting a group of strangers who will affect your well being, is at the same time exciting and anxiety producing for both students and teacher. Some teachers handle their anxiety by postponing it, simply handing out the syllabus and leaving. This does not convey the idea that class time is valuable, nor does it capitalize on the fact that first day excitement can be constructive. If you have prepared as suggested in Chapter 2, you're in good shape; the students will be pleased that the instruction is under control, and focusing on meeting the students' concerns can not only help you quell your own anxiety but also make the first class interesting and challenging.

Other things being equal, anxiety is less disruptive in situations where stimulus events are clear and unambiguous. When the students know what to expect they can direct their energy more productively. An important function of the first day's meeting in any class is to provide this structure; that is, to present the classroom situation clearly, so that the students will know from the date of this meeting what you are like and what you expect. They come to the first class wanting to know what the course is all about and what kind of person the teacher is. To this end, the following concrete suggestions are offered.

One point to keep in mind both the first day and throughout the term is that yours is not the students' only class. They come to you from classes in chemistry, music, English, physical education, or rushing from their dormitory beds or from parking lots. The first few minutes need to help this varied group shift their thoughts and feelings to you and your subject.

You can ease them into the course gradually or you can grab their attention by something dramatically different, but in either case you need to think consciously about how you set the stage to facilitate achieving the course objectives. Even before the class period begins you can communicate nonverbally by such things as arranging the seats in a circle and putting your name on the board, or chat with early arrivals about what class they have come from or anything else that would indicate your interest in them.

Breaking the Ice

You will probably want to use the first period for getting acquainted and establishing goals. You might begin by informally asking freshmen to raise their hands, then sophomores, juniors, seniors, or out-of-staters. This gives you some idea of the composition of the class and gets students started participating.

You might then ask all class members (including yourself) to introduce themselves, tell where they're from, mention their field of concentration, and answer any questions the group has. Or you can ask each student to get acquainted with the persons sitting on each side and then go around the class with each student introducing the next or each repeating the names of all those who have been introduced—a good device for promoting development of rapport and for helping you learn the names too.

Having established a degree of freedom of communication, the class can discuss the objectives of the course. It seems helpful to list these on the board as class members suggest them or react to your suggestions. After class record them so that the class may periodically refer to them and check progress. Note that these are only a first approximation that can be altered and rephrased as the class becomes aware of new needs during the course.

Problem Posting*

The technique of posting problems is not only a useful icebreaker, but one of value whenever it is useful to stimulate interest and assist students in communicating their problems to one another. This may be the case not only at the beginning of the course, but also after a lecture or other classroom method has aroused anxiety or defensiveness. The technique

---

* This technique is one I learned from Norman R. F. Maier, described in his book, _Problem-solving discussions and conferences: leadership methods and skills_ (New York: McGraw-Hill, 1963).

may also be useful to you when you wish to avoid answering questions immediately yourself. This might be because you don't wish to establish an atmosphere in which you dominate, because you wish to lay more groundwork, or because you don't wish to reinforce or to engage in a colloquy with a particular questioner whose concerns are not likely to contribute toward achievement of the goals of the class as a whole.

Do these potentialities intrigue you? All you need do is to say something like, "Let's see if we can get all the questions out so that we can see what they are and how to handle them."

If it is the first class meeting, you might say, "Let's see what problems you'd like to have us tackle during the course. What sorts of concerns do you think that we might deal with?" or "What kinds of things have you heard about this course?"

The instructor's task then becomes that of understanding and recording briefly on the blackboard the problems contributed by the group. This means that you must be ready to accept all contributions whether or not you yourself feel they are important. To test your understanding of the problem it may be useful to restate the problem in different words. Restatement may also be useful in removing emotional loading or in bringing out implicit feelings. When you feel that a question is ambiguous or too general, it is helpful to ask for an illustration or to ask other group members to help you understand.

As contributions begin to slow down, suggest stopping. But, if possible, the posting should not be ended before there has been a good pause, since some of the most deeply felt problems will not come out until the students have seen that the teacher is really accepting and non-critical. This is a point where sensitivity is particularly important, for one can often see the visible signs of conflict about whether or not to raise an emotion-laden problem. If such a problem does come out and elicits a new batch of problems, forget about the suggested ending and get the problems out.

It is important in problem posting to maintain an accepting, non-evaluative atmosphere. Thus, if other members of the group argue that someone's contribution is not really a problem or that the real problem is different from that stated, the teacher needs to make it clear that even though not everyone agrees about a given problem, anything that is a problem for any member of the group is entitled to be listed. Disagreement should be used to get additional problems out rather than to persuade a group member to withdraw his contribution.

Inevitably some discussion will come out about solutions. While this should not be abruptly censored, if it becomes involved or lengthy the teacher may point out that the task of dealing with the problems comes later.

By the end of the problem posting the class normally has become better acquainted, has become used to active participation, has taken the first step toward developing an attitude of attempting to understand rather than compete with one another, has reduced the attitude that everything must come from the teacher, has learned that the teacher can listen as well as talk (and is not going to reject ideas different from his or her own), and, I hope, has begun to feel some responsibility for solving its own problems rather than waiting for them to be answered by the instructor.

The Course Outline

From problem posting it is a natural transition to an introduction of ways to tackle the problems. The instructor here faces a dilemma. You need to give students some notion of what to expect. You need to give them a sense that you have worked to prepare for the course and will continue to work to help them learn, but you also want to leave students with a sense of their own responsibility for achieving course goals. Thus, in presenting a course outline, a summary of your evaluation and grading plans and other aspects of the course structure, you need to communicate their relevance to the problems raised by the students, your responsiveness to them, and a sense of willingness to change as the course develops.

Ambiguity may excite some students, but for most it simply arouses anxiety. As we saw in Chapter 2, a simple way to reduce some of that anxiety is to distribute a mimeographed course schedule.

Introducing the Teacher

In presenting the course outline and mechanics you also give the students some notion of the kind of person that you are. Although I am not recommending a complete personality change without benefit of at least short-term psychotherapy, three characteristics seem to be especially appreciated by the student: 1) enthusiasm and willingness to work to make the course worthwhile, 2) objectivity (the students will call it "fairness"), 3) a sympathetic attitude toward the problems of the students. If these characteristics apply to you at all, or if you think they do, let the students know it.

Presenting a syllabus is one demonstration that you have made an investment in the course. Obviously you want to be open to student input, but in my experience students resent much more than an authoritarian teacher the teacher who says, "This is your class," and leaves completely to the student the organization and structure of the course. As we shall see in Chapter 5, student-centered discussion is an effective teaching method, but students often interpret a student-centered beginning as evidence that the instructor is lazy and uninterested in the course.

Promoting the notion that you are objective or fair can best be handled in connection with marks and the assignment of grades. For this reason, we will postpone direct discussion of the topic until later. But remember that a large part of the students' motivation in the classroom situation is (perhaps unfortunately) directed toward the grades they hope to get from the course. The very least that students can expect of you is that this mark will be arrived at on some impartial basis.

The simplest way to show students that you are objective and fair is to let the students know that you are willing to meet and advise them. Indicate your office hours. In addition to this, students appreciate it if you are willing (and have the time) to spend a few minutes in the classroom after each class answering specific questions. Such queries most often concern questions of fact that can be answered briefly and would hardly warrant a trip to your office at a later time in another building, even if the student could be counted on to remember the question for that long. If your time permits, adjournment to a convenient snack bar or lounge may give students with special interests a chance to pursue them and get to know you better.

The first class is not the time to make sure the students understand your inadequacies and limitations. Frankly admitting that you don't know something is fine after the course is under way, but apologies in advance for lack of experience or expertise simply increase student insecurity.

Introducing the Textbook

To continue with the discussion of the first meeting of the class, we turn now to the presentation of the textbook(s). Here the most serious question that arises concerns possible disagreement between the textbook and the materials you intend to present in your lectures. Unfortunately this is a matter that cannot always be solved simply by judicious selection of text materials. In some cases, there is simply no book available that presents certain material as you would like to have it presented. In others, the textbook is decided upon by someone other than yourself, and you have to make the best of it. In the case where disagreement is inevitable, the students have a right to know which version to accept as TRUTH and what they are supposed to do about such discrepancies on examinations. By facing the situation squarely, you can not only escape from the horns of this dilemma, but also turn it to your advantage. Explain that rival interpretations stand or fall on the basis of pertinent evidence and plan to give your reasons for disagreeing with the textbook. This procedure will accomplish two things: 1) it will give the student the notion that your opinions are based upon evidence, and 2) it will frequently point up current problems in theory that often have great appeal for the serious student.

Avoid a tirade against the author. This may serve as an emotional catharsis for the instructor, but for the student, any severe criticism you raise may generalize to the textbook as a whole. Of, if the student is not convinced by your argument, it may generalize to much of what you have to say.

Questions

Even in a large lecture it seems well to interrupt these first descriptions of the course for questions. Some of the questions will be designed as much to test you as to get information. Often the underlying questions are such things as:

➺ "Are you rigid?"

➺ "Will you really try to help students?"

➺ "Are you easily rattled?"

➺ "Are you a person as well as a teacher?"

➺ "Can you handle criticism?"

In general, it is good to respond to the surface content and not to the indirect one in this first class before trust has been built up. Nevertheless, an awareness of the feelings behind the questions may help temper your responses.

Finally, ask students to take two minutes at the end of class, to write their reactions to the first day (anonymously). This accomplishes two things! 1) It indicates your interest in learning from them and starts building a learning climate in which they have responsibilities for thinking about their learning and influencing your teaching. 2) It gives you feedback, often revealing doubts or questions students were afraid to verbalize orally.

SUPPLEMENTARY READING

Kenneth E. Eble, *The craft of teaching* (San Francisco: Jossey-Bass, 1976), Chapter 9.

PART II

Discussion Methods

CHAPTER 4 / Organizing Effective Discussions

Discussion methods are among the most valuable tools in the teacher's repertoire. Often teachers in large classes feel that they must lecture because discussion is impossible. In fact discussion techniques can be used in classes of all sizes. This is not to say that small classes are not desirable—generally they *are* more effective, but large classes should not be allowed to inhibit the teacher's ability to stimulate student thinking and participation.

The type of discussion method used will determine the extent to which particular roles are dominant.

Discussion is probably not effective for presenting new information the student is already motivated to learn, but discussion techniques seem particularly appropriate when the instructor wants to do the following:

1. Help students learn to think in terms of the subject matter by giving them practice in thinking.

2. Help students learn to evaluate the logic of, and evidence for, their own and others' positions.

3. Give students opportunities to formulate applications of principles.

4. Help students become aware of and formulate problems using information gained from readings or lectures.

5. Use the resources of members of the group.

6. Gain acceptance for information or theories counter to folklore or previous beliefs of students.

7. Develop motivation for further learning.

8. Get prompt feedback on how well objectives are being attained.

Why should discussion be the method of choice for achieving such objectives? The first justification is a very simple extrapolation of the old adage, "Practice makes perfect." If instructors expect students to learn how to integrate, apply, and problem solve, it seems reasonable that students should have an opportunity to practice these skills. Most important, learning should be facilitated if this practice is accompanied by feedback so that the students can identify their errors and successes.

Further, I would expect learning to be most effective if there is sufficient guidance to ensure some successes. Experiments on learning motor skills reveal that guidance is most helpful in the early stages of learning, suggesting that the instructor should play a more directive role at the beginning of a course than at its end.

Problems in Teaching by Discussion

In discussion groups the instructor is faced with several problems:

1. Getting participation in the discussion.

2. Making progress (or making the student aware of the progress) toward course objectives.

3. Handling emotional reactions of students.

The type of discussion method used will determine the extent to which particular roles are dominant. In Chapter 5 I shall review some of the evidence on the relative effectiveness of different types of discussions, but first I will describe a middle-of-the-road discussion method particularly useful in problem solving.

Developmental Discussion

The term "developmental discussion" was coined by Professor Norman R. F. Maier (1952) to describe a problem-solving discussion technique in which the teacher breaks problems into parts so that all group members are working on the same part of the problem at the same time. One of the reasons discussion often seems ineffective and disorganized is that different members of the group are working on different aspects of the problem and are thus often frustrated by what they perceive as irrelevant comments by other students. In developmental discussion the teacher tries to keep the students aware of the stage of discussion that is the current focus. Typical stages might be:

1. formulating the problem
2. suggesting hypotheses
3. getting relevant data
4. evaluating alternative solutions.

Typically, an early step in developmental discussion is to get information relevant to the problem for discussion. Such information can be supplied by a lecture, by reading, or by group members. In this technique teachers should feel free to give information or raise questions. Often an appropriate problem for developmental discussion is the application or implications of particular principles or findings presented by lectures or reading.

Like other discussion methods, developmental discussion implies active participation of group members. In developmental discussion, participation is directed to a definite goal. However, this does not imply a type of discussion leadership in which the leader manipulates the group to follow the steps and reach a predetermined goal. Rather the leader helps the group progress by dividing the problem up into parts that can be solved in steps. In short, developmental discussion is not nondirective, but neither is it autocratic.

Breaking a Problem into Subproblems ═══════════

One of Maier's important contributions to effective group problem solving, as well as to teaching, is to point out that groups are likely to be more effective if they tackle one aspect of a problem at a time rather than skipping from formulation of the problem, to solutions, to evidence, to "what-have-you," as different members of the group toss in their own ideas. In developmental discussion the group tackles one thing at a time.

One of the first tasks is likely to be a *clarification of the problem*. Often groups are ineffective because different participants have different ideas of what the problem is, and group members may feel frustrated at the end of the discussion because "the group never got to the real problem."

A second task is likely to be, "What do we know?" or, *"What data are relevant?"*

A third task may be, *"What are the characteristics of an acceptable solution?"*—for example, "What is needed?"

A fourth step could be, *"What are possible solutions?"*, and a fifth step may be to *evaluate these solutions* against the criteria for a solution determined in the previous step.

The developmental discussion technique can be used even in large groups, since there are a limited number of points to be made at each step regardless of the number of participants. Maier and Maier (1957) have shown that developmental discussion techniques improve the quality of decisions as compared with freer, more nondirective discussion methods.

Skills in Leading Discussion

In a developmental discussion the teacher attempts to guide a discussion along a certain line, but not to push it beyond the group's interest and acceptance. Obviously this requires skill in initiating discussion, getting student participation, appraising group progress, asking questions, and overcoming resistance.

Starting Discussion

After a class has been meeting and discussing problems successfully, there is little problem in initiating discussion, for it will develop almost spontaneously from problems encountered in reading, from experiences, or from unresolved problems from the previous meeting. But during the first meetings of new groups, the instructor may need to assume the initiative in beginning the discussion.

Starting discussion with a common experience   One of the best ways of starting a discussion is to provide a concrete, common experience through presentation of a demonstration, film, or role playing. Following such a presentation it's easy to ask, "Why did———?"

Such an opening has a number of advantages. Since everyone in the group has seen it, everyone knows something about the topic under discussion. In addition, by focusing the discussion on the demonstration, the instructor takes some of the pressure off anxious or threatened students who are afraid to reveal their own opinions or feelings.

However, you will not always be able to find the demonstration you need to introduce each discussion, and you may be forced to turn to other techniques of initiating discussion. One such technique is Problem Posting, which was discussed in Chapter 3. But the most commonly used technique is the question.

Starting discussion with a question   The commonest discussion opener is the question, and the commonest error in using a question to open discussion is not to allow students time enough to think. Ten seconds seems a long period of silence for the instructor, but it is very little for students trying to recall relevant information, to relate it to the question, and to formulate a lucid answer. For this reason it is often helpful to give students a few minutes to write out their thoughts about the question before beginning the oral discussion.

There are times when it is appropriate to check student background knowledge with a series of brief factual questions, but more frequently you want to stimulate problem solving. One common error in phrasing questions for this purpose is to ask a question in a form conveying to students the message, "I know something you don't know and you'll look stupid if you don't guess right." Rather than dealing with factual questions, discussions need to be formulated so as to get at relationships, applications, or analyses of facts and materials. Solomon, Rosenberg, and Bezdek (1964) found that teachers who used interpretation questions were effective as measured by gains in student comprehension. A question of the type, "How does the idea that——apply to——?" is much more likely to stimulate discussion than the question, "What is the definition of——?" Dillon (1982) reports that teachers often foil discussion by questions. Questions require answers which teachers follow by more questions requiring answers. Teacher statements, on the other hand, elicit discussion. The secret is not to avoid questions or to lecture in statements, but rather to listen and to reflect upon what is heard. Questions are tools for teaching, but as Dillon demonstrated they can interfere with, as well as facilitate achievement of teaching goals. What happens depends upon the question and its use.

A question may arise from a case or it may be a hypothetical problem. It may be a problem whose solution the instructor knows; it may be a problem which the instructor has not solved. In any case it should be a problem that is meaningful to the students and, for the sake of morale, it should be a problem they can make some progress on. And even if the teacher knows an answer or has a preferred solution, the students should have a chance to come up with new solutions. The teacher's job is not to sell students on a particular solution, but rather to listen and to teach them how to solve problems themselves.

A common error in question phrasing is to frame the question at a level of abstraction inappropriate for the class. Students are most likely to participate in discussion when they feel that they have an experience or idea that will contribute to the discussion. This means that discussion questions need to be phrased as problems that are meaningful to the students as well as to the instructor. Such questions can be devised more easily if you know something of the students' background. An experiment by Sturgis (1959) showed that knowledge of student background makes a significant difference in a teacher's effectiveness as measured by students' learning.

Another error in raising questions is to ask your question before finding out about the students' problems. Often a good question fails to elicit responses because students are hung up on some prior problem.

Suppose you ask a question and no one answers, or the student simply says, "I don't know." Discouraging as this may be, it should not necessarily be the end of the interaction. Usually the student can respond if the question is rephrased. Perhaps you need to give an example of the problem first; perhaps you need to suggest some alternative answer; perhaps you need to reformulate a prior question. More often than not you can help the students discover that they are more competent than they thought.

Types of questions* Critical questions examine the validity of an author's arguments or discussion. Being so critical that students feel that their reading has been a waste of time is not helpful, but presenting an alternative argument or conclusion may start students analyzing their reading more carefully, and eventually you will want students to become critical readers who themselves challenge assumptions and conclusions.

Comparative questions, as the name suggests, ask for comparisons between one theory and another, one author and another, one research study and another, etc. Such questions help students determine important dimensions of comparison.

---

* I came upon these three types of questions in the *Teaching Assistants Handbook* of Northwestern University.

Connective questions involve attempts to link material or concepts that otherwise might not seem related. One might, for example, cut across disciplines to link literature, music, and historical events.

Starting discussion with a controversy A third technique of stimulating discussion is to cause disagreement. Experimental evidence is accumulating to indicate that a certain degree of surprise or uncertainty arouses curiosity, a basic motive for learning (Berlyne, 1960). Some teachers effectively play the role of devil's advocate; others are effective in pointing up differences in point of view.

I have some concerns about the devil's advocate role. I believe that it can be an effective device in getting students to think actively rather than accept passively the instructor's every sentence as "Truth." Yet it has its risks, the most important of which is that it may create lack of trust in the instructor. Of course, instructors want students to challenge their ideas, but few want their students to feel they are untrustworthy, lying about their own beliefs.

A second danger in the "devil's advocate" role is that it will be perceived as manipulative. Students may feel (with justification) that the instructor "is just playing games with us—trying to show how smart he is and how easily he can fool us."

A third danger is that the devil's advocate role will be used as a screen to prevent students from ever successfully challenging the instructor. In this use the instructor, whenever the student wins an argument, simply says, "Well, I just presented that position to see if you could see its weakness."

Not only are all of these possible problems infuriating for the student, but they maintain a superior-subordinate relationship antithetical to the sort of learning environment that this book is plugging for. If the best classroom is one in which both students and teacher are learning, a role that provides armor against the instructor's learning is bad.

Yet the devil's advocate role can be effective. Its success depends a good deal upon the spirit with which it is played. My own compromise solution is to make it clear when I'm taking such a role by saying, "Suppose I take the position that———" or, "Let me play the role of devil's advocate for a bit."

In any case the instructor should realize that disagreement is not a sign of failure but may be used constructively. When rigid dogmatism interferes with constructive problem solving following a disagreement, the instructor may ask the disagreeing students to switch sides and argue the opposing point of view. Such a technique seems to be effective in developing awareness of the strengths of other positions.

As Maier has shown in his studies of group leadership, one barrier to effective problem solving is presenting an issue in such a way that participants take sides arguing the apparent solution rather than attempting to solve the problem by considering data and devising alternative solutions. Maier suggests the following principles for group problem solving.*

1. Success in problem solving requires that effort be directed toward overcoming surmountable obstacles.

2. Available facts should be used even when they are inadequate.

3. The starting point of the problem is richest in solution possibilities.

4. Problem-mindedness should be increased while solution-mindedness should be delayed.

5. Whether disagreement leads to hard feelings or to innovation depends on the discussion leadership.

6. The "idea-getting" process should be separated from the "idea-evaluation" process because the latter inhibits the former.

What Can I Do About Nonparticipants?

In most classes some students talk too much and others never volunteer a sentence. What can the teacher do?

Unfortunately, most students are used to being passive recipients in class. To help them become participants I try to create an expectation of participation in the discussion section. You can start to do this in the first meeting of the course by defining the functions of various aspects of the course and explaining why discussion is valuable. In addition to this initial structuring, however, you must continually work to increase the students' awareness of the values of participation. Participation is not an end in itself. For many purposes widespread participation may be vital;

---

* N. R. F. Maier, *Problem-solving discussions and conferences* (New York: McGraw-Hill, 1963).

for others it may be detrimental. But you want to create a climate in which an important contribution is not lost because the person with the necessary idea did not feel free to express it.

What keeps a student from talking? There are a variety of reasons— boredom, lack of knowledge, general habits of passivity—but most compelling is a fear of being embarrassed. When one is surrounded by strangers, when one does not know how critical these strangers may be, when one is not sure how sound one's idea may be, when one is afraid of stammering or forgetting one's point under the stress of speaking— the safest thing to do is keep quiet.

What can reduce this fear? Getting acquainted is one aid. Once students know that they are among friends, they can risk expressing themselves. If they know that at least one classmate supports an idea, the risk is reduced. For both these reasons the technique of subgrouping helps; for example, you can ask students to discuss a question in pairs or small groups before asking for general discussion.

Asking students to take a couple of minutes to write out their answers to a question can help. If a student has already written an answer, the step to speaking the answer is much less than answering a question when asked to answer immediately. Even the shy person will respond when asked, "What did you write?"

Rewarding infrequent contributors at least by a smile helps encourage participation even if the contribution has to be developed or corrected. Calling students by name seems to encourage freer communication. Seating is important too. Rooms with seats in a circle help tremendously.

Getting to know the nonparticipant is also helpful. For example, I have found that it is helpful to ask students to write a brief life history indicating their interests and experiences relevant to the course. These autobiographies help me to gain a better knowledge of each student as an individual, to know what problems or illustrations will be of particular interest to a number of students, and to know whom I can call on for special information. One of the best ways of getting nonparticipants into the discussion is to ask them to contribute in a problem area in which they have special knowledge.

The technique of asking for a student's special knowledge deals directly with one of the major barriers to class discussion—fear of being wrong. No one likes to look foolish, especially in a situation where mistakes may be pounced upon by a teacher or other students. One of the major reasons for the deadliness of a question in which the teacher asks a student to fill in the one right word—such as, "This is an example of what?"—is that it puts the students on the spot. There is an infinity of wrong answers, and obviously the teacher knows the one right answer; so why should the student risk making a mistake when the odds are so much against the student? And even if the answer is obvious, why look like a stooge for the teacher?

One way of putting the student in a more favorable position is to ask general questions that have no wrong answers. For example, you can ask, "How do you feel about this?" or, "How does this look to you?" as a first step in analysis of a problem. Students' feelings or perceptions may not be the same as yours, but as reporters of their own feelings, they can't be challenged as being inaccurate. While such an approach by no means eliminates anxiety about participation (for an answer involves revealing oneself as a person), it will more often open up discussion that involves the student than will questions of fact. "Problem Posting," the technique discussed in Chapter 3 as a method for establishing objectives during the first day of class is an example of a discussion technique minimizing risk for students. It can be useful in introducing a new topic, at the conclusion of a topic, or for analysis of an experiment or a literary work. An added advantage is that it can be used in large groups as well as small ones.

Another technique for reducing the risk of participation for students is to ask a question a class period before the discussion and ask students to write out answers involving an example from their own experience.

All of these techniques will still not make every student into an active, verbal participant. Two group techniques can help. One is "buzz groups"; the other is the "inner circle" technique.

Buzz Groups One of the popular techniques for achieving student participation in groups is the buzz session. In this procedure, classes are split into small subgroups for a brief discussion of a problem. Groups can be asked to come up with one hypothesis that they see as relevant, with one application of a principle, or an example of a point. In large classes I march up the aisles saying "Odd," "Even," "Odd," "Even" for each row and ask the "odd" rows to turn around to talk to the "even" row behind, forming themselves into groups of four to eight. I tell them to first introduce themselves to one another and then to choose a person to report for the group. Next they are to get from each member of the group one idea about the problem or question posed. Finally they are to come up with one idea to report to the total class.

The Inner Circle In using the inner circle technique I announce that at the next class meeting we are going to have a class within a class, with half the students acting as the discussion group and the other half as observers. If the classroom has moveable chairs, I then arrange the seating in the form of two concentric circles. I may explain that I want to give some of the quieter members of the class a chance to express their ideas. I am impressed that students who are normally silent will talk when they feel the increased sense of responsibility as members of the inner circle.

The Discussion Monopolizer

If you have worked on nonparticipation effectively, the discussion monopolizer is less likely to be a problem, but there will still be classes in which one student talks so much that you and the other students become annoyed. As with nonparticipation, one solution is to raise with the class the question of participation in discussion—"Would the class be more effective if participation were more evenly distributed?"

A second technique is to have one or more members of the class act as observers for one or more class periods, reporting back to the class their observations. Perhaps assigning the dominant member to the observer role would help sensitivity.

A third technique is to use buzz groups with one member chosen to be reporter. Often the monopolizer will not be chosen to report.

A direct approach should not be ruled out. Talking to the student individually outside class may be the simplest and most effective solution.

Patience

You should not expect an immediate response to every question. If your question is intended to stimulate thinking, give the students time to think. A few seconds of silence may seem an eternity, but a pause for thought may result in better discussion than a quick answer generated out of a desire to avoid silence. In some cases you may plan for such a thoughtful silence by asking the students to think about the question a few seconds and then write down one element that might help answer the question. Such a technique increases the chance that the shyer or slower students will participate, since they know what they want to say when the discussion begins. In fact you may even draw one in by saying, "You were writing vigorously, Ronnie, what's your suggestion?"

Appraising Progress

One of the important skills of discussion leaders is the ability to appraise the group's progress and to be aware of barriers or resistances that are blocking learning. This skill depends upon attention to such clues as inattention, hostility, or diversionary questions.

Skill at appraising is of little avail if instructors don't respond to the feedback they receive. In some cases you may need to respond only by interposing a guiding question or by emphasizing a significant contribution. In other cases you may need to summarize progress and restate the current issue or point out the stumbling block or diversion that has stopped progress. In extreme cases, you may have to stop the discussion to begin a discussion of the reasons for lack of progress.

How Can You Have a Discussion
if the Students Haven't Read the Assignment?

It's hard to have a discussion if students haven't studied the material to be discussed. What to do?

If there are extenuating circumstances, you (or a student who is prepared) can summarize the needed points. Alternatively you can give students a few minutes to scan the material before beginning the discussion. If used often, however, such strategies may discourage out-of-class preparation.

If the problem persists, present it to the students. What do they suggest? One likely proposal is a short quiz at the beginning of class— which usually works. However, you'd like to have students motivated to study without the threat of a quiz. Usually the quiz can be phased out once students find discussion really requires preparation and that the assignments are more interesting as they develop competence.

Barriers to Discussion

A primary barrier to discussion is the students' feeling that they are not learning. Occasional summaries during the hour not only help students chart their progress, but also help smooth out communication problems. A summary need not be a statement of conclusions. In many cases the most effective summary is a restatement of the problem in terms of the issues resolved and those remaining.

Probably one of the most common barriers to good discussion is the instructor's tendency to tell students the answer or to put the solution in abstract or general terms before the students have developed an answer or meaning for themselves. Of course, teachers can sometimes save time by tying things together or stating a generalization that is emerging. But all too often they do this before the class is ready for it.

Another barrier to discussion is agreement. Usually instructors are so eager to reach agreement in groups that they are likely to be happy when the students are agreeing. But agreement is not the objective of most educational discussions. Students come to class with certain common naive attitudes and values. While the attitudes they hold may be "good" ones, they may be so stereotyped that the students fail to develop an understanding of the complex phenomena to which their attitudes apply. The teacher's task is often directed not so much toward attitude change as toward increased sensitivity to other points of view and increased understanding of the phenomena to which the attitude applies. As I suggested earlier, the instructor may sometimes need to assume a role of opposition.

When you oppose a student's opinions, you should be careful not to overwhelm the student with the force of the criticism. Your objective is to start discussion, not smother it. Give students an opportunity to respond to criticisms, examining the point of view that was opposed. Above all, avoid personal criticism of students.

Handling Arguments

In any good discussion conflicts will arise. If such conflicts are left ambiguous and uncertain, they, like repressed conflicts in the individual, may cause continuing trouble. One of the teacher's functions is to help focus these conflicts so that they may contribute to learning.

Reference to the text or other authority may be one method of resolution, if the solution depends upon certain facts.

Using the conflict as the basis for a library assignment for the class or a delegated group is another solution.

If there is an experimentally verified answer, this is a good opportunity to review the method by which the answer could be determined.

If the question is one of values, your goal may be to help students become aware of the values involved.

In any case it should be clear that conflict may be an aid to learning, and the instructor need not frantically seek to smother it.

Sometimes students will dispute your statements or decisions. Such disagreements may sometimes be resolved by a comparison of the evidence for both points of view, but since teachers are human, they are all too likely to become drawn into an argument in which they finally rest upon their own authority. To give yourself time to think as well as to indicate understanding and acceptance of the students' point, I suggest listing the objections on the blackboard. (Incidentally, listing evidence or arguments is also a good technique when the conflict is between two members of the class.) Such listing tends to prevent repetition of the same arguments.

The Two-Column Method

Another of Maier's techniques, the two-column method, is a particularly effective use of the blackboard in a situation where there is a conflict or where a strong bias prevents full consideration of alternate points of view. Experimental studies (Hovland, 1957) suggest that when people hear arguments against their point of view, they become involved in attempting to refute the arguments rather than listening and understanding. Disagreement thus often tends to push the debaters into opposite corners in which every idea is right or wrong, good or bad, black or white. The truth is often more complex and not in either extreme.

The two-column method is designed to permit consideration of complications and alternatives. As in problem posting, leaders using this technique suggest that before the issues are debated before the group, all the arguments on each side be listed on the board. The leader then heads two columns, "Favorable to A" and "Favorable to B" or "For" and "Against," and then asks for the facts or arguments group members wish to present. The instructor's task is to understand and record in brief the arguments presented. If someone wishes to debate an argument presented for the other side, the instructor simply tries to reformulate the point so that it can be listed as a positive point in the debater's own column. But even though an argument is countered or protested it should not be erased, for the rules of the game are that the two columns are to include all ideas that members consider relevant. Evaluation can come later.

When the arguments have been exhausted, discussion can turn to the next step in problem solving. At this point the group can usually identify areas of agreement and disagreement and in many cases it is already clear that the situation is neither black nor white. Now the issue becomes one of *relative* values rather than good vs. bad. When discussion is directed toward agreements, some of the personal animosity is avoided, and some underlying feelings may be brought to light. The next stages of the discussion are thus more likely to be directed toward constructive problem solving.

Challenges and disagreements may be an indication of an alert, involved class. But the instructor should also be aware of the possibility that they may be symptoms of frustration arising because the students are uncertain of what the problem is or how to go about solving it.

Teaching Students How to Learn Through Discussion

I have already implied that classes don't automatically carry on effective discussions. To a large extent students have to learn how to learn from discussions just as they have to learn how to learn from reading. How can this occur?

Some of the attributes are already apparent. For example, one skill is clarification of what it is the group is trying to do. Developmental discussion carries this to the extent of specifying subgoals for each stage of the discussion. One of the skills in learning through discussion is developing sensitivity to confusion about what the group is working on and asking for clarification. For teachers this implies presenting their own goals for the discussion and encouraging students to participate in formulating the group's goals.

A second attribute is the students' development of a willingness to talk about their own ideas openly and to listen and respond to others' ideas. It is important for students to realize that it is easy to deceive themselves about their own insights or understandings and that verbalizing an idea is one way of getting checks upon and extensions of it. Teachers can encourage development of listening skills by asking one group member to repeat or paraphrase what another said before responding to it.

A third skill is planning. Discussions are sometimes frustrating because they are only getting under way when the end of the class period comes. If this results in continuation of the discussion outside the class, so much the better, but often learning is facilitated if students learn to formulate the issues and determine what out-of-class study or follow-up is necessary before the group breaks up.

A fourth skill is building on others' ideas in such a way as to increase their motivation rather than make them feel punished or forgotten. Often students see discussion as a competitive situation in which they win by tearing down other students' ideas. As Haines and McKeachie (1967) have shown, cooperative discussion methods encourage more effective work and better morale than competitive methods.

A fifth attribute is sensitivity to feelings of other group members. Students need to become aware of the possibility that feelings of rejection, frustration, dependence, and so on, may influence group members' participation in discussion. Sometimes it is more productive to recognize the underlying feeling than to focus on the content of an individual's statement.

A sixth attribute is skill in evaluation. If classes are to learn how to discuss effectively, they need to review periodically what aspects of their discussion are proving to be worthwhile and what barriers, gaps, or difficulties have arisen. Some classes reserve the last five minutes of the period for a review of the discussion's effectiveness.

Leadership Functions

While I advocate the sharing of leadership responsibilities with other members of the group, I have already indicated some of the duties I believe the teacher should perform when necessary. These include:

1. Calling the meeting to order and introducing the topic for discussion.
2. Clarification of goals during the discussion.
3. Summarization.
4. Mediation and clarification of differences.

In addition, the teacher needs to be particularly aware of two leadership functions not discussed in the previous section: 1) agenda setting, and 2) giving minority views a chance to be heard.

If the agenda is set at the preceding meeting, the group can be better prepared for the current meeting. Agenda setting, like other leadership functions, can be shared with the group, and should be flexible enough so that it can be changed when the group wishes. Keeping the agenda a secret may spare the instructor the embarrassment of having students complain that only half the day's agenda was completed, but if students understand the agenda, their cooperation can be of much value to the struggling teacher.

One problem faced by the discussion leader is the student who dominates discussion or the clique that carries the ball. It may be that in some discussion classes, the instructor's fear of exerting too much control over the class has resulted in failure to ensure that minority points of view were given an adequate hearing. Research suggests that effectiveness of group problem solving depends upon the leader's ability to obtain a hearing for minority opinion (Maier and Solem, 1952).

Taking Minutes or Notes

Boris (1983) suggests that a student be assigned each day to keep the "minutes" of the day's discussion and that each class period be initiated with a reading of the minutes. Such a procedure is probably particularly useful for the student taking the minutes but it also has the value of starting the class with a review of where they have been so that there is a sense of building from one class period to the next.

In Conclusion

The teachers' own needs are more evident in the conduct of discussion than in a lecture, for skillful discussion leading requires a quick awareness of individual and group needs. Instructors must, at least occasionally, relinquish their spots in the limelight and banish the temptation to make the discussion a little lecture.

In general, if an instructor is enthusiastic, friendly, and obviously interested in the subject, students also will be. Let me emphasize again that both lecture and discussion may have advantages at certain points in a course. Skillful teachers will choose the method best adapted to their objectives rather than rigidly sticking to one method only.

SUPPLEMENTARY READING

J. T. Dillon, *Teaching and the art of questioning* (Bloomington, IN: Phi Delta Kappa Educational Foundation, 1983).
Barbara Scheider Fuhrmann and Anthony F. Grasha. *A practical handbook for college teachers* (Boston: Little, Brown, 1983), Chapter 6.

CHAPTER 5 | *Student-Centered Discussion Methods*

Discussion may be ill adapted for communicating information because the rate of communication from instructor to student is slow. However, not all information is eagerly received. When information encounters intellectual or emotional resistance, discussion methods may be necessary in order to bring the source of resistance to light. If students have misunderstandings or misconceptions, it is important that they come out and be corrected.

Moreover, if students are to achieve application, critical thinking, or most higher cognitive outcomes, it seems reasonable to assume that they should have an opportunity to practice application and critical thinking and to receive feedback on the results. Group discussion provides an opportunity to do this. While computers and simulations may also be programmed to provide prompt and realistic feedback, a group discussion permits presentation of a variety of problems and enables a number of people to gain experience in integrating facts, formulating hypotheses, amassing relevant evidence, and evaluating conclusions. In fact, the prompt feedback provided by the computer may actually be less effective than a method in which students are encouraged to discover solutions for themselves with less step-by-step guidance (Della-Piana, 1956). Since problem solving ordinarily requires information, instructors might expect discussion to be more effective for groups with more information than for those lacking in background. Some support for this hypothesis is provided by a study on the learning of children visiting a museum. Melton, Feldman, and Mason (1936) found that lectures were more effective than discussions for children in grades five, six, and seven, but discussions were more effective for eighth graders.

Lectures place the learner in a passive role, and passive learning is less efficient than active. We would expect discussions to promote more active learning. Bloom and his colleagues at Chicago used recordings of classes to stimulate students to recall their thought during class (1953). As predicted, they found that discussion stimulated more active thinking than lecture classes did. Krauskopf (1960) substituted written for oral responses to the tape recordings and found that rated relevance of thoughts was positively correlated to achievement, accounting for variance in achievement beyond that accounted for by ability.

The idea that discussion methods should help overcome resistance to learning is difficult to verify. Essentially, the argument is that some desired learning encounters emotional barriers preventing it from affecting behavior. For example, psychology students may learn that "cramming" is not effective, but not change their study methods because their anxiety about grades is so great that they don't dare try anything different. In such circumstances experiments on attitude change suggest that instructors must either bring about changes in underlying attitude and motivation, or they must change students' perceptions of the instrumental relationship between their beliefs and their motives. Psychotherapists believe that expressing one's attitude in a nonthreatening situation is one of the steps in the process of change. A group discussion may provide such opportunities for expression as well as give opportunities for other group members to point out other relationships.

In addition, most attitudes influencing learning have some interpersonal antecedents and are stabilized by a person's perception of the attitudes of other liked persons. Group discussion may facilitate a high degree of liking for the instructor and for other group members. It also permits more accurate assessment of group norms than is likely in other techniques of instruction. Consequently change may follow.

In fact, while individual instruction would be advantageous for many teaching purposes, group processes can provide a real advantage in bringing about changes in motivation and attitudes. Lewin (1952) showed in his classic experiments on group decision that it is sometimes easier to change a group than an individual.

Not all discussions actually are superior in these respects, for discussions range from monologues in which occasional questions are interposed to bull sessions in which the instructor is an interested (or bored!) observer. Nevertheless, a good deal of research has attempted to compare the effectiveness of differing discussion techniques.

Student-Centered vs. Instructor-Centered Teaching

A wide variety of teaching methods are described by the labels "student-centered," "nondirective," "group-centered," or "democratic" discussion. Proponents of these various methods have in common the desire to break away from the traditional instructor-dominated classroom and to encourage greater student participation and responsibility. Table 5–1 lists some of the ways in which student-centered methods differ from the traditional "instructor-centered" class.*

From the standpoint of theory, student-centered teaching in its more extreme forms might be expected to have some serious weaknesses, at least in achieving lower level cognitive goals. With the instructor giving little information, feedback, or structure, it is apparent that a heavy burden falls upon the group members to carry out any of these functions.

Thistlethwaite (1960) found that National Merit Scholars check "allowing time for classroom discussion" as one of the outstanding characteristics of the teachers who contributed most to their desire to learn. Other characteristics mentioned included "modifying course content to meet students' needs and interests," "treating students as colleagues," and "taking a personal interest in students." Another trait was "providing evaluations reassuring the student of creative or productive potentialities."

The advocates of student-centered or group-centered teaching also introduced another category of objectives, not usually considered in traditional classes—the goal of developing skills in group membership and leadership. The group-centered teacher might argue that even if group-centered teaching were no more effective than traditional methods in achieving the usual course objectives, it is so important that students learn to work effectively in groups that it may even be worth sacrificing some other objectives in order to promote this kind of growth.

Since student-centered teachers often stress group cohesiveness, a possible explanation for the contradictory results in some experiments may be found in the studies of group cohesiveness and productivity in industry (for example, Seashore, 1954). These studies indicate that it is not safe to assume that a cohesive group will be a productive one. Cohesive groups are effective in maintaining group standards, but may set either high or low standards of productivity. Since cohesive groups feel less threatened by management than less cohesive groups, it may be difficult to change their standards. Thus, in creating "groupy" classes instructors may sometimes be helping their students develop strength to set low standards of achievement and maintain them against instructor pressures, or at least to develop group goals different from their normal academic goals.

---

* A good summary and critical evaluation of studies in this area may be found in R. C. Anderson (1959).

TABLE 5–1 / *Dimensions upon Which Student-Centered and Instructor-Centered Methods May Differ*

Student-Centered	Instructor-Centered
Goals	
Determined by group (Faw, 1949)	Determined by instructor
Emphasis upon affective and attitudinal changes (Faw, 1949)	Emphasis upon intellectual changes
Attempts to develop group cohesiveness (Bovard, 1951 (a,b)	No attempt to develop group cohesiveness
Classroom Activities	
Much student participation (Faw, 1949)	Much instructor participation
Student-student interaction (McKeachie, 1951)	Instructor-student interaction
Instructor accepts erroneous or irrelevant student contributions (Faw, 1949)	Instructor corrects, criticizes, or rejects erroneous or irrelevant student contributions
Group decides upon own activities (McKeachie, 1951)	Instructor determines activities
Discussion of students' personal experiences encouraged (Faw, 1949)	Discussion kept on course materials
De-emphasis of tests and grades (Asch, 1951)	Traditional use of tests and grades
Students share responsibility for evaluation (Ashmus and Haigh, 1952)	Instructor evaluates
Instructor interprets feelings and ideas of class member when necessary for class progress (Axelrod, 1955)	Instructor avoids interpretation of feelings
Reaction reports (Asch, 1951)	No reaction reports

Another factor may account for the fact that some researchers report student enthusiasm for student-centered teaching while others report hostility. Horwitz (1958) found that aggression toward the teacher increased when the teacher exercised authority arbitrarily; for example, refused to abide by the students' decision about teaching methods after telling them that their vote would count. The same method was not resented when the instructor indicated that he would make the final decision. This is important because the limits of student power are often ambiguous in student-centered classes.

While scores on objective final examinations seem to be little affected by teaching method, student-centered methods were superior in adjustment as reported by Asch (1951), Faw (1949), and Zeleny (1940). The classes compared by Bovard (1951a and b) and McKeachie (1951) differed in the degree to which interaction between students was encouraged and in the degree to which the class made decisions about assignments, examinations, and other matters of classroom procedure. Like other experimenters, Bovard and McKeachie found that the groups did not differ in achievement as measured by the final examination. However, two clinical psychologists evaluated recordings of the class discussions that followed the showing of the film, "The Feeling of Rejection." Both clinicians reported that the "group-centered" class showed much more insight and understanding of the problems of the girl in the film. Similarly Wieder (1954) found that a nondirectively taught psychology class tended to produce more reduction in prejudice than conventional classes.

Patton (1955) felt that an important variable in group-centered classes was the students' acceptance of responsibility for learning. He compared traditional classes to two classes in which there were no examinations, no lectures, and no assigned readings. Students in the experimental classes decided what reading they would do, what class procedure would be used, what they would hand in, and how they would be graded, so that they had even more power than had previous experimental groups. At the end of the course, these classes, as compared to the control group, 1) felt the course was more valuable, 2) showed greater interest in psychology, and 3) tended to give more dynamic, motivational analyses of a problem of behavior.

But giving students power can't work if students will not accept responsibility; so Patton also obtained individual measures of acceptance of responsibility within the experimental classes. As hypothesized, he found that the degree to which the student accepted responsibility was positively correlated with gain in psychological knowledge, gain in ability to apply psychology, interest in it, and rating of the value of the course.

Gibb and Gibb (1952) reported that students who were taught by their "participative-action" method were significantly superior to students taught by traditional lecture-discussion methods in role flexibility and self-insight. In the participative-action method class, activities centered around "sub-grouping methods designed to increase effective group participation." The instructor, who played a constantly diminishing role in the decisions and activities of the group, gave training in role playing, group goal setting, problem centering, distributive leadership, evalution of individual performance by intra-group ratings, process observing, and group selection, evaluation and revision of class activities.

Gibb and Gibb also provide support for the assumption that group-centered teaching can facilitate development of group membership skills. They found that in nonclassroom groups the participative-action students were rated higher than other students in leadership, likableness, and the group membership skills. Di Vesta's results tend to support this (1954), and Anderson and Kelly (1954) report that members of student-centered groups are characterized by positive attitudes toward themselves as participants.

Additional evidence for the effectiveness of small group discussion is cited in Chapter 12, "Project Methods and Independent Study." A number of studies suggest that small group discussion without a teacher present can be an effective educational method.

Another bit of support for less directive teaching is Thistlethwaite's finding (1959) that there is a significant negative correlation between a college's productivity of Ph.D.'s in natural science and the directiveness of teaching methods used. His finding (1960, p. 67) of a positive correlation for National Merit Scholars between their desire to learn and the flexibility and permissiveness of their teachers lends additional support to student-centered teaching.

In one of our own studies (McKeachie et al., 1978) instructors whose students did best on achievement tests of critical thinking (with intelligence controlled) tended to be described as follows: "He listened attentively to what class members had to say." "He was friendly." "He was permissive and flexible." "He explained the reason for criticism." "Things are explained clearly." "He is skillful in observing student reactions." Both the Thistlethwaite and these results, then, support the value of student-centered teaching for motivation and critical thinking.

Student-Centered Teaching: Conclusions

The results of the spate of research on student-centered teaching methods support the theory with which this discussion began. I had suggested that student-centered teaching might be ineffective in achieving lower-order cognitive objectives. There seem to be few instances of such a loss. Students apparently can get information from textbooks as well as from the instructor. But I had also predicted that any superiority of student-centered discussion methods would be revealed in higher level incomes. As Table 5–2 indicates, differences in ability to apply concepts, in attitudes, in motivation, or in group membership skills have been found between discussion techniques emphasizing freer student participation compared with discussion with greater instructor dominance. The differences favor student-centered methods.

TABLE 5–2

Reference	Course	Student-Centered vs. Instructor-Centered Criteria		
		Factual Exam	*Higher Exam Cognitive*	*Attitude, Motivation*
Faw (1949)	Psychology	*S		S
Asch (1951)	Psychology	*I		S
Deignan (1956)	Psychology			S
Bovard (1951a & b)	Psychology		S	S
McKeachie (1951)	Psychology		S	S&I
Patton (1955)	Psychology		S	*S
Carpenter (1959) & Davage (1958; 1959)	Psychology	*S	*S	*S
Anderson & Kelly (1954)	Psychology			S
McKeachie (1954)	Psychology			S
Wieder (1954)	Psychology			S
Guetzkow, Kelly, & McKeachie (1954)	Gen. Psych.	I		S

Reference	Course	Student-Centered vs. Instructor-Centered Criteria		
		Factual Exam	_Higher Cognitive_	_Attitude, Motivation_
Bills (1952)	Gen. Psych.	I		*S
Lyle (1958)	Gen. Psych.	I	S	
Perkins (1950)				S
Gibb & Gibb (1952)	Gen. Psych.			*S
Johnson & Smith (1953)	Intro. Psych.			S (2 classes)
Smith (1954)	Intro. Psych.			
Maloney (1956)	Educ. Psych.			S
Rasmussen (1956)	Educ. Psych.			S
Moore & Popham (1959)	Educ. Psych.			S
Landsman (1950)	Human Development			S
Di Vesta (1954)	Human Relations			S
Slomowitz (1955)	Grad. Counseling			S
Krumboltz & Farquhar (1957)	"How to Study Course"			
Burke	College Freshman Orientation	I		
Jenkins (1952)	English			
Wispe (1951)	Social Relations	ATI		
Ashmus & Haigh (1952); Haigh & Schmidt (1956)	Child and Adolescent Psych.			S
Zeleny (1940)	Sociology			S

I   = Instructor-Centered Superior
S   = Student-Centered Superior
ATI = Attribute-Treatment Interaction
*   = Difference significant at .05 level or better. All other results are the actual direction of the difference in the experiment.

The choice of instructor-centered vs. student-centered discussion thus appears to depend upon your goals. The more highly you value outcomes going beyond knowledge acquisition, the more likely that you will prefer student-centered methods.

SUPPLEMENTARY READING

R. D. Mann, S. M. Arnold, J. Binder, S. Cytrynbaum, B. M. Newman, B. Ringwald, J. Ringwald, and R. Rosenwein, *The college classroom: conflict, change, and learning* (New York, Wiley, 1970).

CHAPTER 6 ⫽ *Six Roles of Teachers*

There are many varieties of discussion. Some discussions primarily involve group problem solving; some are gripe sessions; some may be pep meetings; some may provide practice in integrating and applying information gained from textbooks or lectures. The instructor's role will vary depending upon which of these or other functions the discussion is serving. The roles are most apparent in discussion classes, but every class places demands upon teacher behavior which result in role behavior that has much in common whatever teaching method is used.

Solomon Cytrynbaum, working with my colleague Richard Mann in our research on college teaching, has suggested the following categorization of teacher roles:*

1. The teacher as expert.
2. The teacher as formal authority.
3. The teacher as socializing agent.
4. The teacher as facilitator.
5. The teacher as ego ideal.
6. The teacher as person.

He describes them as follows:

The Teacher as Expert

"Looked at from one perspective, the teacher is connected to the students in his classroom because to some extent and in some form or other he stands before them as an expert. The core of his goal is to transmit whatever information, analytic perspectives, or critical viewpoints he wishes

* The following sections in this chapter are excerpted from W. McKeachie, J. Milholland, and R. Mann et al., *Research on the characteristics of effective teaching.* Final Report to the Bureau of Research, Office of Education, on Project No. 05950, Grant No. OE–4–10–001, Dept. of Psychology, University of Michigan, Ann Arbor, 1968. A more accessible and detailed account may be found in R. D. Mann et al., *The college classroom* (New York: Wiley, 1970).

the students to acquire in that course. His relevance for that situation flows directly from the fact that he knows something the students do not know yet. Whether his expertise be displayed by means of a lecture, by means of answering questions, or by the act of correcting or validating what a student has said, his interests revolve around the effort to achieve one or more of what Bloom has described as the educational objectives within the cognitive domain.

"To complete the picture, we must ask about the roles and activities of the student while he is connected with the teacher as expert. While the student in the large lecture course relates to the teacher as expert primarily by taking notes, the student's activities are not necessarily passive and accepting. Whether the student is asking a highly technical question or is quarreling with a teacher over how to prove a particular Euclidian theorem, he is operating within the ground rules of this aspect of total task if he is at that moment responding to the teacher in his capacity as expert. The student's response may include uncertainty ("What did you say the three causes of the Peloponnesian War were?") or discouragement ("I just can't get this stuff.") or any of a number of emotions. It is simply a matter of convenience to note first how the classroom interaction might look when all is going relatively smoothly.

"Beyond specifying the kinds of goals and activities which characterize this aspect of the total task, it might be useful to note some of the satisfactions and motives which propel and sustain these activities. Perhaps the core of the matter is best approached by way of the concept of competence. For the teacher the issue of competence includes both his ability to comprehend and organize the relevant intellectual material and his capacity to present this material clearly and convincingly. Questions of the teacher's ability to remain well informed on new developments in his area, as well as his ability to make creative and critical judgments concerning the main trends in his field, bear directly upon the teacher's competence as an expert. From the student's perspective the issue of competence is no less relevant. One may wish to refer to the student's curiosity or to his intrinsic love of knowledge, or one may wish, in the line of analysis suggested by McClelland to consider the student's need for achievement, which in this case would center around his concern for meeting his own internal standards of excellence with respect to the mastery of the relevant intellectual material. However, it is well to remember that this and each other aspect of the total task is sustained not only by positive or approach motivation but by negative or avoidance motivation as well. One need only think back to the experience of sitting in a lecture hall listening to words whose meaning seemed totally beyond one's grasp to know that the fear of appearing stupid to others and to oneself makes its contribution to the college classroom. Not only are the students chasing after the goal of confidence and greater knowledge; they are seeking to avoid one of the many disasters inherent in the process of education—the realization that one is over one's head, that certain kinds of information cannot be acquired with a reasonable expenditure of effort. By the same token, it would be misleading to assert that the teacher is driven only by the positive motivation of wishing to be competent in his own eyes. It would seem fair to assume that no teacher can indefinitely reveal his ignorance or his lack of preparation without experiencing shame and discomfort in dealing with his students.

The Teacher as Formal Authority

"The second aspect of the task is defined by a series of activities and functions in which the teacher serves in the capacity of formal authority. Viewed from the perspective of the larger social structure within which the college classroom is located, the teacher is an agent not only of instruction but of control and evaluation. The Registrar's office expects the grade sheet within some number of hours after the final examination. Beyond certain poorly defined limits one class may not disrupt the activities of another, nor may one student disrupt the learning of another student. Assignments, standards of excellence, and deadlines are all matters of concern, however they may be resolved. The pressures upon the teacher to perform the traditional functions of the formal authority come from many sources. Future employers, professional schools, and Deans' offices all express some need for a meaningful and averageable estimate of the student's performance.

"Some educators view the grading system as a deterrent to self-deception regarding one's ability or one's performance; others seem to view it as the ultimate weapon against the students' inherent slothfulness. Beyond noting these functions it may be useful to remember that, given a choice, most people would rather be the evaluator than the evaluated, and would rather be one up than one down. Even if one intends to be "the good guy" and delegate or deny one's power, it is relevant that one enters the situation with one's power clearly established and institutionalized.

"We would not wish to imply by the above remarks that the teacher's activities and his capacity as formal authority serve only the institution and/or the needs of the teacher. Given the traditional institutional structure within which the student operates, it is very much in the students' interest to know what the teacher expects and what the teacher will reward. And even if the traditional educational structure were removed, there may well be sound pedagogical reasons why learning is more effective in an interpersonal situation where the students ascribe legitimacy and power to a teacher, who then would proceed to make clear demands and to distribute objectively based rewards for excellence. However one feels about the latter point, it is at least true that, given the existence and consequences of the grade sheet, many of the students' concerns center around the dual emphasis on the assignment and the evaluation of the students' intellectual activity.

"We would include within the activities relevant to the teacher as formal authority all those instances of moment-by-moment control over the classroom which derive ultimately from the teacher's power to banish the student from the classroom in the interest of maintaining an environment in which the other students could learn. While this ultimate power might never be invoked, the fact remains that it is typically within the teacher's power to define what is relevant for class discussion, who shall speak in class, and what kinds of behavior are unacceptably disruptive. It follows, then, that we would include within the set of activities initiated by students within this definition of the task not only the familiar requests for clarity regarding assignments and grades but also those activities which address the issue of the teacher's control over the classroom interaction. Students may indicate their acceptance of this control by requesting permission to speak or by complaining about the irrelevance of other students' digressions, or by efforts during office hours to have the teacher control a particularly annoying fellow class member.

"We have already discussed several of the pressures which can impel the teacher to take over various functions of the formal authority, and we have implied that among the teacher's fears in the classroom one often finds the fear of "losing control of the class." It does not take much experience with college classrooms to recognize that some students are motivated by their desire for a good grade. While some teachers seem to spurn this source of the students' motivation, referring to it as "extrinsic" motivation or "grade grubbing," their scorn often conveys the impression that they feel capable of making somewhat deeper interpretations regarding the underlying dependency or passivity of the students in their classes. There is little doubt that a lifetime of educational experience has suggested to some students either that the teachers know best or that it is the better part of wisdom to act as if they did. Be that as it may, it is in our interest here to indicate those other forces which impel students to want the teacher to fulfill his functions as formal authority. These forces vary considerably from student to student. When, for whatever reason, the student has little energy available for a particular course, to have a teacher specify clearly what is expected often seems far preferable to having a teacher create an open-ended situation in which the student feels guilty for anything less than total absorption in the course. Even students who will eventually find other sources of motivation sometimes find it useful to focus initially upon the teacher's demands and standards. To emphasize that there are other motives than dependency which underlie the student's involvement with the teacher as formal authority is not to deny the relevance of dependency needs among college students. Nor would we deny that there are students who stubbornly cling to the notion that the teacher's evaluations constitute the sole criterion of success or failure. Our intention in the above discussion has been simply to indicate that there are many sources for such student activities as attempting to clarify what is expected, attempting to anticipate what will be on the final exam, and attempting to use the teacher as the final arbiter of what is acceptable classroom behavior.

The Teacher as Socializing Agent

"The third aspect of the task facing the classroom can be understood only if one realizes two things about the context in which education takes place. First, the teacher is not only in possession of certain intellectual material; he is also a member of various overlapping collectivities with respect to which the students are either outsiders or marginal members. Furthermore, the goals toward which the students are striving typically extend in time far beyond the particular classroom and the particular course. The teacher is a member of the community of scholars as accredited by a particular professional and academic discipline, and he is, as well, a member of an institution that may be highly relevant to the occupational aspirations of a given student. The teacher resembles in some sense the gatekeeper, the one who does or does not pass the individual student along to the next plateau or the next screening process. It is soon apparent to the students that acceptability within the standards of the discipline or even within the standards of the community of intellectuals involves more than the ability to master the intellectual material.

"If we wish to talk seriously about the actual state of affairs in American education, and not simply about how it should be, we must realize that many students are discouraged from being majors in a given department or from going on to graduate work because individual faculty members operate on the assumption that acceptability involves matters of temperament, value commitment, and many other factors. When the faculty member tells the student that going on in his field does not seem to be that student's "cup of tea," he may be responding every bit as much to the student's conception of the good life as to his capacity for intellectual attainment. In a very real sense a college teacher is a recruiting officer whose job includes encouraging, discouraging, and training students to "go on."

"To the extent that undergraduate programs are adapted to this aspect of college education, they tend to become highly "pre-professional." The student is encouraged to take courses which would be useful to him in graduate school. He is engaged in discussions of the underlying commitment to science or humanism or beauty which seems to the faculty member to be a necessary condition for acceptance into training programs at a higher level. But we should not overlook the socializing activities of the teacher whose relevant reference group is the more broadly defined community of scholars. While a particular teacher may shun the more explicit forms of creating "little graduate students," he may feel very strongly about the extent to which the university is an appropriate place only for those who share their political or social values.

"From the student's perspective, the potential letter of recommendation may be a more salient reward to be obtained from the teacher than the grade in that one course. Some students declare that they would like to get into the world, however broadly or narrowly defined, inhabited by the teacher; that is, students sense that they would like to test out whether they could get in, or whether it would be satisfying if they attempted to move in that direction. For understandable reasons students may have mixed emotions about the fact that the teacher controls access to further training and membership in "the elect." Some may seize eagerly upon any opportunity to join with the faculty member as junior members of the circle while others may resist any attempt on the teacher's part to ensnare them into the pre-professional pathway. In either case they are contending with the issue of the teacher as socializing agent.

"The students make their contribution to the establishment of this aspect of the total task. For many students, to imagine their future in terms of a particular occupational goal is to crystallize their still-developing interests and passions; for others, it makes concrete and reachable a future that assures them the necessities and pleasures of life. And then there are many students who are motivated primarily by their alienation from or rejection of the life style associated with their parents, their community, or their peers.

"Thus the teacher and the students may in various ways be bound together within the socialization process. For the student to try on the discipline or profession which the teacher represents may involve him in the acquisition of sacred artifacts or the awkward mimicry of an accepted intellectual pose. Fortunately for the student most teachers overlook these ungainly beginnings. A faculty member may remark to a colleague that such and such a bright undergraduate seems to be "coming into the field," although he may feel constrained to conceal his sense of pleasure at this indication that his field has proved capable of attracting yet another valuable recruit.

The Teacher as Facilitator

"Different teachers tend to conceive of the most troublesome impediments to learning in different ways. Some view the student as capable of productive intellectual effort only to the extent that such impediments as fear of failure, self-abasement in the face of authority, or discouragement in the face of excessively high standards are removed. Others, who operate more like administrators than like therapists, address themselves to the situational impediments: the students do not know how to use the library system; they find it difficult, without assistance, to gain access to the field experiences which would make their intellectual work more salient; or they need someone to fight for them in their battle for ungraded or more socially relevant courses. In whatever form it takes it is clear that the teacher as facilitator tends to respond primarily to the student's own definition of his goals. The student's goals may be quite divergent from the teacher's goals, but then for one person to facilitate the learning and development of another often involves a recognition of the substantial differences between individuals in terms of what they value and what they are seeking. If we were to capture the pedagogical fervor which often underlies some teachers who strongly emphasize the facilitator functions, we would note the teacher's rejection of any effort to "impose" his answers and even his questions upon the students who need more than anything else to develop questions and answers that are relevant to their own lives. The prototypic behaviors associated with the teacher as facilitator would include a fair amount of listening and efforts on the teacher's part to clarify in everyone's mind what a particular student is trying to say.

"The student, or, more properly, that aspect of all students which connects with the teacher as facilitator may be characterized as one whose personal agenda includes not only finding out more about the course material but also finding out more about himself. Thus the student asks: "What am I interested in? What am I good at? What are my ideas about a particular event or body of knowledge? Why am I in this classroom?" One senses here that the student's performance in class is partly expressive, driven by a need to articulate new ideas and to develop some sense of ownership vis-à-vis old and borrowed knowledge. Probably the most relevant words within this aspect of teaching and learning are creativity and independence. Over and over again the students test out in relation to the teacher whether they can be creative, as opposed to restricted within the teacher's definition of what is appropriate; and independent, as opposed to functioning as the perfect robot. However, the path to functioning creatively and independently turns out to have snares and pitfalls which have nothing to do with the teacher. Some have to do with the inherent difficulty of the material or with the difficulty of gaining access to it; some have to do with the pre-existing limitations or immaturities of the particular learner.

"There are few interpersonal dramas more intricate than the one created by a student who wishes help but only if it entails no loss of independence on his part. The teacher may often sense that the student, hidden among the various efforts to appear supremely confident and self-reliant, is trying to tell him that he is having a hard time getting started on a paper, that he suffers from recurrent perceptions of himself as stupid, or that he is far more anxious than he seems about how the teacher will receive the fruits of his labor. The teacher often feels caught in the cross-currents between wanting to respond to the pleas and wanting to preserve whatever mutual respect had thus far developed. The point we make here is that the pressures on the teacher to perform as facilitator may begin with pressures to remove various constraints, but the situation often moves to the point where to facilitate is to assist a student over the real and imaginary barriers which block him from his goals. But here, as well, the pressures are complex. As the history of man has indicated in numerous arenas, unremitting oppression is sometimes easier to bear than conditional autonomy. Thus many of the pressures on the teacher test either what limits he places upon the students' freedom or whether the teacher, despite his apparent openness, is basically patronizing or manipulating the students. The teachers do not always pass these tests, and one sometimes wonders whether any human being could pass some of the tests constructed by students. It is clear that from the perspective of the student as well as from that of the teacher, it is not unusual to find intense and mixed feelings regarding the desirability of granting or achieving freedom.

The Teacher as Ego Ideal

"Thus far we have described the teacher in his capacities as expert, formal authority, socializing agent, and facilitator. We would turn now to an aspect of the teacher's total function which may or may not overlap with any or all of the previously discussed aspects of teaching. We would point here to the fact that the teacher may play an essentially heroic or charismatic role in the classroom and in so doing may end up serving in the capacity of ego ideal for the student Some teachers will accomplish this by emphasizing their expertise, and some will accomplish it by emphasizing their high status within the student's chosen field, but clearly it is possible for a teacher to play the role of expert or socializing agent without becoming in any meaningful sense a part of the students' ideal. Perhaps the key attributes of the teacher as ego ideal are his commitment, or, as it is sometimes referred to, his enthusiasm. Some teachers who function primarily as facilitators convey, by their devotion to an underlying educational philosophy and by their capacity to be patient and helpful, certain qualities which cause some students to identify strongly with them. We cite this particular example because it is all too easy to associate the ego ideal with the flamboyant lecturer whose performances amount to an intellectual and interpersonal _tour de force_.

"Viewed from the most general perspective, it would seem that one very important cue to which students respond when they accept their teacher as an ego ideal is any indication that the teacher enjoys what he is doing. Not only does he evidently enjoy teaching, but he seems to find something in that situation which is personally liberating. He seems to have more than enough energy for the task at hand, more than enough self-confidence, and a belief that the activity or the ideas involved are sufficiently worthwhile to care deeply about them. What this suggests is that an important aspect of being a teacher is the extent to which one's values or one's ideals are engaged. Why do some students report that the enthusiasm of a particular teacher was contagious and caused them to work unusually hard in that course? One answer might be that students and teachers alike are striving to make their life and the activities in which they engage congruent with their developing sense of what is important and what is satisfying. The presence of a person who can so unconflictedly involve himself in a particular body of ideas or a particular kind of teaching sets in motion various responses; some students are alienated by the teacher's exuberance, some are envious and resentful, but some find in that teacher at that moment someone with whom they can identify and who can serve for them as an ideal.

"Faculty members tend to be rather uncharitable about those of their colleagues who attract large numbers of students to their lectures and usually they allege that the consequences of the teacher's activities must be integral to the cause of his performance. That is, since he attracts so many students, he must be doing anything and everything to attract students. He must be a showman or an entertainer, he must be driven by a somewhat excessive desire to have students identify with him. The point here is not that these inferences are always wrong, but rather that they are usually quite incomplete. One must ask what the satisfactions are for the teacher who is functioning as ego ideal. Teachers have internal audiences, composed of significant others whose standards of judgment are important to them. One reason why a particular teacher's performance may be in fact so attractive for others is that the performance also satisfies the teacher's own standards of excellence, and thus one part of his entire performance involves the communication of his pleasure with himself. He acts as if he feels brilliant, more fully alive, more patient and sensitive, i.e., capable of satisfying whatever standards of self-judgment are applicable at that moment.

The Teacher as Person

"The sixth and last aspect of the teacher-student relationship which we would like to isolate and discuss involves the development of a mutually validating relationship. Beyond the fact that the teacher knows more about the field than the student, beyond the fact that the teacher has certain rights and duties which flow from his position in the larger system, beyond the fact that the teacher is a gatekeeper to the various collectivities of which he is a part, beyond the fact that the teacher can sometimes be of use to the student who is formulating and pursuing his own goals, and beyond the fact that the teacher can upon occasion find the energy and skill to satisfy his own standards of excellence, beyond all these facts remains the inescapable fact that the teacher is also a person. The array of goals toward which the teacher strives is not completely accounted for by referring to the fact that he is the teacher. Every social role places constraint upon the extent to which personal gratifications may be obtained within that relationship, without at the same time destroying the foundations of the role or relationship itself. If the new teacher takes too seriously the implications of various snide remarks to the effect that teacher X "just wants to be liked by all his students," he might get the impression that wanting to be liked is out of bounds if one wishes at the same time to be a teacher. One might be tempted to conclude that being a good teacher and being liked are incompatible goals, but it would seem more appropriate to conclude that there may be limits beyond which wanting to be liked will impair a teacher's performance. But what about within those limits?

"We would allege that the teacher and the students alike have a fundamental interest in having themselves, and not simply their course-related selves, validated within the relationship that is developing in the classroom. Basic human and interpersonal issues, issues of trust and misperception, created by people who want to be seen as similar in some respects, or who want to be respected although dissimilar, issues of trustworthiness and affection—in short, the full range of human needs—are very much a part of the classroom.

"Consider the efforts by teachers and students to indicate that they continue to exist beyond the classroom. The implication is that each is telling the other that if he continues to be seen solely in terms of his activities within the classroom then the relationship cannot help but remain a highly limited and less than ideal arrangement. Teachers sneak in little anecdotes about their own days as students or their families or their political activities. Students allude to their summer vacations and their weekends and their religion and their skirmishes with the law. Each is involved in a process of asserting that he would like more of himself to be validated than simply that part of him which joins with the others in the pursuit of the course goals.

"The other parts of oneself, for both the teacher and the students, are not simply those parts which are outside the classroom. Equally important are those feelings and reactions which, while not explicitly part of the agenda for class discussion, press upon one's consciousness. Thus an individual in the classroom may be impelled to break through the task-oriented discussion to comment upon an absurdity which has just occurred to him or to express irritation or a sudden burst of pleasure. Each such attempt is a commentary upon the extent to which the speaker wishes to expand the range of legitimate activity to include other more subjective or emotional reactions to what is going on.

"We would not want to leave the impression that these communications of emotion and "outside-the-class" identity are irrelevant to the manifest task of teaching and learning. If one of the latent goals of the teacher as ego ideal is to convey the relevance of the course material to what is worthwhile and exciting in life, the latent function of the teacher as person is to convey that the intellectual matters under discussion are not irrelevant to the conduct of a life that is within the range of the students in the class. To the extent that the teacher can convey how he came to be interested in these matters, or how his interests are sustained by their application to issues of concern to him in his "everyday life," the student can come to understand the relevance of the teacher's career and knowledge to the student's own interests and personal needs. While one can imagine that a passionate and thoroughly admirable professor may inspire students to join the quest for his version of the Holy Grail, one can also imagine that students are affected by hearing of the haphazard route by which some academics found their way into the field. Some of the reasons why a career is chosen or an interest sustained are far from the stylized versions selected for inclusion in the "Lives of Great Men" mythologies. Watson's route to the formulation of a model for the DNA molecule is full of recognizable human motives and chance occurrences: an unwillingness to study certain fields of mathematics, personal friendships, the coincidences of time and place, and so forth. One senses in his narrative, as in the performance of many teachers in their capacity as persons, that even marvelous achievements are attainable when one hears how large a role good fortune and human frailty have played all along the way. One also senses in such performances a real reluctance to convey only the admirable parts of the process, as if the teacher (or Watson) were impelled not to create a myth when in fact reality is far more humorous (and attractive) than the myth of the genius striking directly toward the Nobel Prize could ever be. Thus the teacher as person is not only addressing his own need to recognize the self he is portraying by his performance. He is also performing a vital task of puncturing the various mythic constructions which students may develop, and the net effect of this is both to decrease the awe in which he is held and to increase the extent to which his interests reveal him to be an ordinary mortal in pursuit of a recognizable and manageable set of goals.

"Furthermore, as the teacher begins to make possible these kinds of information about himself he is also enabling the student to be "all there" and to work on the integration of his disparate elements in an accepting or trust-inducing interpersonal environment.

"Table 6–1 summarizes some of the contrasting goals and prototypic behaviors which characterize each of the six aspects of the teacher's total function."

TABLE 6–1

The Teacher's Roles	Major Goals	Characteristic Skills	Major Sources of Student Motivation (and Fear)
Expert	To transmit information, the concepts and perspectives of the field	Listening, scholarly preparation, class organization and presentation of material: answering questions	Curiosity, need for achievement; intrinsic interest in content (fear of being/appearing stupid; fear of being snowed)
Formal authority	To set goals and procedures for reaching goals	Defining structure, and standards of excellence; evaluating performance	Dependency; getting a good grade (fear of flunking, of being lost and pursuing irrelevant activities)
Socializing agent	To clarify goals and career paths beyond the course; to prepare students for these	Clarifying rewards and demands of the major, the field, and academic	Need to clarify one's interests and calling; desire to be "in" (fear of being rejected by field or having options reduced)

TABLE 6–1 (Cont.)

The Teacher's Roles	Major Goals	Characteristic Skills	Major Sources of Student Motivation (and Fear)
Facilitator	To promote creativity and growth in student's own terms; to help overcome obstacles to learning	Bringing students out, sharpening their awareness of their interests and skills; to use insight and problem solving to help students reach goals, avoid blocks	Self-discovery and clarification to grow in desired direction (fear of being/becoming a puppet or grade-grubber; fear of not developing a clear and useful identity)
Ego ideal	To convey the excitement and value of intellectual inquiry in a given field of study	Demonstrating the ultimate worthwhileness of, or personal commitment to one's material/educational goals	The desire to be turned on; the desire for a model, a personification of one's ideals (fear of being bored, unmoved, and cynical)
Person	To convey the full range of human needs and skills relevant to and sustained by one's intellectual activity; to be validated as a human being; to validate the student	Being self-revealing in ways which clarify one's totality beyond the task at hand; being trustworthy and warm enough to encourage students to be open as well	The desire to be known as more than a student; the desire to have one's life cohere (the fear of being ignored or treated as a "product")

Basic Skills:
Lecturing, Testing,
and Grading

CHAPTER 7   *Lecturing*

The lecture is probably the oldest teaching method and still the method most widely used in American colleges and universities. Through the ages a great deal of practical wisdom about techniques of lecturing has accumulated. It is probable that the most effective lecturers utilize this accumulated wisdom plus their own talents in ways that are close to maximally effective. Effective lecturers combine the talents of scholar, writer, producer, comedian, showman, and teacher in ways that contribute to student learning. Nevertheless, it is also true that few college professors combine these talents in optimal ways and that even the best lecturers are not always in top form.

Why have lectures survived since the invention of print? Why have they persisted in the face of the intrusions of radio, television, computers, and other media? Is the lecture an effective method of teaching? If it is, under what conditions is it most effective? These questions will be answered not only in the light of research on the lecture as a teaching method, but also in terms of analyses of the information-processing techniques used by students in learning from lectures.

Research on the Effectiveness of Lectures

A large number of studies have compared the effectiveness of lectures with other teaching methods. Table 7–1 shows that when measures of knowledge are used, the lecture proves to be as efficient as other methods. Alternatively, in those experiments involving measures of retention of information after the end of a course, measures of transfer of knowledge to new situations, or measures of problem solving, thinking, or attitude change, or motivation for further learning, the results tend to show differences favoring discussion methods over lecture.

TABLE 7–1 / *Lecture vs. Discussion*

Reference	Course	Factual Exam	Higher Level Cognitive	Attitude Motivation
Spence (1928)	Educ. Psych	*L		
Remmers (1933)	Elem. Psych	L		
Husband (1951)	Gen. Psych	L (5 classes)		
Lifson et al. (1956)	Gen. Psych	L=D		*D
Ruja (1954)	Gen. Psych Philosophy	*L (4 classes) D (2 classes)		
Elliott (1951)	Elem. Psych			D
Casey & Weaver (1956)	Human Devel. & Behavior			D
Beach (1960)	Social Psych	D		*D
Hill (1960)	Anthropology (15 classes)	D		D
Bane (1925)	Education (5 experiments)	L(3) D(2)	*D(5)	
Solomon et al. (1964)	Government (24 classes)	L	D	
Gerberich & Warner (1936)	Government	L		
Barnard (1942)	Science (6 classes)	L	*D	*D
Barnard (1936)	(2 classes)	L=D		
Dawson (1956)	Elem. Soil Sci. (6 classes)	L	D	
Lancaster et al. (1961)	Physics	D		
Warren (1954)	Physics	D		

L = Lecture Superior
D = Discussion Superior
* = Difference significant at .05 level or better. All other results indicate only the direction of difference in the experiment.

For What Are Lectures Effective?

We do not need to lecture when concepts are available in printed form at an appropriate level for our students. In general, print presents information in a form which can be covered more rapidly and in a way more accessible for retrieval than lectures. Students using printed materials can choose their own rate of learning: they can review, they can skip; they can vary the order. The lecturer thus starts with some serious handicaps; however, not all information is available in printed form. For example, most printed sources available to college and university teachers for assignment to students are at least several years out of date by the time they are available for assignments. Lectures are particularly appropriate for helping students get up-to-date information on current research and theories relevant to topics they are studying. Moreover, lecturers may sometimes usefully summarize material scattered over a variety of printed sources, thus providing a more efficient method of conveying information than if students were to be assigned to cover these sources by their own reading. Finally, a lecturer can adapt material to the background and interests of a particular audience—material which in printed form is at a level or in a style not well suited to a particular class.

Lectures also can provide structures to help students read more effectively. In fact the lecture may help students learn to read. Readability of material depends on the expectations brought to material by the reader. Thus, appropriate lectures can build structures and expectations that help students read material in the given subject-matter area more effectively.

Lectures also have indirect values apart from their cognitive content. Many lectures have important motivational functions. By helping students become aware of a problem, of conflicting points of view, or of challenges to ideas they have previously taken for granted, the lecturer can stimulate interest in further learning in an area. Moreover, the lecturer's own attitudes and enthusiasm have an important effect upon student motivation. Research on student ratings of teaching as well as on student learning indicates that the enthusiasm of the lecturer is an important factor in effecting student learning and motivation. Not only is the lecturer a model in terms of motivation and curiosity, the lecturer also models ways of approaching problems, portraying a scholar in action in ways that are difficult for other media or methods of instruction to achieve. In fact there is some evidence suggesting that one of the advantages of live professors is the tendency of people to model themselves after other individuals whom they perceive as living, breathing human beings with characteristics that can be admired and emulated (see Chapter 6, for example).

Finally, there are values in lecturing for professors themselves. While there is little direct evidence on the point, there is certainly anecdotal evidence, as well as supporting psychological theory, suggesting that preparing and delivering a lecture is an important factor in the professor's ability to integrate and retrieve the subject matter.

How Can Lectures Be Improved?

The message of this chapter is that one way of improving lectures is to think about how students process lectures. What are students trying to do during a lecture?

As one looks at students at a lecture and observes their behavior, the most impressive thing one notices is the passive role students have in most classrooms. Some students are having difficulty in staying awake; others are attempting to pass the time as easily as possible by reading other materials, counting lecturer mannerisms, or simply doodling and listening in a relatively effortless manner. Many students are taking notes.

Attention

One of the factors determining students' success in information processing is their ability to attend to the lecture. Attention basically involves focusing of one's cognitions upon those things which are changing, novel, or motivating. We know that individuals have a limited capacity for attending to the varied features of their environment. The individual's total capacity for attention may vary with the degree of activation or motivation. At any one time part of the capacity is devoted to the task at hand (in this case listening to the lecturer), part is monitoring other aspects of the classroom, and part of the attention capacity may be available for other uses—in other words, it is simply spare capacity.

Hartley and Davies' (1978) review notes that studies of the attention of students during lectures find that, typically, attention increases from the beginning of the lecture to ten minutes into the lecture and decreases after that point. They found that after the lecture students recalled 70 percent of the material covered in the first ten minutes, and only 20 percent of the material covered in the last ten minutes.

One of the characteristics of a passive lecture situation in which a lecturer is using few devices to get students to think actively about the content of the lecture is that attention tends to drift. Probably all of us have had the experience of listening to a speaker and finding with a start that we have not heard the speaker for some time because our attention has drifted on to thoughts that are tangential to the lecturer's theme. Bloom's (1953) studies of students' thinking during lectures and discussion indicated that more of students' thoughts were relevant to the content during lectures than during discussions, but that there was less active thinking in lectures than in discussions.

What Can Be Done to Get Attention?

In determining how to allocate attention, students use various strategies. Any lecturer knows that one way of getting attention is to precede the statement by the phrase, "This will be on the test." In addition, students listen for particular words or phrases that indicate to them that something is worth noting and remembering. Statements that enumerate or list are likely to be on tests and thus are likely to be attended to.

Changes in the environment recruit attention. The ability of changes to capture attention can work to the advantage of the lecturer. Variation in pitch, intensity, and pace of the lecture, and visual cues such as gestures, facial expression, movement to the blackboard, the use of demonstrations or audio-visual aids—all of these recruit and maintain attention to the lecture.

Auditory attention is directed to some extent by visual attention. As the eyes move, auditory attention tends to shift as well. Distracting movements in the classroom are thus likely to cause students to fail to recall what the lecturer has said. On the positive side, there is some evidence that students' comprehension is greater when the students can see the speaker's face and lips. Thus attempts of colleges and universities to conserve energy by reducing the lighting level may also reduce the students' abilities to maintain attention and learn from the lecture.

I indicated above that at most times when students are not highly motivated there is spare capacity of attention available. This spare capacity is very likely to be used for daydreaming or other tasks which may become more engrossing than listening to the lecture. Hence motivation is important in holding student attention. Keeping lectures to student interests, giving examples that are vivid and intriguing, building suspense toward a resolution of a conflict—these are all techniques of gaining and holding attention. Anxiety is a motive with potential negative effects. There is a good deal of evidence that students who are high in anxiety about tests are likely to fail to pay attention to the test while they are taking it because they are distracted by thought of failure (Wine, 1971). It seems likely that such anxiety about achievement may also distract a student listening to a lecture. In fact some of the very cues used by the lecturer, such as "this will be on the test," may also cue anxious thoughts about the likelihood of failing the test, about the consequences of failing in college and the resulting disappointment of family. Thus, while heavy emphasis upon tests and grades may cause some students to increase the amount of attention devoted to the lecture, it may also negatively affect others to the degree that their thoughts turn to the consequences of success or failure.

Should Students Take Notes?

Note taking is one of the activities by which students attempt to keep attentive, but note taking is also an aid to memory. "Working memory," or "short term memory," is a term used to describe the fact that one can hold only a given amount of material in mind at one time. When the lecturer presents a succession of new concepts, students' faces begin to show signs of anguish and frustration; some write furiously in their notebooks, while others stop writing in complete discouragement. Note taking thus is dependent upon one's ability, derived from past experience (long term memory), to understand what is being said and to hold it in working memory long enough to write it down. In most cases, when queried about their listening or note-taking habits, students report that they are primarily concerned about getting the gist of the lecture in order to be prepared for an examination. To do this they try to extract significant features from the lecture, to distill some of its meaning.

Hartley and Davies (1978) reviewed the research on note taking and student information processing during lectures. They report that students believe that there are two purposes for taking notes: One is that the process of taking notes will in itself help later recall; the other is that the notes provide external storage of concepts which may be reviewed when needed. The research results indicate some support for both beliefs.

Several studies show that students who take notes remember material better than a control group not taking notes even though the note takers turned in their notes immediately after the lecture. Note taking involves elaboration and transformation of ideas, which increases meaningfulness and retention (Peper and Mayer, 1978; Weiland and Kingbury, 1979). But note taking has costs as well as benefits. Student strategies of note taking differ. Some students take copious notes; others take none. We know that student information processing capacity is limited; that is, people can take in, understand, and store only so much information in any brief period of time. Information will be processed more effectively if the student is actively engaged in analyzing and processing the information rather than passively soaking it up.

Students' ability to process information depends upon the degree to which the information can be integrated or "chunked." No one has great ability at handling large numbers of unrelated items in active memory. Thus when students are in an area in which there are new concepts or when the instructor is using language that is not entirely familiar to the students, students may be processing the lecture word by word or phrase by phrase and lose the sense of a sentence or of a paragraph before the end of the thought is reached. This means that lecturers need to be aware of instances in which new words or concepts are being introduced and to build in greater redundancy as well as pauses during which students can catch up and get appropriate notes.

Snow and Peterson (1980) pointed out that brighter students benefit more from taking notes than less able students. We believe that this is because the less able students cannot, while they write their notes, keep what they hear in their memories, so that their note taking essentially blocks them from processing parts of the lecture. But this is not simply a matter of intelligence; rather a student's ability to maintain materials in memory while taking notes and even to process and think about relationships between one idea and other ideas depends upon the knowledge or cognitive structures the student has available for organizing and relating the material. Thus the background of the student in the area is probably more important than the student's level of intelligence.

Some faculty members hand out prepared notes or encourage the preparation of notes for students to purchase. Hartley's research, as well as that of Annis (1981), suggests that a skeletal outline is helpful to students but with detailed notes students relax into passivity. It is better simply to provide an overall framework which they can fill in by selecting important points and interpreting them in their own words. Because student capacity for information processing is limited and because students cannot stop and go over again a confusing part of a lecture, you need to build more redundancy into your lectures than into writing, and you need to build in pauses where students can catch up and think rather than simply struggle to keep up.

How Do Students Process the Content of a Lecture?

Let us assume that students are allocating attention appropriately to the lecture. This alone, however, does not ensure that the content of the lecture will be understood, remembered, and applied appropriately. Even though students are trying to meet the demands of the situation, they may differ in the ways they go about processing the words that they have heard. Marton and Säljö (1976a,b) and other researchers at the University of Goteborg have used Craik and Lockart's (1972) differentiation of surface versus deep processing to describe differences in the way students go about trying to learn educational materials. Some students process the material as little as possible, simply trying to remember the words the instructor says and doing little beyond this. This would be described by Marton as "surface processing." Other students try to see implications of what the lecturer is saying, try to relate what is currently being said to other information either in the lecture or in their own experience and reading. They elaborate, they translate the instructor's words into their own. They may question. This more thoughtful and more active kind of listening is what Marton and Säljö refer to as "deep processing." Experienced students can probably vary their strategies from verbatim memory to memory of concepts, depending upon the demands of the situation. Obviously there are times when exact recall of what the lecturer said is important, but, in general, "deep processing" is more likely to yield long-term memory and retrieval of the kind of knowledge needed for solving problems.

Strategies of surface processing or deep processing are probably not fixed, and lecturers may be able to help their students process more material at a deep level, and, in addition, help students to learn from lectures more effectively. Pointing out relationships, asking rhetorical questions, or asking questions to be answered by class members are ways of encouraging active thought. Teachers can also ask for examples of how students apply concepts to their own experiences, thus encouraging all students to realize that it is important to try to think about how concepts relate to oneself. One can train students to write better notes by collecting student notes, evaluating the degree to which they summarize, translate, and show relationships as opposed to simply representing more or less verbatim accounts.

Planning the Lecture Series

A typical lecture strives to present a systematic, concise summary of the knowledge to be covered in the day's assignment. Chang, Crombag, van der Drift, and Moonen (1983, p. 21) call this approach "conclusion oriented." _Don't do it!_ The lecturer's task in university teaching is not to be an abstracter of encyclopedias, but to _teach students to learn and think._

I have been a conclusion oriented lecturer for 35 years and I am now trying to move toward a style of lecturing that provides a model of cognitive _activity_ rather than cognitive results. I believe that most of our lectures should involve analyzing materials, formulating problems, developing hypotheses, bringing evidence to bear, criticizing and evaluating alternative solutions—revealing methods of learning and thinking.

One of the implications of the theoretical approach we have taken is that what is an ideal approach to lecturing early in a course is likely to be inappropriate later in the course. As we noted earlier, the way students process verbal material depends on the structures that not only enable them to process bigger and bigger chunks of subject matter but also give them tacit knowledge of the methods, procedures, and conventions used in the field and by you as a lecturer. For, intentionally or not, you are teaching students how to become more skilled in learning from your lectures.

Because this is so, one should at the outset of a course go more slowly, pause to allow students with poor short-term memory to take notes, and give more "everyday" types of examples early in the term. Pausing to write a phrase or sketch a relationship on the blackboard will not only give students a chance to catch up, but also provide visual cues that can serve as points of reference later. Later in the term students should be able to process bigger blocks of material more quickly.

Preparing Your Lecture Notes

One of the security-inducing features of lectures is that one can prepare a lecture with some sense of control over the content and organization of the class period. In lectures the instructor is usually in control, and this sense of controlled structure helps the anxious teacher avoid pure panic.

But no matter how thoroughly one has prepared the subject matter of the lecture, one must still face the problem of how to retrieve and deliver one's insights during the class period. If one has plenty of time and is compulsive, one is tempted to write out the lecture verbatim. Don't! Or if you must (and writing it out may be useful in clarifying your thoughts), don't take a verbatim version into the classroom. Few lecturers can read a lecture so well that students stay awake and interested.

At the same time few teachers can deliver a lecture with no cues at all. Hence you will ordinarily lecture from notes. Most lecturers use an outline or a sequence of cue words and phrases.

Day (1980) has studied lecture notes used by professors at over 75 colleges and universities. She notes that extensive notes take the instructor out of eye contact with students so that students fall into a passive, nonquestioning role. Day suggests the use of graphic representations to increase teaching flexibility and spontaneity. Tree diagrams, computer flow charts, or network models enable a teacher to have at hand a representation of the structure that permits one to answer questions without losing track of the relationship of the question to the lecture organization. Pictorial representations using arrows, faces, Venn diagrams, or drawings that symbolize important concepts may not only provide cues for the instructor but can also be placed on the blackboard to provide additional cues for students. Color coding your notes with procedural directions to yourself also helps. I have a tendency to run overtime, so I put time cues in the margin to remind me to check. I also put in directions to myself such as,

➤ "Put on blackboard,"—(usually a key concept or relationship)

➤ "Ask students for a show of hands,"

➤ "Put students in pairs to discuss this."

You may not feel at home with all of these possibilities, but some experience with hybrids of graphic and verbal cues will probably facilitate your effectiveness as a lecturer. Whatever your system, indicate *signposts* to tell students what is ahead, *transitions* that tell students when you are finishing one topic and moving to the next, _key points_ or _concepts,_ and _links_ such as "consequently," "therefore," and "because."*

Organization of Lectures

In thinking about lecture organization, most teachers think first about the structure of the subject matter, then try to organize the content in some logical fashion, such as building from specifics to generalization or deriving specific implication from general principles.

Some common organizing principles used by lecturers are: cause to effect; time sequence (for example, stories); parallel organization such as phenomena to theory to evidence; problem to solution; pro versus con to resolution; familiar to unfamiliar; and concept to application.

Leith (1977) has suggested that different subjects are basically different in the ways in which progress is made in the field. Some subjects are organized in a linear or hierarchical fashion in which one concept builds upon a preceding one. In such subjects one must follow a particular sequence of ideas in order to reach a sophisticated level. Other subject matters are organized more nearly in the manner of a spiral or helix in which the path from one level to the next is not linear but rather depends upon accumulating a number of related ideas before the next level can be achieved; and any of the related ideas at one level need not precede other ideas at that level. Still other subject matters are organized in the fashion of networks in which one may start at different points of the network and go in various directions. One may build up a network equally well by starting at any one of a number of places and proceeding through a variety of sequences to arrive at comprehension of the subject matter.

The logical structure of one's subject should be one factor determining the lecture organization, but equally important is the cognitive structure in the students' minds. If we are to teach our students effectively, we need to bridge the gap between the structure in the subject matter and structures in the students' minds. As is indicated in all of the chapters in this book, the learner's mind is not _tabula rasa_. The teacher is not making impressions on a blank slate. Rather our task in teaching is to

---

* These four types of signposts are discussed in the book by George Brown, _Lecturing and explaining_ (London: Methuen, 1979).

reorganize existing student cognitive structures or to add new dimensions or new features to existing structures. Thus the organization of the lecture needs to take account of the student's existing knowledge and expectations as well as the structure of the subject matter.

The Introduction

One suggestion for organization is that the *introduction* of the lecture should point to a gap in the student's existing cognitive structure or should challenge or raise a question about something in the student's existing method of organizing material in order to arouse curiosity (Berlyne, 1954a,b). There is a good deal of research on the role of prequestions in directing attention to features of written texts. Prequestions in the introduction of a lecture may help students to discriminate between more and less important features of lectures. For example, before a lecture on cognitive changes in aging, I ask, "Do you get more or less intelligent as you get older?" "What is a fair test of intelligence for older people?" Such questions may also help to create expectations which will enable the students to allocate their information processing capacity more effectively. If students know what they are expected to learn from a lecture, they learn more of that material (sometimes at the expense of other material; Royer, 1977).

Body of the Lecture

In organizing the *body* of the lecture, the most common error is probably that of trying to include too much. As we have stressed throughout this chapter, students' information-processing capacities are limited, and a lecturer who is expert in the field is likely to overestimate the students' ability to grasp large blocks of material and to see relationships. An explanation that would be perfect for advanced students may be incomprehensible to beginning students. Lecturers very often overload the students' information processing capacity so that they become less able to understand than if fewer points had been presented. David Katz (1950), a pioneer Gestalt psychologist, called this phenomenon "mental dazzle." He suggested that just as too much light causes our eyes to be dazzled so that we cannot see anything, so too, too many new ideas can overload processing capacity so that we cannot understand anything.

It seems likely that students will differ in their ability to benefit from particular kinds of sequences. As Greeno and his colleagues have shown

(Larkin, Heller, and Greeno, 1980), some students do better when they are given a sequence of generalizations first and specific drill and practice sequences second, while other students do better when the specifics lead to generalizations.

Whatever the structure one uses, it is clear from research that highlighting the structure and giving students cues to the nature of organization that one is using is helpful to many students, particularly those who are lower in intelligence or more anxious (Snow and Peterson, 1980). Davis's studies of outstanding lectures (1976) indicated that professors known as outstanding lecturers did two things; they used a simple plan and many examples.

Periodic Summaries Within the Lecture

From our knowledge of students' note-taking behavior and from our theory of information processing, it seems likely that students would be better able to learn from lectures if there were periodic summaries of preceding material. These give students a chance to catch up on material covered when they were not tuned in and also give them a check upon possible misperceptions based upon inadequate or misleading expectations. Moreover, such summaries can help make clear to students transitions from one theme to another so that they are aided in organizing the material not only in their notes but in their minds.

Probably one of the greatest barriers to effective lecturing is the feeling that one must cover the material at all costs. While it may seem irrational to cover material when students are not learning from it, one should not underestimate the compulsion one feels to get through one's lecture notes. A remedy for this compulsion is to put into the lecture notes reminders to oneself to check the students' understanding—both by looking for nonverbal cues of bewilderment or of lack of attention and by raising specific questions that will test the students' understanding.

The Conclusion

In the conclusion of the lecture, one has the opportunity to make up for lapses in the body of the lecture. Encouraging students to formulate questions or asking questions oneself can facilitate understanding and memory. By making the oral headings visible once again, by recapitulating major points, by proposing unanswered questions to be treated in the reading assignments or the future lectures, and by creating an anticipation of the future, the lecturer can help students learn. Having suggested all this, I must admit that my own greatest problem as a lecturer is that I never seem to be ready for the conclusion until it is already past time to dismiss the class.

Lecture and Discussion

Lecture has often been compared in effectiveness with discussion. Since discussion offers the opportunity for a good deal of student activity and feedback, it could, according to theory, be more effective than lecture in developing concepts and problem-solving skills. However, because the rate of transmission of information is slow in discussion classes, I would expect lecture classes to be superior in attaining the objective of teaching knowledge. In this section I propose to review the research comparing lecture and discussion methods and then suggest a combination of both.

Unfortunately, although there have been many research studies of the lecture method as compared to discussion or other methods, not all have used independent measures of the different types of outcomes suggested above. The results of the experiments, however, are generally in line with my hypotheses. For example, using tests of information, Remmers (1933) found slight but nonsignificant differences favoring learning in large lecture groups as compared with that in small (35–40 student) recitation sections. Spence (1928) obtained similar results comparing lecture and discussion technique in classes of over one hundred students. Ruja (1954) found that the lecture was superior to discussion as measured by a test of subject-matter mastery in a general psychology course. In the other two courses in his experiment there were no significant differences in achievement, nor were there differences in changes in adjustment in any of the courses. Similarly, Solomon, Rosenberg, and Bezdek (1964) found that among 24 teachers of evening college courses in American Government those who stressed lectures tended to produce higher achievement on a factual test but not on a test of comprehension. Husband (1951) found no significant difference in achievement of students in large (200 student) lectures versus those in small (50 student) recitation classes, but in five out of six semesters, the lecture group was nonsignificantly superior. In these and other experiments, the information measured by the examination could be obtained from a textbook; in only one was a discussion group smaller than 35 students used.

When we turn to measures of more complex outcomes, the results favor discussion. In one of the earliest comparisons of lecture and discussion, Bane (1925) found little difference between the methods on measures of immediate recall, but a significant superiority for discussion on a measure of delayed recall. Hirschman (1952) compared the effectiveness of presenting written materials followed by discussion and rereading using a measure of concept learning. The reading-discussion method resulted in superior ability to identify examples of the concepts presented.

In quite a different type of experiment Barnard (1942) compared the effectiveness of a lecture-demonstration teaching method with that of a problem-solving developmental discussion in a college science course. The lecture-demonstration method proved superior on a test of specific information, but the discussion method proved to be superior on measures of problem solving and scientific attitude. Likewise Dawson (1956) found problem-solving recitation and lecture-demonstration methods to be equally effective in a course in elementary soil science as measured by a test of recall of specific information, but the problem-solving method was significantly superior as measured by tests of problem-solving abilities.

Other evidence favoring discussion was the experiment of Elliott (Beardslee, Birney, and McKeachie, 1951), who found that students in his discussion groups in elementary psychology became interested in electing more additional courses in psychology than did students in a large lecture. Similarly, Casey and Weaver (1956) found no differences in knowledge of content but superiority in attitudinal outcomes (as measured by the Minnesota Teacher Attitude Inventory) for small discussions as compared to lectures. (Results of studies comparing lecture and discussion are summarized in Table 7–1.)

What this adds up to is the use of lecture for communicating information and modeling problem solving and discussion for practicing problem-solving skills. One way of doing this is to schedule separate lecture and discussion periods. Another is to incorporate both discussion and lecture in the same class period.

Distribution of Lecture and Discussion Time

Many universities and large colleges use a method of distributing class meetings between lectures and discussions. This administrative arrangement is supported by a study in the teaching of psychology in which discussion meetings were substituted for one-third of the lectures (Lifson et al., 1956). There were no significant differences in achievement. However, the partial discussion method, as compared with the all lecture method, resulted in more favorable student attitudes that persisted in a follow-up study two years later.

Warren (1954) compared the effectiveness of one lecture and four recitations to two lectures and three demonstrations per week. In one out of five comparisons the four-recitations plan was superior while the other comparisons found nonsignificant differences. Superior students tended to prefer the two-lecture plan while poorer students did not. On the other hand, in Remmers's comparison (1933) of two lectures and one recitation vs. three recitations, the poorer students tended to do better in the lecture-recitation combination. Students preferred the all-recitation classes. In Klapper's study (1958), most NYU students preferred a combination lecture-discussion method to all lectures or all discussions. Iowa students preferred all group discussion or a combination of lecture and discussion to lectures alone (Becker et al., 1958).

In a course in which the instructors must not only give information but also develop concepts, the use of both lectures and discussions would thus seem to be a logical and popular choice.

Sometimes you will be unable to schedule separate small group discussions. Do not despair. Discussion is possible in large groups. As we shall see in Chapter 20 there are many practical methods for achieving the advantages of discussion in large groups.

The Lecturer: A Summary

What is the role of the lecturer in higher education? The research results I have cited provide little basis for an answer. Nevertheless, they do not contradict, and sometimes they support, my earliest notions that the lecture is sometimes an effective way of communicating information, particularly in classes where variations in student background, ability, or interest make feedback to the lecturer important. We have also shown that the organization and presentation of lectures may influence their effectiveness in achieving application of knowledge or in influencing attitudes. Discussion, however, may be more effective than lecturing in achieving some of the higher level cognitive and attitudinal objectives.

Good lecturers probably do intuitively many of the things we have suggested. Becoming conscious of what is going on in the students' heads as we talk, being alert to feedback from students through their facial expressions, nonverbal behavior, or oral comments, adjusting one's strategies in reference to these cues—these will help the lecturer learn and help students to learn from the lecturer more effectively.

SUPPLEMENTARY READING

A very practical guide to lecturers is George Brown's handy paperback, _Lecturing and explaining_ (London: Methuen, 1980).

CHAPTER 8 *Tests and Examinations*

Most instructors in colleges with traditional grading systems deplore the emphasis students place upon getting a good grade. Usually instructors attempt to minimize this aspect of the course by stating that the important thing is what the students learn, not what grade they make. While such words may be accepted intellectually, motivationally the grade remains the most important aspect of the course for most students. Since grades in large courses are determined to a great degree by test scores, tests are among the most frustrating aspects of the course to many students, and arouse a great deal of overt and covert aggression. If teachers attempt to go beyond the usual practice of asking simply for memory of information from the textbook or lectures, they are immediately deluged with the complaint, "These are the most ambiguous tests I have ever taken!"

Reducing Student Aggression

To most beginning teachers the aggression that students direct against them after a test is very disturbing. It is likely to impair the rapport of the instructor with the class and may actually be a block to learning. Hence, devices for reducing the aggression seem to be worthwhile.

The most obvious solution to the problem is to reduce the frustration involved in taking tests. An aid in this area is to emphasize the contribution the course can make to the long-range goals of the students, so that the need of a good grade is not the only one involved in the situation. Emphasizing the educational and diagnostic value of tests is one application of this principle. Yet, no matter how much the instructor emphasizes long-range goals, the tests are going, in a large measure, to determine the student's goals. Do you want the students to memorize details? Then give the usual memory-of-details test.

The first step in constructing a test is to list your goals for the course. Not all goals can be measured by a test. (New attitudes and interests, for example, are not measured by classroom achievement tests.) Once you have specified objectives you can determine how many test items embody each category of objective. You'll probably be surprised to find out how many of your test items pile up in certain categories.

One way of helping to maintain a balance is to construct a grid, listing objectives along the side of the page and content areas along the top. If you then tally items as you write them, you can monitor the degree to which your test adequately samples the objectives and content desired.

Because some course examinations emphasize recall of facts, many students demand _teaching_ that emphasizes memorization of facts. One student wrote on a slip evaluating me, "The instructor is very interesting and worthwhile, but I have rated him low because he doesn't give us enough facts. The sort of job I get will depend on my grades, and I have little chance of beating other students out for an A unless I can get a couple of pages of notes each period."

Students may object at first to tests requiring them to think, but if you emphasize that the tests will measure the students' abilities to use their knowledge, you can greatly influence their goals in the course. This is indicated by a student comment we received: "More of the course should be like the tests. They make us apply what we've learned." Marton and Säljö (1976b) showed that questions demanding understanding rather than memory of detailed facts resulted in differing styles of studying for later tests and better retention.

Admittedly it is more difficult to devise measures of the more complex, higher-level objectives. Yet the very effort to do so will, I believe, have an influence on student motivation and learning. Moreover, consideration of these objectives may help you break out of the conventional forms of testing. For example, in my classes in introductory psychology, the desired goals include developing greater curiosity about behavior, awareness of dimensions of behavior that might ordinarily be ignored, and increased ability to describe and analyze behavior objectively. To get at this I have sometimes used a film as a stimulus, with the test questions having to do with the students' reactions to the film; or I have asked students to leave the classroom for fifteen minutes and then return and report on some interesting behavior they have observed. I have brought in collections of journals and asked students to find an article of interest and to write their reactions to it. I have asked for analyses of newspaper items to get at the degree to which students can read critically. Using materials with somewhat greater apparent relevance to course objectives than typical test items is more fun for the students taking the test—and more fun to grade.

When to Test

Because tests are so important in operationalizing goals and influencing student methods of learning, I like to give a test early in the term—after the third or fourth week of a fourteen-week semester. To reduce the stress, I weight the test very little in determining the final grade, perhaps a third of a comparable hour test given later in the term. Such an early test gets students started, rather than delaying their studying until the conventional midterm examination, and it will help you to identify problems early while they are still remediable. Thus, this test should demand the style of learning you expect and needs to be constructed carefully, even though its purpose is more motivational and diagnostic than evaluative.

I usually also give midterm and final examinations, but the amount and frequency of tests should depend upon the background of your students. In a freshman course in an area new to students, frequent short tests early in the term facilitate learning, as demonstrated in the Keller Plan (see Chapter 21). Generally, however, I want to wean students from studying for tests, so that they become lifelong learners who will be able to evaluate their own learning. This implies less frequent testing as learners become more experienced. It probably also implies questions requiring broader integration and more detailed analysis as the learners advance. For this reason my tests are all cumulative; that is, they cover material previously tested as well as material learned since the last test.

Test Construction

This is not the place to engage in an extended discussion of test-construction theory. However, let me confess that from the students' point of view, tests and marks are frequently the most important part of the instructor's job. Because of this, these topics deserve some consideration.

Choosing the Type of Question

The instructor who is about to give an examination is in a conflict situation. There are two time-consuming procedures involved in the administration of an examination: the first is the construction of the examination; the second is the grading. Unfortunately, it appears to be generally true that the examinations that are easiest to construct are the most difficult to grade and vice versa. Essay examinations that can be made up in a few minutes require hours to grade. Multiple-choice examinations, which can be constructed by an experienced item builder at the rate of three to five items an hour, can be corrected at the rate of about twenty to thirty seconds for a sixty-item test. Short-answer examinations fall somewhere between these two extremes.

Teachers often choose questions solely in terms of class size, using multiple-choice tests for large classes, short-answer questions for medium-sized classes, and essay questions for small classes. Class size is obviously an important factor, but I urge that your educational goals take precedence. This almost always implies use of some essay questions, problems, or other questions requiring analysis, integration, or application.

Problems   In mathematics, science, and some other disciplines a test typically consists of problems. The value of problems depends upon the degree to which they elicit the sort of problem-solving skills that are your goals. Some problems are too trite and stereotypic to have much value as indicators of whether or not students understand the steps they are following. In other cases the answer depends to such a large extent on tedious calculations that only a small sample of problems can be tested. In such cases you might provide calculations leading up to a certain point and ask the student to complete the problem or you might use a multiple-choice question about the proper procedure.

Short-answer tests   An example of a short-answer item might be this: "Give one example from your own experience of the concept of elaboration." In responding a student might describe an experience in explaining a concept to another student or in thinking of the relationship of a fact to a general principle.

Such a question is restricted enough that it is not often difficult to judge whether the expected answer is there. Furthermore, such questions can be presented in a format that allows only a small amount of space for the answer. The student's tendency to employ the "shotgun" approach to the examination is thus inhibited. Short-answer questions permit coverage of assigned materials without asking for petty details. Unfortunately, many short-answer questions test only recall of specific facts.

Short-answer questions can get at other than informational outcomes. If you are trying to develop skill in analysis or diagnosis, for
example, you may present case material or description of an experiment
and ask the students what questions they would ask. You can then provide additional information that the students can use in an analysis. Or
a short-answer question can ask students to solve a problem or propose
a hypothesis relevant to information learned earlier. An example is the
following question from a course on the psychology of aging:

> 1. Given the *differences* in ways in which men and women ex-
> perience middle age, and the fact that depression rises as a psy-
> chiatric symptom in middle age, how might the *causes* of the
> depression differ for men and women at this time in life?

Essay tests   Although the short-answer examination is very useful
in certain situations, I would recommend that, if possible, you include
at least one essay question on examinations in most college courses.
Whether or not essay tests are valid measures, experiments indicate that
students study more efficiently for essay-type examinations than for objective tests (Monaco, 1977; McClusky, 1934; d' Ydewalle et al., 1983).

Whatever the values of essay tests as evaluation devices, you should
also take into consideration their potential educational value. Particularly
where the tests can be returned with comments, essay examinations may
give students practice in organized, creative thinking about a subject and
an opportunity to check their thinking against the standards of someone
with more experience and ability in the field. Moreover, they may, as we
suggested earlier, orient students to work toward objectives beyond
memorization of details. Johnson (1975) demonstrated that when marginal comments on earlier tests emphasized creativity, creativity on the
final exam was improved.

Finally, if you read the examinations yourself (or at least some of
them), you get some excellent information on what students are learning.
While the teacher can also learn from students' responses to objective
tests, the impact on the teacher of what students are learning seems to
be greater and more vivid in reading essay tests.

True-false tests   Although true-false examinations are rather easy
to make up, I'm not sure what they measure, and don't advocate their
use. This is partly a concession to student opinion. Students can usually

figure out reasons why any particular item can be either true or false. Because of this, the true-false test tends to enhance the frustration which is inherent in the test-making situation anyway.

   **Multiple-choice tests**   It is improbable that most teachers can adequately measure all their objectives with a test made up entirely of multiple-choice questions. Nonetheless, for some purposes multiple-choice items are useful. They can measure both simple knowledge and precise discrimination. Items need not be entirely verbal. Louis Berman of the University of Illinois, Chicago, has worked out a number of items using cartoons, sketches, graphs, and diagrams, which students feel are more interesting than all-verbal questions. Some students with low verbal ability do better on these questions than on the usual ones.

   Good multiple-choice questions are difficult to construct. (As a matter of fact, the greater your experience in their construction, the more you realize how long it takes per item to construct a reasonably fair, accurate, and inclusive question.) Because of this difficulty, the construction of such items is probably not worthwhile unless they will be administered to several hundred students, either in a single year or in successive years. Here are some useful hints for their construction.

1. Teachers' manuals that are provided for many textbooks contain multiple-choice items. You will not be able to rely on a manual as the source of all your questions, because it will not often contain enough good questions of this sort.

2. A second source of such items is the students themselves. This is not a particularly satisfactory source of test questions because only about 10 percent of the items thus received will be usable. They are typically from obscure passages in reading materials; where they are not, they are apt to be duplicated by many students. However, this technique is a rather successful pedagogical device because it gets the students to read their assignment more analytically. It also gives the instructor a good index of what the students are getting out of the various sections of their reading and gives you a chance to remind them of the goals of the course going beyond memory of details.

3. Item analysis may be useful in improving the questions, but I have found that the best suggestions for improvement came from students themselves in their discussion of the test. It seems almost criminal

to waste this experience with items; therefore I recommend a permanent file. I have found it to be a good procedure to keep items on 5″ × 8″ file cards, one item per card, rather than on sheets of paper. This system permits easy filing and the discard of individual items that have been unsatisfactory without the use of scissors and paste. New items can be filed in the proper subject area. This card size permits revision of the item if it has turned out to be confusing.

4. If you have a problem, but no good distractor (incorrect alternative), give the item in short-answer or essay form and use the students' own responses for alternatives for a later use of the item in multiple-choice form.

5. Multiple-choice questions typically have four or five alternatives. Rather than wasting your and your students' time with extra alternatives that don't test a discrimination that is important, use only as many alternatives as you can construct making meaningful discriminations. Costin (1972) has shown that three-choice items are about as effective as four-choice.

6. For measuring understanding, I like questions that require the student to predict the outcome of the situation rather than those that simply ask the student to label the phenomenon.

7. General rules.
   a. The item as a whole should present a problem of significance in the subject-matter field.
   b. The item as a whole should deal with an important aspect of the subject-matter field, not with a minor element that is of significance only to the expert.
   c. The item as a whole should be phrased in language appropriate to the subject-matter field.
   d. Items that attempt to measure understanding should include an element of novelty, but too much novelty is likely to make the problem too hard. Trick questions should be avoided.

8. Rules for stating the problem.
   a. There must be a single central problem.
   b. The problem should be stated briefly but completely; the problem should not test the student's ability to understand complex sentence structure except when the teacher is deliberately measuring that ability.

   c. The problem should be stated in a positive, not a negative form. Somehow, even intelligent adults often fail to see a "not" in reading a sentence.

   d. It should be possible to understand the problem without reading the alternatives.

   e. Generally speaking, the test is more interesting if the questions are worded in concrete rather than abstract terms. Such items are particularly worthwhile if you wish to measure ability of the student to apply concepts to concrete situations.

9. Rules for developing the suggested solutions.

   a. The suggested wrong answers should represent errors commonly made by the students being tested, not popular misconceptions among the public at large.

   b. The right answer should be unquestionably right, checked by two or three independent experts.

   c. The suggested answers should be as brief as possible.

   d. The position of the right answers should be scattered.

   e. Numerical answers should be placed in numerical order.

   f. Even wrong alternatives should not contain words unfamiliar to students.

   g. Use "All of the above" and "None of the above" rarely. Usually they are tossed in when you can't think of another good distractor.

   h. The right answer should not be given away by irrelevant clues. A few examples of commonly occurring irrelevant clues are: 1) alternatives that include absolute terms such as "always" and "never" are rarely right answers, 2) alternatives that are longer and more elaborate than the others are frequently right answers, 3) if the lead of the item is an incomplete statement, then alternatives that do not complete it grammatically are obviously wrong.*

Even if you don't pre-test the item on students, it is worthwhile to have someone take the test before it is in its final form. If you can persuade a skilled test-taker who doesn't know the subject matter to take the test, you will probably be surprised at how many he or she gets right simply from cues you've provided in the questions.

---

 * Many of the foregoing rules are derived directly or indirectly from notes taken in the "Test Construction" class of Dr. R. M. W. Travers. For a more detailed exposition, see his book, _How to make achievement tests_ (New York: Odyssey Press, 1950).

How Many Questions Should I Use?

Obviously the number of questions depends upon the type and difficulty of question. I prefer to give tests without a time limit, but the constraints of class scheduling usually require that you clear the classroom so that the next class can begin. Thus, you must plan the length of the exam so that even the slower students have time to finish before the end of the period. As a rule of thumb I allow about a minute per item for multiple-choice or fill-in-the-blank items, two minutes per short-answer question requiring more than a sentence answer, ten or fifteen minutes for a limited essay question, and a half-hour to an hour for a broader question requiring more than a page or two to answer.

Instructions to the students   The test instructions should indicate whether or not students are to guess, what the time limit is, and any other directions that define the nature of the expected responses. Emphasizing in the multiple-choice test introduction that the students should choose the *best* answer may help prevent lengthy discussion with the student who can dream up a remote instance in which the correct alternative might be wrong.

In taking a multiple-choice examination, the student has a right to know whether there is a penalty for guessing. For the typical classroom examination, there is no point in a correction for guessing.

Particularly in the case of multiple-choice examinations, I have found that a good morale builder is spending fifteen minutes or so before the first examination in telling the student how to take a multiple-choice quiz.

Some of the points which I make in such a lecture follow:

Taking Multiple-Choice Tests

The student taking a multiple-choice examination is essentially in the same position as a poker player. The object is to get into a position where you are betting on a sure thing. If this is impossible, at least make your bet on the choice where the odds are in your favor. In poker, you are obviously in the strongest position if you know exactly what the opponent has; and in the examination situation, you are also in the strongest position if you know the material. There is no substitute for study. At the same time, it is unlikely you will be absolutely certain of all the right answers. In these cases certain techniques may help.

What I recommend (to the student) is this: Go through the examination a first time and answer all of the items you know. In addition to getting a certain amount of the examination done without wasting too much time on single, difficult items, it is frequently true that going through the complete test once in this way will suggest the answers to questions that might have been difficult had they been answered in serial order. When you have gone through the test once in this fashion, go through it again and answer any questions that are now obvious. There will still usually remain a few questions that have been left unanswered. It is in connection with these that certain tricks may be useful.

First of all, if the item is multiple choice, do not simply guess at this stage of the game. See whether it is not possible to eliminate some of the choices as incorrect. In a four-choice, multiple-choice item, the probabilities of getting the answer right by pure guesswork are one in four; if you can eliminate two of them, your chances are fifty-fifty. So take advantage of the mathematics of the situation.

Once some of the answers are eliminated, there are still better ways of answering the questions than pure guesswork. One of these is to choose the answer that you first thought was right. A second is to choose one of the middle alternatives. If you have no notion at all as to the right answer, and if the "b" or "2" choice is one of the possibilities, use it. There are two reasons for this advice: 1) it gives you a rule of thumb by which you can answer all highly doubtful items, thus eliminating anxiety-building, trial-and-error behavior, and 2) it takes into account instructor behavior in constructing items.

When instructors set out to make up a multiple-choice item, they usually have 1) a bit of information for which they want to test, 2) a notion as to what is the right answer, and 3) one or more "seductive" alternatives. The tendency is, in listing choices, to make the first choice one of the seductive alternatives, the second choice the right answer, and the remaining choices anything else that they can think of. Most instructors have a feeling that the right answer sticks out if it is first or last. Hence the correct answer on instructor-made tests tends to be in the middle.

Once the examination has been answered completely, it is a good idea to go through the whole thing again to check your choices on the various items to make sure that they are the ones you still regard as correct and to make sure that you have made no clerical errors in recording them on the separate answer sheets. In this connection, it is worthwhile to point out the common misconception that, when you change your answers, you usually change from right answers to wrong ones. As a matter of fact Mueller and Wasser (1977) review eighteen studies demonstrating that most students gain more than they lose on changed answers.

Taking essay tests   My instructions for essay exams are simpler. They include the following:

> Outline your answer before writing it. This provides a check against the common error of omitting completely one part of the answer. If a question completely baffles you, start writing on the back of your paper anything you know that could possibly be relevant. This starts your memory functioning and usually you'll soon find that you have some relevant ideas. If you are still at a loss, admit it and write a question you can answer and answer it. Most instructors will give you at least a few points more than if you wrote nothing.

Some will perhaps want to question whether it is wise to give away the secret of examination construction in the way in which this discussion obviously does. The answer to this question depends upon your purposes in giving the examination. If you want to test for "test-taking" ability, you will not want to give the students these hints. If you are interested in eliminating this as a source of variation, an orientation lecture of the kind that we have described is well advised. At any rate, it seems to have the effect of giving the students the notion that you are not out to "outsmart" them, but that you are interested in helping them get as high a grade as their learning warrants. In this connection, it is a good idea to point out to the class that the instructor is not out to trick the student through the use of various kinds of sophistry in the examination, that ordinarily the answer that they think is the right one will be the right one, and that any attempt to read more into a particular answer than initially appeared to be there is a mistake.

I also warn students that their grade will be affected by their writing. Even if I intended not to grade on writing ability, my judgment is negatively influenced when I have to struggle to read poor handwriting or surmount poor grammar and sentence structure. Moreover since I believe that every course is responsible for teaching writing, writing will enter into our grading. It is amazing to me that when I forget to mention writing, the essays are much less readable than when I announce that writing counts. Apparently my students can spell, punctuate, and write clearly if they need to, but don't bother if it isn't expected.

Research by McKeachie, Pollie, and Speisman (1955) and by Smith and Rockett (1958) has demonstrated that on multiple-choice tests the instruction "Feel free to write comments" with blank space by each question for the comments results in higher scores, especially for anxious students.

Administering the Test

Handing out a test should be a simple matter. Usually it is, but in large classes, simple administrative matters can become disasters. It is hard to imagine how angry and upset students can become while waiting only ten minutes for the proctors to finish distributing the test forms. And if this doesn't move you, imagine your feelings when you find that you don't have enough tests for all of the students. (It has happened to me twice—deserving a place among my worst moments in teaching!)

How can you avoid such problems?

1. If you are having tests mimeographed, ask for at least 10 percent extra—more if the test is administered in several rooms. (Some proctor always walks off with too many.) This gives you insurance against miscounting and against omitted or blank pages on some copies.

2. Unless there is some compelling reason to distribute the tests later, have your proctors pass out the tests as students come in the room. This protects students from mounting waves of panic while they wait for the test to be distributed.

3. Minimize interruptions. Tell students before the exam that you will write announcements, instructions, or corrections on the blackboard. Some exam periods are less a measure of achievement than a test of the students' ability to work despite the instructor's interruptions.

Cheating

In this section, I discuss how to handle cheating. It is never pleasant or easy. To coin a phrase, "An ounce of prevention is worth a pound of cure."

It may be hard for you to believe that your students would ever cheat—"Maybe other students cheat, but not mine!" Unfortunately studies of cheating behavior invariably find that a significant percentage of students report that they have cheated. I believe that most students would rather not cheat, but the pressures for good grades are so intense that many students feel that they, too, must cheat if they believe that other students are cheating. In my experience the most common excuse given by a student caught cheating is that other students were cheating and that the teacher didn't seem to care, at least not enough to do anything to prevent or stop cheating. Many students thus feel less stress when an examination is well managed and well proctored.

Preventing Cheating

"O.K., so we want to prevent cheating. What can we do?"

An obvious first answer is to reduce the pressure. While you can't affect the general academic atmosphere that puts heavy emphasis on grades, you can influence the pressure in your own course, for example, by providing a number of opportunities for students to demonstrate achievement of course goals, rather than relying upon a single examination.

A second answer is to make reasonable demands and write a reasonable test. Some cheating is simply the result of frustration and desperation arising from assignments too long to be covered adequately or tests requiring memorization of trivial details. In some cases cheating is simply a way of getting back at an unreasonable, hostile teacher.

A third answer is to develop group norms supporting honesty. I frequently give my classes a chance to vote on whether or not we will conduct the tests on the honor system. I announce that we will not use the honor system unless the vote is unanimous, since it will not work unless everyone feels committed to it. If the vote is unanimous, I remind the students of it on the day of the exam and ask whether they still wish to have the test under the honor system. While I haven't collected data on the success of this approach, I've never had a complaint about it. Nevertheless, only a minority of classes vote for the honor system.

If the honor system does not work, what else can be done?

One principle is to preserve each student's sense that he or she is an individual with a personal relationship both with the instructor and with other students. Students are not as likely to cheat in situations in which they are known as in situations in which they are anonymous members of a crowd. Thus, if a large course has regular meetings in small discussion or laboratory sections, there is likely to be less cheating if the test is administered in these groups than if the test is administered en masse. Moreover, if it is in their regular classroom they will perform better (Metzger et al., 1979).

But even in small groups cheating will occur if the instructor seems unconcerned. Graduate student teaching assistants often feel that any show of active proctoring will indicate that they do not trust the students. There is certainly a danger that the teacher will appear to be so poised to spring at a miscreant that the atmosphere becomes tense, but it is possible to convey a sense of alert helpfulness while strolling down the aisles or watching for questions.

The most common form of cheating is copying from another student's paper. To reduce this I usually ask to have a large enough exam room to enable students to sit in alternate seats. I write on the board before students arrive, "Take alternate seats." Some students fail to see the sign, so in large exams you not only need two proctors at each door passing out exams, but at least one more to supervise seating.

In the event that you can't get rooms large enough to permit alternate seating, you probably should use two or more alternate forms of the test. Houston (1983) found that scrambling order of items alone did not reduce cheating. Since I prefer to have items on a test follow the same order as the order in which the material has been discussed in the course, I scramble the order of items only within topics and also scramble the order of alternatives. I typically write separate sets of essay questions for the two tests. Since it is difficult to make two tests equally difficult, you probably will want to tabulate separate distributions of scores on each form of the test.

Whether you use one form or two, don't leave copies lying around your office or the typist's office. One of our students was nearly killed by a fall from a third-floor ledge outside the office where he hoped to steal the examination, and janitors have been bribed to turn over the contents of wastebaskets thought to contain discarded drafts of the test.

All this advice will not eliminate cheating. It is a sad commentary on our educational system that it occurs, but recognizing and preventing problems is likely to be less unpleasant than ignoring it.

Handling Cheating

Despite preventive measures, almost every instructor must at some time or other face the problem of what to do about a student who is cheating. For example, as you are administering an examination you note that a student's eyes are on his neighbor's rather than his own paper. Typically you do nothing at this time, for you don't want to embarrass an innocent student. But when the eyes again stray, you are faced with a decision about what to do.

Most colleges have rules about the procedures to be followed in case of cheating. Yet instructors are often reluctant to begin the procedure. The reasons for instructor reluctance vary. Sometimes it is simply uncertainty about whether or not cheating really occurred. Students' eyes do wander without cheating. Answers may be similar simply because two students have studied together. "If the student denies the charge, what evidence do I have to support my accusation?"

Again, unwillingness to invoke the regulations concerning cheating may be based upon distrust of the justice of the eventual disposition of the case. Cheating is common in colleges; few teachers have not been guilty themselves at some stage in their academic careers. Thus, most of us are understandably reluctant to subject the unfortunate one who gets caught to the drastic possible punishments that more skillful cheaters avoid. Such conflicts as these make the problem of handling a cheater one of the most disturbing of those a new teacher faces.

Unfortunately I've never been completely satisfied that I handle the problem adequately; so my "advice" should, like the rest of the advice in this book, be regarded simply as some ideas for your consideration rather than as dicta to be accepted verbatim.

First, let me support the value of following your college's procedures. Even though it may not be long since you were taking examinations yourself, your role as a teacher requires that you represent established authority rather than the schoolboy code that rejects "tattlers." Moreover, your memories of student days may help you recall your own feelings when you saw someone cheating and the instructor took no action.

Further, student or faculty committees dealing with cheating are not as arbitrary and impersonal as you might expect. Typically, they attempt to get at the cause of the cheating and to help students solve their underlying problems. Being apprehended for cheating may, therefore, actually be of real long-term value to the students.

There still remain cases where the evidence is weak and you're not even quite sure whether or not cheating actually occurred. Even here I advise against such individual action as reducing a grade. If you're wrong, the solution is unjust. If you're right, you've failed to give the student feedback which is likely to change his behavior. In such cases I advise calling the chairman of the committee handling cheating cases, the student's counselor, or some other experienced faculty member. It's surprising to find how often your suspicions fit in with other evidence about the student's behavior. Even when they don't, advice from someone who has additional information about the student will frequently be helpful.

Finally, let's return to the case of the straying eyes. Here you haven't time for a phone call to get advice; your decision has to be made now. Rather than arousing the whole class by snatching away the student's paper with a loud denunciation, I simply ask the student unobtrusively to move to a seat where he'll be less crowded. If he says he's not crowded, I simply whisper that I'd prefer that he move. So far no one's refused.

Scoring the Test

Once the test has been constructed and administered, the next problem is scoring it. One of the main advantages of the multiple-choice examination is that scoring can be extremely rapid even without the benefit of electric scoring equipment. Although fairly efficient scoring can be achieved without the use of separate answer sheets, such answer sheets are very useful. They can be obtained through the IBM company at about one cent each, or they can be mimeographed or lithoprinted. Unless you plan to use several thousand answer sheets a year, the IBM sheets are quite satisfactory and not too expensive. The advantage of the separate answer sheet is that it can be scored simply by placing a stencil, cut from one of the answer sheets, over the student's paper. In the stencil, you will punch holes in the space where the correct answers would be. All empty spaces on the student sheet are counted as wrong answers. The stencil, marked with the correct answers, can be punched out easily. Several potential stencils (five or six) can be stapled together and punched out simultaneously. Such a stencil can also be used for the correction of true-false examinations if, on the separate answer sheets, you instruct the student to use the "a" choice for true and the "b" choice for false.

If you mimeograph your own answer sheet, my experience indicates that an answer sheet set up in the form

1.   a   b   c   d   e
2.   a   b   c   d   e

is easier for students to follow and instructors to correct than answer sheets of the forms

1.   (b)
2.   (d)

or

	a	b	c	d	e
1.	( )	( )	( )	( )	( )
2.	( )	( )	( )	( )	( )

Grading Essay Questions

I recommend that you use essay questions because of their powerful effect upon the way students study, but there is a drawback. Instructors don't grade essay tests very reliably.

One of the problems is that standards vary. First papers are graded differently than later papers; a paper graded immediately after several poor papers is graded differently from one graded after several good papers.

There are six procedures you can initiate to improve your evaluation of essay examinations—but they entail work.

1. Read all or several of the examinations in a preliminary fashion to establish some notion of the general level of performance.

2. Write (or choose after reading several papers) models of excellent, good, adequate, and poor papers to which you can refer to refresh your memory of the standards by which you are grading. This technique is particularly useful if an assistant is helping to grade or if grading is carried out over a period of time.

3. Establish a set of grading criteria. One of the problems in using essay exams and in assigning term papers is that students feel that the grading represents some mysterious, unfathomable bias. The more that you can write helpful comments on the paper, the more the

mystery is dispelled. (I say more about this in Chapter 10, "Term Papers and Teaching Writing.")

Both for your own guidance and that of the students, develop a set of criteria. Having identified papers of differing levels of excellence, compare them to determine what the distinguishing features were. The more completely you can identify and describe these, the less trouble you will have in defending your grades to irate students (or sometimes parents!) and the more help you can be to students who want to do better.

4. Give a global grade—not several subgrades which are summed. Your overall impression is likely to be more reliable than the sum of grades on such elements as content, organization, originality, etc. Don't simply give points for each concept or fact mentioned. This simply converts the essay into a recall test rather than measuring higher level goals of integration and evaluation.

5. Read essay exams without knowledge of the name of the writer.

6. Do your grading in teams. My teaching assistants and I gather after administering a test. We bring in draft model answers for each question. We discuss what we expect as answers on each question. We then establish two-to-three-person teams for each essay question. Each team then picks eight–twelve test papers, and these are circulated among the team members, with each team member noting privately his or her grade for the question. The team then compares grades and discusses discrepancies until they have reached consensus. A second group of tests is then graded in the same way with grades compared and discrepancies discussed. This procedure continues until the team is confident that they have arrived at common criteria. From this point on, each member grades independently. When a team member is not sure how to grade a paper, it is passed to another team member for an opinion.

We stay with the grading until all the papers are done, but we make a party of it to alleviate fatigue and boredom. Funny answers are read aloud. Sandwiches are brought in from a delicatessen. Teams help other teams for a change of pace or to balance the workload.

Grading papers is still time-consuming but does not become the sort of aversive task which makes for procrastination and long delays in providing feedback to students.

Helping Students Learn from the Test

The most important function of testing is *not* to provide a basis for grading. Rather tests are an important educational tool. Not only do they direct students' studying, but they can provide important corrective feedback. The comments written on essay tests are far more important than the grade.*

What kind of comments are helpful? First of all rid yourself of the usual teacher's notion that most inadequacies are due to a lack of knowledge so that improvement rests simply on supplying the missing knowledge. Rather we need to look for cues that will help us identify the students' structures of representation of knowledge. Usually the students' problems arise from a lack of ability to see relationships, implications, or applications of material. There is always some discrepancy between the structure of knowledge in the student's mind and that in the instructor's. Students construct their own knowledge based on their individual past experiences and their experiences in the course. Thus comments on essay items are more likely to be helpful if they help students find alternative ways of looking at the problem rather than simply noting that something is wrong.

Comments that provide correction and guidance may not achieve their purpose if students become so discouraged that they give up. Thus the motivational as well as the cognitive aspects of comments needs to be considered. Misconceptions need to be identified, but not in overwhelming number. Encouragement and guidance for improvement should set the overall tone.

Assigning a Test Grade

Whatever scoring method is used, there is often a question as to whether some more refined score should be calculated. In addition to scores that are corrected for guessing, the choices include percentile ranks, standard scores, or some combination of these, such as scores corrected for guessing and then put into standard scores. In general, it seems to me that, except for the statistical practice for the instructor imparted by these arithmetic maneuvers, the use of special scores is of little value. There

---

* This holds true except for the final course examination. In my experience few do more than look at the grade on a final examination.

are two reasons for this: 1) nothing in the way of validity is gained, and 2) students have difficulty interpreting refined scores. In the case of corrections for guessing, to take one case, the correlation between corrected and uncorrected scores is usually in the very high nineties, so high that the time required to compute the corrected scores is exorbitant.

Again, the chief argument against the use of standard scores is that you gain very little by going through a rather tedious arithmetic manipulation (even if you make an assistant do it). If the standard deviations of the scores obtained on all of the tests that you give during a course are the same, the simple addition of all of the test scores for each student is the exact arithmetic equivalent of adding or averaging standard scores.

If the standard deviations are radically different from test to test, this arithmetic equivalence does not hold. This leads to the question of what is the main source of such variations in examination scores. By far the largest source of such variation is the length of examinations, long examinations tending to produce larger standard deviations than short ones. When you give a long examination, it is almost always true that you consider the materials covered by the long examination to be more important than those covered by the short one. In this event, you would probably want to weight the long examination more heavily in the computation of a final mark than the short one. Simply adding test scores will do exactly this. The proportional weight will vary as the ratio of the standard deviations.

Add to all of this the fact that each additional arithmetic step presents one more opportunity for arithmetic and clerical error, and it becomes fairly obvious that the use of the various corrections and scalings has little to recommend it.

Grading on the Curve: Don't Do It!

Grading based upon relative achievement in a given group may encourage an undesirably high degree of competition. Despite the absence of absolute standards in any very objective sense, I believe that attempts to avoid competitive grading systems are worthwhile. Grading on the curve stacks the cards against cooperative learning, because helping classmates may lower one's own grade.

The problem of grading "on the curve" seems to arouse the most heated discussion around standards for assigning failing grades. Logically, it would seem that an instructor should be able to designate some minimal essentials, mastery of which would be necessary for a passing grade. Keller Plan courses, programmed courses, and contract courses typically specify mastery of certain materials. As I shall show in the next chapter, so-called mastery grading has some serious pitfalls, but at least some attempt to get away from strict "grading on the curve" is likely to be helpful for class morale.

I tell my students that I'll grade in terms of percentage of a possible score. Thus if a test has 150 possible points, I say:

If you make 140 or over (93% +), I'll guarantee an A

$$
\begin{array}{ll}
135 \text{ to } 142 \ (90\% \ +) & A- \\
131 \text{ to } 134 \ (87\% \ +) & B+ \\
125 \text{ to } 130 \ (83\% \ +) & B \\
120 \text{ to } 124 \ (80\% \ +) & B- \text{ etc.}
\end{array}
$$

If everyone gets over 140 points, everyone will get an A, and I'll be very pleased if you all do well.

I tell the students that I may grade more generously than the standards I have announced but will promise not to be tougher than announced. As it turns out, my distribution of grades has never turned out to be more generous than that of my colleagues—which may indicate that I'm not teaching as effectively as I'd like.

Returning Test Papers

Returning test papers to students promptly is much appreciated by the students and conforms to traditional learning principles. However, if you don't plan to discuss the papers, don't hand them back at the beginning of the hour, or you risk loss of attention the rest of the hour.

Students do like to have their examinations back. In the case of multiple-choice examinations, developed through a considerable amount of hard work, you may not want to let them have them, because you may want to use the items another year. But you can do this: Return separate answer sheets so that your marking and arithmetic can be checked. Allow the students to have copies of the examination while you go through the test. If you do these things, certain questions arise. Does such a procedure destroy the validity of the item in future tests? Does the student profit from such experience? These are experimental questions to which we have only partial answers, but evidence suggests that validity is not lost and that students do learn from their corrected papers (McClusky, 1934). Although you may not wish to spend class time quibbling over some individual items, you should make known your willingness to discuss the test individually with students who have further questions.

On questions that many students missed, I recommend this sort of procedure:

> When you read a particular question, do not merely read the stem of the question or answer the question with the correct choice. Instead, read the stem and each of the choices. For each of the incorrect choices give your reasons for regarding it as incorrect.

This procedure gives you the "jump" on the chronic criticizer. It is more difficult to maintain that a given choice is right under these circumstances than it would be if you had said nothing about the various alternatives and students could argue that the correct alternative was not completely correct. But there will be cases in which a legitimate argument arises. If some ambiguities have gotten through the screening process, and an item is really capable of two equally correct interpretations, admit it and change scores. But remember that you can't escape aggression simply by changing scores, because every time you admit a new right answer, the students who originally had the question right are likely to feel injured.

Accepting students' suggestions for better wording of items reduces their aggressiveness. You can prevent some aggression from being directed against yourself if you have items explained by the students who got them right. However, you should not call upon the same student to explain every difficult question or you may simply be substituting another scapegoat for yourself.

For essay tests I try to describe what we expected in a good answer and the most common inadequacies. I may read an example of a good answer (without identifying the student), and I might construct a synthetic poor answer to contrast with the good one.

One of the techniques for returning tests that seems to reduce much aggression was, I believe, first used in the classes of Dr. N. R. F. Maier. Instructors using this technique break the class into small groups of five to eight students for discussion of the test. Each group discusses the test for part of the class period. When they have finished, unresolved questions are referred to the instructor as the expert. This method seems to permit dissipation of the aggressions aroused and limit arguments to points where there are several aggrieved students.

What about the student who comes to your office in great anger or with a desperate appeal for sympathy but with no educationally valid reason for changing the test grade? First of all, listen. Engaging in a debate will simply prolong the unpleasantness. Once you have heard the student out, if you have decided not to change the grade, try to convert the discussion from one of stonewall resistance to problem solving. Try to help the student find alternative modes of study that will produce better results. "What can we do to help you do better next time?" Encourage the student to shift from blaming you or the test toward motivation to work more effectively.

But there is a technique that will reduce the number of students coming into your office in a state of high emotion. Deborah Keller-Cohen asks students coming to see her with complaints about grades to write a paragraph describing their complaint or point-of-view. She declares her willingness to go over the test of anyone who brings in such a paragraph, noting that she may change the grade either positively or negatively. She reports that this technique has a calming effect, resulting in fewer un-founded complaints and more rational discussion with those who do come in.

While these suggestions may save the instructor some bitter mo-ments, they cannot substitute for the time (and it takes lots) devoted to the construction of good tests.

What Do You Do About the Student Who Missed the Test?

In any large class some students are absent from the test. Their excuses vary from very legitimate to very suspicious, but making that discrimi-nation is not always easy. The usual solution is to offer a make-up test.

Make-up tests can involve a good deal of extra work for the instruc-tor. If you devise a new test, you may have trouble assigning a norm with which to grade on the make-up comparable to grades on the original test. If you use the same test that the students have missed, you cannot tell how much the student has learned about the test from students who took it at the scheduled time. Hence, I don't usually give make-ups except for the final exam. I simply use marks from the tests the student did take to determine the grade, counting the missed test neither for nor against the student. Most students are happy not to have to make up a test, but I encourage them to take the test for practice.

SUPPLEMENTARY READING

The following books contain both theory and practical advice on test construction·

R. M. W. Travers, *How to make achievement tests* (New York: Odyssey Press, 1950).

N. E. Gronlund, *Constructing achievement tests,* 3rd ed. (Englewood Cliffs, NJ: Prentice-Hall, 1982).

W. A. Mehrens and I. J. Lehmann, *Measurement and evaluation in education and psychology* (New York: Holt, Rinehart & Winston, 1973).

CHAPTER 9

The A B C's of Assigning Grades

Grading is currently in the news.* Grade inflation, contract grading, mastery grading—all of these stimulate heated discussion and cries of dismay. My own ideas of grading have become somewhat clearer as I have talked to my teaching assistants about grading policies and thought through why some of the new grading systems make me uneasy.

First let us agree that grades are fundamentally a method of communication. Through the grade a professor is presumably trying to communicate something to someone else. The question then becomes, "What does the professor intend to communicate to whom?"

When one puts grading into this context, three things become apparent:

1. What professors communicate by a grade depends upon the meaning of the grade to the person reading it—the effect that it has on that person.

2. Evaluation is a great deal more than giving a grade. In teaching, the major part of evaluation should be in the form of comments on papers, responses to student statements, conversations, and other means of helping students understand where they are and how to do better. A professor giving a grade is communicating to several groups—the student, professors teaching advanced courses, graduate or professional school admissions committees, prospective employers, and so on.

3. Professors cannot change the meaning of grades unilaterally. While the grade may have a new meaning for the professor, those reading the grade will interpret it in terms of the meanings they have tradi-

---

* The following section is largely derived from my article in the *AAUP Bulletin*, 1976, 62, 320–322.

tionally assigned to grades, unless the professor specifically interprets for them the new meaning he or she wishes to assign to a grade. Even if he asserts, "The grade means what I mean it to mean," the readers' interpretations will be colored by their previous experiences with grades, and they are likely to be disturbed, or to feel that they are being misled, when the professor uses grades in new ways. This explains the strong emotional reaction to "grade inflation," "all A" grading, or other practices deviating from the traditional meaning.

What is that traditional meaning? What are grades used for? I suggest that the person reading a grade typically wants information with respect to some decision involving a judgment about the students' *future* performance. Mastery systems of grading, pass-fail grading, and other alternative systems are resisted because they are not efficient conveyors of the information useful in predicting future performance.

What Do Students, Professors, and Employers Want from Grades?

Students want to be able to use grades to assist them in decisions such as the following:

1. Will I do well if I take additional courses in this field?

2. Should I major in this field? Does it represent a potential career in which I'm likely to be successful?

3. Do I have the skills and ability necessary to work independently in this field—learning more, solving problems, able to evaluate my own work?

4. What kind of person am I?

Professors advising the student or determining admissions expect the grade to tell them:

1. Does this student have the motivation, skills, knowledge, and ability needed to do well in advanced courses (insofar as the type of problems dealt with in the earlier course are relevant to the demands of the advanced courses or program)?

2. What kind of person is this? What does the pattern of grades tell us about this student's ability and work habits?

Similarly, prospective *employers* want to use grades to assist in decisions about whether or not the student will do well in the job.

1. How well will the student be able to solve problems on jobs related to the area of his or her coursework?

2. Does the overall pattern of grades indicate that this is the sort of person who will do well in our organization?

From this analysis it seems evident that grades are used not just as a historical record of what has happened, but also as information about what the student can do in situations outside the class for which the grade was awarded. For the users the grade is not so much historical as potentially predictive.

Do Grades Provide Information Useful for Decision Making?

One of the arguments against conventional grading is that grades are invalid; that is, they do not provide useful information for the major purposes for which they are usually used.

Most critics would grant that grades are useful for decisions about whether a student is likely to be able to succeed in an advanced course or in a further academic experience such as graduate or professional school, but they do not believe that they provide useful information for students or for potential employers.

Teachers assume that grades have some informational and motivational value for students. Critics argue that punishment and failure are not likely to be conducive to achieving the goal of continued enjoyment of learning, and that the threat of low grades is a crutch used to help inadequate teachers. I think that there is much truth in this argument. Yet uniformly positive feedback is not necessarily the most effective method of motivating all students. In fact there is much evidence that such a pattern of reinforcement sometimes diminishes motivation. Psychological research has demonstrated that human beings seek information about their competence and will choose activities that give information upon which to build a sense of competence and self-esteem. While the research on grading is not conclusive, it does suggest that conventional grading is conducive to achievement.

What about information for employers? Probably most personnel psychologists would agree that the best predictor of success on a job is successful performance on a similiar job. For a young person entering the job market, there is often no record of previous performance on comparable jobs. The employer must then make a decision on the basis of other information such as interviews, letters of recommendation, biographical data, family background, and test scores. Each such source is only partially adequate. Insofar as the new job involves at least some expenditure for training, it seems likely that grades, representing the result of skills applied in study, learning, and problem solving, will add some information, albeit incomplete, that will be useful for making the decision.

Because grades are commonly used in combination with other variables, however, one should not expect them to correlate with success for those selected. This is not simply a problem that only the top students were selected; it is a simple mathematical truism that when one uses several selection criteria, each of which has some validity, one should expect low positive, zero, or even negative correlations between any one selection variable and the ultimate criteria of performance. This occurs because one will select some people low in other important attributes because they have high grades. Thus the common criticism that grades don't predict later performances is largely invalid because most of the studies cited have been carried out in situations where grades have already been used in selection.

Contract Grading

In contract grading students and instructors develop a written contract about what the student will do to achieve given grade levels. Contracts typically specify papers to be written, books to be read, projects to be completed, and so forth. With respect to the contract system of grading, it seems to me that the problem basically is that students often gain points, not for achievement, but rather for carrying out those activities, such as writing papers or reading books, that _should_ be conducive to achievement. Thus, rather than measuring learning, you assess whether the student has engaged in activities that are the means to learning. I suspect that this means that in many cases there is a considerable gap between the points the student has earned and the points a similar student would earn if the student's achievement were assessed. If contract grading is used, criteria for quality as well as quantity of achievement are needed.

Assigning grades on the basis of the quantity of work done rather than the degree of competence achieved is not a problem restricted to contract grading. Many instructors subtract points for absences, tardiness, or other things they dislike. In psychology classes, points are sometimes added for participation in research studies, a very dubious practice unless it involves some assessment of what the students learned from research participation.

Competency-Based Grading

In "Mastery" or "Competency-Based" systems, the student is graded on a pass-fail basis for achieving "mastery" or "competence" in terms of carefully specified objectives. The real core of the problem may be in the use of the word "mastery". The mastery concept essentially emphasizes reaching a particular finish line. In fact, however, most educational purposes in higher education have no end point, but are extensive in breadth and depth of their possibilities. An achievement examination in a course is ordinarily designed to *sample* a domain of problems to solve, or concepts, or generalizations, that the students will be able to generalize to a larger domain. The more limited the definition of those achievements that the students should "master," the less valid a test or grade is in terms of its ability to assess the students with respect to other problems, other concepts, or other generalizations in the total domain.

For example, suppose I give my students a list of five problems at the beginning of the semester and say, "My objectives are that you should be able to solve these five problems." In this situation most students will master the problems but differ substantially in their ability to solve other problems within the same general categories. Five problems that have *not* been specifically studied during the course would be more likely to be a reasonable sample of future problems students might encounter than five problems the students have already memorized, and a larger sample of problems from the domain would be likely to be even better.

Giving students the option of choosing among several test questions or problems on a test means that one is not getting an unbiased sample of what the students can do.

Letting students turn in papers or book reports over and over again until they do them correctly is a fine teaching technique. However, the student who writes an acceptable book report after ten trials is probably less able to write a new report acceptably than the student who does it right in the first place. Thus the grade on such a rewritten paper should not be counted as equivalent to that of a paper that has not been rewritten.

Nonetheless, mastery learning has positive features. It forces the teacher to think about goals and it focuses students' learning. Moreover such a focus results in better retention (Glasnapp et al., 1978).

Pass-Fail Grading

During the 1960s there was a good deal of push toward the use of "pass-fail" grades rather than the conventional A, B, C, D, E. While the arguments for some such change seem persuasive, there is little evidence that pass-fail grading has positive effects (Lempert, 1972; Bronfenbrenner, 1972).

Assigning Grades

Because grades represent to many students a fearsome, mysterious dragon, anxiety can sometimes be reduced by encouraging the students to participate in planning the methods by which grades will be assigned. Students usually can recognize the need of the instructor to conform to college policy in grade distribution, but the dragon seems less threatening if they have helped determine the system by which they are devoured (or rewarded).

Some instructors have gone as far as to let students determine their own grades or to have groups of students grade one another. I like the idea that students should develop the capacity for self-evaluation, but I recognize that many students resist this procedure, either through modesty or fear that they'll underrate themselves. If you use it, I'd suggest thorough discussion of the plan with students and an agreed-upon, well-defined set of criteria that all students should use. Even if student participation is not possible, anxiety seems to be reduced if you explain the system you use and give your reasons for using this system.

In giving test grades early in a course, two general approaches are sometimes advocated. One of these is to make these grades lower than those one intends to give at the end of the course. This should reduce the number of complaints about final grades. The other approach is to use these grades to motivate students to work harder. This may mean that you use many plus and minus grades. A plus or minus indicates to the students that the grade may be shifted either way and presumably reduces the chance that they'll coast.

You might also ask students to hand in their own estimates of their grades as an aid to knowing how to motivate them, and also in order to develop their abilities for self-evaluation. Atkinson and Litwin's (1960) theory of motivation suggests that the highest motivation to achieve occurs when the probability of success is moderate. This probably explains the finding of Means and Means (1971) that low grade-point-average students achieved more when told that they had done well on an aptitude test, while high grade-point-average students did better when told that they had done poorly. In general motivation is not helped simply by giving high grades; nor is it helped by setting very tough standards. Students are most motivated when they feel that they can achieve success with a reasonable effort (Harter, 1978).

In keeping students informed during the course about where they stand, you probably are also aiding them to control much of the anxiety they feel when the grading system is indefinite and unstructured. Sometimes it may seem easier to fight off grade-conscious students by being very indefinite about grades, but student morale is better when the students know the situation with which they must cope.

Whatever your grading strategy, being more generous in assigning grades to tests and papers than in the final distribution of grades guarantees visits from aggrieved students. One way in which you get yourself into this position is by providing opportunities for students to omit questions on an exam, to throw out the lowest test grade, or to submit extra work for a higher grade. Any of these procedures can have some educational justification, but if you expect to finish the course with grades representative of those for similar courses at your college, you need to devise a system of grading in which the constituents of the total grade will come out at an appropriate level in relation to the standards of grading at your college or university.

Professors sometimes devise systems of grading that allow students to drop out any test scores below A and are then surprised that their grade distribution is not comparable to that of other courses. You will find that your colleagues are not convinced that the students' level of achievement has improved so greatly in your class that they all deserve grades higher than those earned in other classes.

Grading on the Curve: A Mild Reprise ═══════

In the last chapter we talked about grading a test on the curve. Now we extend our discussion to final course grades. One of the persisting controversies in college teaching is whether to grade "on the curve" or in terms of an absolute standard. In fact, these two positions are probably not as far apart as the argument would indicate. Even teachers who grade on the curve are influenced in setting their cutoff points between grades in terms of their feelings about whether this was a good or poor class. And similarly, teachers who do not grade on the curve set their standards in terms of what previous experience leads them to regard as reasonable accomplishment in the course. As I indicated in the preceding chapter, I believe that grading on the curve is educationally dysfunctional. If possible your grades should, both in the students' eyes and in actuality, be more nearly based on absolute standards than on relative standing in this particular class.

The use of an absolute standard is easier if you have formulated your major and minor objectives and tested their achievement. Travers (1950) proposed one set of absolute standards:

➤ A : All major and minor goals achieved.

➤ B : All major goals achieved; some minor ones not.

➤ C : All major goals achieved; many minor ones not.

➤ D : A few major goals achieved, but student is not prepared for advanced work.

➤ E : None of the major goals achieved.

What Do You Do with the Student Who Wants a Grade Changed? ═══════

My basic strategy is the same as that involved in returning tests—go over the criteria used in grading and the student's record during the term.

If students are worried about their grades in connection with their admission to a specialized school or because they are on probation, I may offer to write a letter to their advisor or other authorities describing their work in detail and pointing out any extenuating circumstances that may have influenced the grade. This may serve to cushion the refusal to change the grade.

In addition, of course, you may try to explain to the students the rationale of grades. Usually this doesn't seem to do much good. Both students and faculty sometimes confuse two possible criteria upon which grades may be based. One of these is the relative amount of *progress* the student has made in achieving the goals of the course; the other is achievement of the goals of the course at the end of the course. In most classes, research has demonstrated a relatively low correlation between these two criteria. If you were to mark solely on progress, the students who came into the course with the least background might still be the poorest students in the class at the end of the course and get an A for their progress. Most employers, registrars, and professors interpret a grade in terms of achievement of course goals; hence, professors who grade solely on the students' progress may send the students into advanced courses or jobs for which they lack the requisite skills and knowledge. However, I find it difficult to assign failing grades to students who have made progress in the course, even though they remain the poorest students in the class. My own solution is to give all but failing grades in terms of achievement of course goals. I give failing grades only to those students who not only demonstrate low achievement, but have also made little progress.

No matter how you grade, some student will be unhappy. The student who has just missed Phi Beta Kappa may feel just as bad as the student who has been asked to leave school. Be sympathetic, but beware! If you begin changing grades, the jungle drums of the campus will soon spread the word.

Don't finish reading this chapter with your own anxiety aroused by the dangers of grading. It is proper that good teachers should be humble as they see how great is the power they have over the happiness of their students by printing a simple A, B, C, or D. Nevertheless, one of the real satisfactions of teaching is giving a good grade to an ordinarily average student who has come to life in your course.

How to Lose Friends and Alienate Students

1. Never give students any idea of what their grades are before the final examination. The shock of seeing an E as the final grade will so stun them that they'll be incapable of protest. Or better yet tell them they

---

* These may look absurd, but they have all happened.

had A's all the way through the course and got an A on the final, but you have too many A's, so you're giving them B's.

2. Tell students that you really think they deserved a higher mark, but that you had to conform to department grading policies and hence had to grade them lower.

3. Tell students that their grades on the final exam were higher than their final grades in the course. (Of course they'll understand that the final examination is only one part of the total evaluation.)

4. Even though your school doesn't record pluses, tell a student that his grade was D +, C +, or B +, rather than a straight D, C, B. He'll gladly accept the fact that the C −, B −, or A − was only three points above him, and will be proud that he did better than anyone else who got a D or C or B.

5. If you make a distribution of total points earned on tests during the term, use large intervals, such as 80 to 90, 90 to 100, etc. When you show a student his position on the distribution, he'll readily see that the person in the next interval above was really much superior.

6. Tell a student that grades are really very arbitrary, and that you could have split the B's from the C's in many different places, and that grades are so unreliable that you really can't distinguish your top B student from your low A student. He'll appreciate the aesthetic value of your choice of a cutting point.

Relevant Research

Not only do instructors control the pleasantness or unpleasantness of a good many student hours, but because of their power to assign grades they can block or facilitate the achievement of many important goals. The importance of this aspect of the teacher's role is indicated by studies of supervision in industry. In one such study it was discovered that workers were most likely to ask a supervisor for help if the supervisor did not have responsibility for evaluating his subordinates (Ross, 1957). This implies that as long as students are anxious about the grades the instructor will assign, they are likely to avoid exposing their own ignorance.

The students' anxieties about grades are likely to rise if their instructor's procedures make them uncertain about what they must do in order to attain a good grade. For many students, democratic methods seem unorganized and ambiguous. In an ordinary course students know they can pass by reading assignments and studying lecture notes, but in a student-centered class they are in a course where the instructor doesn't lecture, doesn't make assignments, and doesn't even say which student comments are right or wrong. The student simply doesn't know what the instructor is trying to do. Thus, if your teaching or grading procedures differ from those your students are used to, you need to be especially careful to specify the procedures and criteria used in grading.

Some instructors have thought that the grade problem might be licked by using a cooperative system of grading. Deutsch (1949) found no differences in learning between students in groups graded cooperatively and those graded competitively, although the cooperative groups worked together more smoothly. Following up Deutsch's work, Haines and McKeachie (1967) also found no significant achievement advantages for students working cooperatively vs. those working competitively for grades, but did find marked differences in group morale. Haines's work suggests that cooperative grading in the discussion can be successfully combined with individual grading on achievement tests.

Complicating the problem of grading is the probability that low grades produce different effects upon different students. As indicated earlier, Atkinson's theory suggests that low grades should be damaging to the motivation of students with low to moderate expectations, but should increase motivation of those with high expectations. Waterhouse and Child (1953) found that frustration produced deterioration in performance for subjects showing high interference tendencies (or anxiety) as measured by a questionnaire, but produced improved performance for those with low interference tendencies.

Considering the importance of grading for both students and instructors, it is regrettable that there is so little empirical research. How do students learn to evaluate themselves? How do they learn to set goals for themselves? Do differing grading procedures facilitate or block such learning? To these questions we have no answers.

Conclusion

To sum up:

1. Grades are communication devices. Instructors cannot unilaterally change their meaning without distorting the communication process.

2. Grading standards differ from college to college and department to department, but there is some shared sense of the meaning of grades.

SUPPLEMENTARY READING

For another view, see S. Ericksen, Grading ≠ evaluation, _Memo to the faculty,_ No. 46 (University of Michigan, Center for Research on Learning and Teaching, 1971).

While I have pointed to problems with typical mastery or contract grading systems, well-designed programs are worth serious consideration. Even conventional grading systems need to establish criteria. A helpful source is M. F. Shaycoft, _Handbook of criterion-referenced testing_ (New York: Garland STPM Press, 1979).

Contracts for contract grading are illustrated in Barbara Fuhrman and Anthony Grasha, _A practical handbook for college teachers_ (San Francisco: Jossey-Bass, 1983).

PART IV

Teaching Techniques, Tools, and Methods

CHAPTER 10 ⫽ Term Papers and Teaching Writing

Term Papers

My experiences with term papers have not always been happy ones. Yet the potential values for students who do a good job are so great that I almost invariably use them in my courses.

When undergraduates are required to turn in a term paper, they seem to face three alternatives:

1. Buy one, or borrow one from a friend or fraternity or sorority file. The student may have this retyped or, if there are no marks on it, simply retype the title page inserting his or her own name for that of the author.

2. Find a book in the library that covers the needed material. Copy it with varying degrees of paraphrasing and turn it in. Whether or not to list this book in the bibliography is a problem not yet adequately covered by student mores, although it is agreed that if it is listed in the bibliography it should be well hidden between two references with Russian (first choice) or German (second choice) authors.

3. Review relevant resources and, using powers of analysis and integration, develop a paper that reveals understanding and original thinking.

Most teachers prefer that their students adopt the third alternative. Few of us, however, have evolved techniques for eliminating the first two.

I start with the assumption that most students would rather not plagiarize. When they plagiarize it is because they feel trapped with no other way out. The trap is typically that the student feels that it is almost impossible to write a paper that will achieve a satisfactory grade. This may be because of self-perception of lack of ability or background. More often it results from a lack of planning so that the student has arrived at the time the term paper is due with little preparation and no paper. The only way out seems to be to find an already-written paper.

How can one help students avoid such a trap? By pacing the student. I try to break the process of writing a term paper into a series of easy steps such as:

1. Finding a topic
2. Gathering sources, or data, or references
3. Developing an outline
4. Writing a first draft
5. Rewriting

I set deadlines for handing in a report at each step. When time permits, I meet with the student to discuss the paper at one of the early steps. In the meeting I not only provide guidance, but I can also offer encouragement and motivation for doing well (and I can sometimes spot and discourage impending signs of plagiarism).

Sandra Powers (1983) uses a technique which neatly breaks up the task of introducing students to a library research paper. Her procedure involves the following tasks:

1. Each student locates a source article and writes a paragraph explaining why this article was chosen.

2. The article and paragraphs are discussed in a small peer group.

3. The student writes a one-page summary of a source article.

4. This paper is discussed and evaluated by the peer group and graded by the teacher. The teacher carefully evaluates one paragraph for writing style, grammar, etc.

5. Students choose a topic and turn in the topic as a question.

6. Each student writes the instructor a one-page letter on "How is my paper going?"

7. The research paper and preceding papers are submitted as a portfolio.

Other techniques I've used are:

1. Include on a test some question that will require the student to use knowledge gained in preparing the term paper.

2. Require students to make oral reports on their papers and answer questions from the class.

If term papers are frequently so inadequate, why would instructors bother to use them? As I see it, term papers attempt to gain two objectives:

1. To provide an opportunity for students to go beyond conventional course coverage and gain a feeling of expertness in a limited area. This is an important way in which students learn to value knowledge and the rational process by which knowledge accumulates.

2. To give students an opportunity to explore problems of special significance to them. In this way instructors hope to capture increased motivation.

Student Reports

Typical student reports to the class are mumbled readings of uninspired papers, not unlike the papers of their professors at the annual meetings of their scientific societies. Like the professor's colleagues, the student's audience is likely to be bored and inattentive.

Sometimes teachers will schedule student reports as a method of saving themselves preparation time. This usually doesn't work. If student reports are to be effective, instructors usually need to schedule conferences with the students reporting and spend time going over both the content and helping the student prepare presentation of the report.

Syndicate Methods

In Great Britain a number of faculty members have used a method of small group teaching which they call the syndicate method. In syndicate methods students are placed in groups of five to eight; each group is given an assignment and the group then reports to the entire class at the completion of the assignment. The method has the advantage of providing more depth on a variety of topics than might be possible if the teacher were to make the assignments to all class members. It also has motivational value in the increased sense of responsibility and in the interaction with peers around an intellectual topic. Both the small group discussion of the assignment and their preparation and presentation of their report are activities which should provide cognitive elaboration resulting in better learning and retention of the material.

The disadvantage of the system is that student reports are not always well presented and the time required may be less efficiently used than with a conventional lecture by the instructor. As with other small group methods success depends a good deal on the instructor's care in preparing assignments and in training group members to work cooperatively in carrying out the assignment and making the report. If the number and quality of the reports suggest some limitations on use of class time, I suggest subdividing the class and letting each group report to half or a third of the class, or announcing topics and letting students choose to listen to those they are most interested in. If it seems likely that some reports will have no audience, one can pair reports in one session, or can ask students to rank their preferences—assigning students to equalize attendance and minimize dissatisfaction.

The Student Log

For a number of years I have required my students to write logs. Originally the logs dealt only with outside reading, but more recently I have broadened them to encourage students to think about psychology in all settings.

Logs are turned in three times during the term. I don't grade them, but I do write extensive comments pressing for active questioning and thinking rather than descriptive summaries. Students clearly improve; whether or not this carries over beyond the course I don't know, but it seems more likely than for some other types of course activity. In any case there is increasing evidence that writing aids learning and problem solving (Beach and Bridwell, 1984). The best description of what I expect is probably contained in the instructions given students which follow.

Writing Logs on Your Reading, Observing, and Thinking

Your assigned readings are designed to give you a basic knowledge of the terminology and concepts used in psychology. You will also be given the opportunity to read about any topic in psychology that especially interests you. You should keep a log of your reading and thinking as described below. In this course you will have four hours in class, two to four hours of assigned reading, and possibly other activities each week. This means that most weeks you should have two to six hours for your free reading and writing. Logs will not be graded but there will be a question on the final examination assessing the skills you have developed.

What to read   You are allowed maximal freedom in selecting readings to enter in your log. Your interest in and profit from what you read is by far the most important criterion of selection. You are encouraged to discard after reading a few pages any material that fails to satisfy either of these criteria.

Chapters of books and journal articles are particularly acceptable for these purposes. At the end of each chapter in the text, there is a list of suggestions for further reading; if you were dissatisfied with your grasp of any particular chapter, or if you just want to learn more about some topic than is available in the text, these "suggestions" are excellent sources. Another method of selection is simply to browse among the books and journals in the library until something catches your interest.

One of the goals of the course is to help you develop skill in reading psychological materials analytically and critically, so that you can learn from reading after you leave college. Thus you are particularly encouraged to use sources that you would be likely to read after college, such as paperback books, _Psychology Today, Scientific American,_ and articles relevant to psychology in newspapers and popular magazines.

Finally, if your position in the course is for any reason precarious, you are encouraged to improve the situation by reading parts of other elementary texts that might illuminate and strengthen your thinking on material covered during the course so far.

Where to find it   The Undergraduate Library has a basic collection of books and the recent volumes of most journals. You will find a wider selection in the General Library. You might find the _Psychological Abstracts_ (the readers' guide to psychological literature) a useful reference to direct you to journal articles concerning the topics of your interest. _The Journal of Experimental Psychology_ and the _Journal of Personality and Social Psychology_ contain fairly concise reports of research projects and their implication. _The Psychological Review_ and _Psychological Bulletin_ contain theoretical articles and reviews of experimental or particular topics, respectively.

What goes in the log   The log is to be in no sense a "paper" in any formal sort of way. It should demonstrate that you have thought about what you have read and experienced. This should and must be accomplished without writing a summary of the reading(s). Rather record your comments, criticisms, evaluations, questions, and insights. How did your reading relate to other material of the course? How did it relate to other psychological concepts or theories with which you are familiar? What interested you? Was the evidence convincing? What hypotheses are suggested to you by this reading or experience?

In addition to writing about reading, write about behavior that you observed, discussions in which you participated, or thoughts you had after class. The log is intended to record your thinking about behavior and experience and about psychology as a field studying behavior and experience.

This kind of report need not be lengthy. A couple of paragraphs should suffice for each reading or event, depending, of course, on how much you have read or thought.

Correcting Papers, Giving Feedback, and Teaching Writing

"I'm teaching physics (or psychology or history). It's the job of the English Department to teach writing. It would be unfair to my students to evaluate their writing. Moreover I've never had any training in teaching writing. I'm not even sure when to insert a comma in my own writing."

Such is the outcry of the professoriate when confronting the proposition that writing should be taught in all courses—across the curriculum.

There is some merit in the outcry. Few faculty members have been taught to teach writing—even fewer than have been taught to teach their own disciplines! But lack of training in teaching has not disqualified us from teaching our own disciplines, and all of us have had substantial experience in writing dissertations, reports, papers, books, and incidental letters. Writing is the very essence of academic life. "Publish or perish" is not an idle phrase. We write.

Most of us recognize good or bad writing when we see it. What we often lack are skills of analysis and diagnosis that will help us identify our students' underlying problems as well as skills in providing correction, feedback, and guidance that will enable students to improve.

In addition to concerns about competence, faculty members have concerns about the time required. If one asks students to write more, how can one conscientiously comment on that writing without an impossible increase in time spent grading?

Here are some suggestions:

1. The professor is not the only person who can provide help on writing. Often peers can provide useful suggestions on their classmates' papers. To help students know what to look for you can provide models—both of well-written papers on a given topic as well as of papers with your own comments about some common problems. Form subgroups of four or five students and have each group read and comment on each other's papers. This not only reduces the burden on the teacher but also helps students to learn to evaluate their own work. You can help this learning by evaluating the evaluations periodically. For example, you might say that each group will determine when each paper in the group is ready to be turned in to you. Or you might ask the group to turn in a first and last version together with their suggestions on the earlier drafts.

2. A ten-page paper is not necessarily twice as valuable as a five-page paper. Short papers can be evaluated in less time than long papers, and may provide sufficient stimulus for student thinking and sufficient opportunity for student feedback.

3. More than one draft of a single paper may be more useful for learning than submission of the final version of a paper. (The problem with the final version of papers is that once a grade has been given students sometimes ignore all other feedback.) Requiring resubmission encourages the student to identify and correct the problems emerging in the earlier drafts.

4. Up to a point, more comments, and more specific comments, lead to greater learning. There are three kinds of qualifications to this statement:
   a. A student can be overloaded with feedback. There is a limited number of things a student can be expected to learn and remedy at one time.
   b. Motivation for improvement is affected by the balance of encouragement vs. criticism. A heavy dose of criticism may cause a student to feel that there is no use in continuing.

  c. The type of comment makes a difference. Simply noting errors is not helpful if the student doesn't know how to correct the errors. Helpful comments provide guidance about how to improve.

5. Establish criteria for evaluation and grading.

As I said in Chapter 8, "Tests and Examinations," a global grade is more reliable than partial grades, but to help students to learn to write and think, grades are of little value. Students need more information about criteria. One method is to read several papers and to make specific notes about the criteria which influenced your judgments about the differences between excellent and poorer papers. An alternative procedure is to develop a set of criteria on rational grounds or in discussion with other instructors. A good example of such a statement of criteria is the following outline developed by Gary LaPree of Indiana University (LaPree, 1977).

A. Content
  1. Introduction
     a. Is the topic novel and original?
     b. Does the author state purpose, problem, or question to be considered?
     c. How does the author convince the reader that the paper is worth reading?
     d. Does the author present a preview of how the problem will be handled?

  2. Body
     a. How are the statements made warranted? (Is there evidence that data collected have been analyzed and the literature reviewed? Are the assumptions logical?)
     b. Presentation of evidence
        1. Is contradictory evidence dealt with adequately?
        2. Are multiple sources considered if available?
        3. Is the evidence discussed relevant to the purpose stated?
        4. Is the argument internally consistent, i.e., does one point follow from another?
        5. Is the argument plausible?

        6. Are the methods chosen for testing the argument convincing?
- c. Suitability of paper's focus
  1. Is the problem chosen focused enough to be adequately covered in the space of the paper?
  2. Is the problem chosen too specific for the author's sources of information?
- d. Background information
  1. Is enough information given to familiarize the reader with the problem?
  2. Is unimportant background material included?
- e. Is the presentation easy to follow and well organized?
- f. Does the author deal with the problem set up in the introduction?

3. Conclusion
   - a. Does the author summarize findings adequately?
   - b. Is the conclusion directly related to the questions asked in the introduction?
   - c. Does the author suggest areas where further work is needed?

B. Connections to class
1. Evidence that class materials have been read and understood.
2. Application of lecture materials and assigned readings to paper.

C. Form
1. Spelling.
2. Grammar.
3. Appropriate use of words: Does the writer use words incorrectly, awkwardly, or inappropriately?
4. Paragraph form: Are ideas presented in coherent order?
5. Footnotes and bibliography: Are borrowed ideas and statements given credit? Is the form of the footnotes and bibliography understandable and consistent?
6. Typing errors: Has the paper been proofread?

    This list of criteria is not intended to be something one considers only after reading a paper but rather as a guide to the teacher's active thought processes while reading student papers and for suggestions to be made to the student. Just as we teach students to read actively—questioning, relating, synthesizing—so we should be actively questioning the writer's thinking and expression as we read.

SUPPLEMENTARY READING

Useful analyses of writing processes and implications for teaching may be found in:

L. W. Gregg and E. R. Steinberg (eds.), *Cognitive processes in writing* (Hillsdale, NJ: Lawrence Erlbaum, 1980). Note especially the chapter by Hayes and Flower.

E. P. Maimon, G. L. Belcher, G. W. Hearn, B. F. Nodine, and F. W. O'Connor, *Writing in the arts and sciences* (Cambridge, MA: Winthrop, 1981).

Alternatives to term papers are discussed in the chapter by Evan I. Farber in Thomas G. Kirk (ed.), *Increasing the teaching role of academic libraries,* New Directions for Teaching and Learning, 18 (San Francisco: Jossey-Bass, 1984).

CHAPTER 11 | *One-on-One Teaching and Counseling*

The principles used in teaching writing are equally valid in the many educational situations in which teacher and student interact one-on-one. Music, art, physical education, dentistry, medicine, social work, and other fields all involve some individualized teaching one-on-one, and every teacher has occasions in which skills in tutoring or one-on-one teaching are needed.

There is relatively little research on one-on-one teaching methods, but several principles mentioned in earlier chapters are relevant:

1. Students are helped by a model of the desired performance. This may be provided by the instructor's demonstration of the technique, by a videotape, or by observation of a skilled performer. Generally speaking, positive examples are more helpful than examples of what not to do. When instructors perform, they should utilize the same techniques they use in presenting other visual aids, particularly in directing the student's attention to crucial aspects of the technique.

2. Students are helped by verbal cues or labels that identify key features of the skill. Students are likely to be distracted by irrelevant details.

3. "Bare bones," simplified simulations or demonstrations are more useful as starting points than complex real-life situations which may overwhelm the student with too many details.

4. Permit students the maximum freedom to experience successful completion of a task or a part of a task, but give enough guidance so that they will not get bogged down in a rut of errors. This implies that the learning experiences of students go from the simple to the complex, with the steps so ordered that each new problem can be successfully solved.

5. Students need practice with feedback.

6. Feedback from the instructor or from peers may provide more information than the student can assimilate. Don't try to correct everything on the first trial.

7. Feedback can discourage students. Try to provide some encouraging feedback as well as identification of mistakes.

8. Feedback that identifies errors won't help if the learner doesn't know what to do to avoid the errors. Give guidance about what to try next.

9. High-level skills are developed through much practice. Simply reaching the point of successful performance once is not likely to achieve the degree of organization and automatization that is necessary for consistent success.

10. Practice with varied examples is likely to be both more motivating and more likely to transfer to out-of-class performance than is simple drill and repetition.

11. Coaching is not simply one-way telling and criticizing. Asking the learners about their perceptions of what they are doing and helping them evaluate their own performance is also important. In teaching self-evaluation, you may model the sort of analysis needed. As you evaluate work, verbalize the process you are using and the basis for your evaluation. Like other skills self-evaluation is learned by practice with feedback. Thus students need many opportunities for self-evaluation with feedback *about their evaluation* as well as about the work being evaluated.

12. Peers can help one another. You don't need to monitor everyone all of the time.

Counseling

Some of your most effective teaching may occur when students come to you with a problem with which they want help. I have already suggested that instructors should establish and keep certain regular office hours for meeting students. In this section I would like to discuss some of the problems that arise in those hours.

First of all, I should warn you that a student's ostensible reasons for coming to you may be quite different from the real reasons. Often students ask about a study problem when their real desire is to know the instructor better. They complain of inadequate study habits when underneath there may be difficulties with their home life. I do not mean that you should disregard the problems the students actually present, but if you are aware of possible underlying factors, you may be more understanding and more effective as a counselor.

Second, you should remember that you do not need to restrict your sources of information to a student's performance in your own class. Helpful information can be gained from the files of the student personnel office. By learning something about a student's background, you can better understand his or her problems.

In addition, remember that counseling need not be restricted to the office. In the classroom the teacher can do much to help individuals by recognizing their potential, by helping them become accepted in the group, and by developing cooperative activities in which they can participate with other class members. Out of the classroom you may be able to get to the real problem more easily over a Coke in the student union than in a more formal office visit.

The most common of student problems is worded something like this, "I study harder for this course than for all my other courses, but I just can't seem to pass the tests." In handling this problem I usually encourage the students to express their own ideas about their difficulties. Sometimes their diagnosis and plans for improvement will be much more accurate than any you can give them. Frequently, simple information on budgeting time, on how the students can ask themselves questions about the assignment, or on getting an overview of a chapter before reading it can be of much help.

In general, the key is to get the students away from reading passively or trying to memorize and instead to questioning, relating, and thinking more actively about the assignment and lectures. Sometimes you can help by getting the students to really use the student workbook often published as an adjunct to the textbook. Even better may be to encourage peer teaching. Chapter 20 will show that even poor students can learn by trying to explain something to a peer. For the theory underlying these suggestions see Chapter 24.*

---

* For further help you might suggest Linda Annis, _Study techniques_ (Dubuque, IA: Wm. C. Brown, 1983); Tim Walter and Al Siebert, _Student success_, 3rd ed. (New York: Holt, Rinehart & Winston, 1984), or James Deese and Ellen K. Deese, _How to study_, 3rd ed. (New York: McGraw-Hill, 1979).

*Educational Counseling** ═══════════════════════

The term educational counseling has been used to refer to three distinctly different types of activity. All of them are inevitable accompaniments of an educational enterprise, but not all of them are equally accepted by faculties as part of their responsibility. The three activities included in educational counseling are 1) program planning, 2) remedial work, and 3) individualized teaching.

Program Planning

The modern university is a complex organization. The student's path through this organization is supposedly mapped by handbooks and catalogs. Unfortunately, most of these documents are, at best, forbiddingly dull and confusingly written. In too many instances they are less than adequate road guides because almost every curriculum has its unwritten requirements. These are preferences for certain sequences of courses or for the choice of one of several alternatives which are so strongly adhered to by the department or college that they become, in effect, requirements for graduation. At the same time, because they are not formal requirements, they exist as part of the folklore rather than as part of the written law.

This state of affairs means that where students are left on their own to select courses, there is great danger of having to extend the normal four-year program because of mistakes in curricular planning. This has given rise to the faculty counselor who is given the responsibility for guiding the students through the intricacies of their chosen curriculum. Often this faculty counselor is expected to double as an amateur professional counselor, one to whom the students can turn for help with any of the other problems that may arise—problems of vocational decision or problems of even more personal import.

The university usually places on this faculty counselor the responsibility for the enforcement of various other regulations governing the students' curricular activities—for example, the number of credits students may elect in a given period, the fulfillment of prerequisites, and the meeting of general requirements for graduation where they exist. The result is that relations between students and faculty are often strained,

---

*Much of this section was written by Professor Edward S. Bordin, The University of Michigan.

for the students going to see the faculty members become a part of a bureaucratic, impersonal processing that they are impatient to pare down to its irreducible essentials. To the faculty members, these duties loom as demeaning, much-to-be-avoided tasks comparable to KP in military service.

The result of all this is that though many catalogs will carry ambitious statements about faculty counseling, conjuring up an image of the wise, genial, pipe-smoking academician in leisurely discussion with the eager, respectful student who avidly gathers up the words of wisdom that are dropped in the course of this conversation, the stark reality of the relationship is too often that of a meeting between a rebelliously impatient student and a harried and disgruntled faculty member.

Remedial Work

As education has become more individualized in its treatment of the student, educators have become more concerned with special learning problems. Consequently, provision is made for specialized individualized help in removing blocks to learning and in improving such varied kinds of skills as reading, spelling, arithmetic, and well-articulated speech. In many universities there are specialists to help students overcome deficits in their methods of study or in the basic skills necessary to academic learning. This remedial work is intended to allow for inadequacies in the students' preparation for college work.

University faculties are not of one mind about the appropriateness of providing this kind of educational service. Many of them see these inadequacies as reflections of the failure of primary and secondary schools to perform their functions adequately and reject any responsibility for helping rescue the unfortunate victim. One is tempted to designate this as a Malthusian philosophy because it is sometimes joined with the attitude that too many unqualified students are coming to college anyhow, so that any influences that will decimate the numbers are to be accepted rather than counteracted.

Where remedial counseling is carried on, there may be considerable variation in the amount of attention devoted to emotional factors in these learning difficulties. There are differences of opinion as to the extent to which emotional and motivational factors are at the roots of learning difficulties or are simply their concomitants. There seems no real need to choose between these two views of the role of emotion in motivation.

One can assume that persons with these learning difficulties will demonstrate symptoms in varying degrees from the one extreme where the difficulties arise primarily from the mechanical sources or cognitive defects, to the other extreme where the difficulty arises because the particular skill has become invested with certain of the emotional conflicts of the individual. To the extent that remedial work is aimed at rectifying what must have been defects in the learning sequences by which a skill was acquired, it is a form of educational counseling, and is close to the work of a teacher. To the extent that remedial work deals with the emotional and motivational factors as sources of the difficulty, it becomes a form of psychological counseling.

Psychological Problems

At some point you will recognize that a student needs psychological counseling. Some of the signs are belligerence, moodiness, excessive worry, suspiciousness, helplessness, emotional outbursts, or depression. Sometimes you will spot symptoms of drug or alcohol abuse. How do you get the student to the help needed? The first step may be to get the student to talk to you. Usually this can be handled by asking the student to come in, perhaps to discuss a paper or test. Typically the student will be aware that things aren't going well, and you can talk about what the student might do. One alternative, obviously, is to seek specialized help such as the reading clinic or counseling service. If the student agrees that this might be a good idea, I've found that it helps to pick up the phone and say, "I'll call to see when they can see you." In fact, most such agencies will at least carry out an initial interview with any student who walks in. But the sense of commitment involved when a faculty member has called seems to make students more likely to follow through than if they simply agree that they'll go in. Even if the student does not immediately get professional help, your concern and support will be helpful and awareness of the availability of professional help may be valuable later.

Potential Suicides

The increasing concern with suicide risk among college students prompts a few words on the early recognition of the kinds of depressed states that accompany such risks. If you were to notice a sudden falling off of a particular student's faithfulness in attending class, you might want to inquire further, especially if you noted signs of neglect of personal grooming and hygiene, lethargy, and any marked weight changes. Your interest in the student should include concern with any other changes he or she has been experiencing including major separations or losses and mood states. You should listen for talk of death or references to suicide or to getting one's personal and legal affairs in order. Your major concern should not be to reach an accurate assessment of suicide risk. A student manifesting any of these characteristics is surely troubled and should be urged to seek whatever professional counseling is available.

Individualized Teaching

The potentially most fruitful and most appropriate interpretation of educational counseling is the one least often defined explicitly and most neglected. When colleges and universities were small communities of a few hundred students and mature scholars, learning and teaching were naturally relatively individualized processes. The size of even the smaller major colleges and universities is such as to no longer make this individualized learning automatic. Even in classes of forty to sixty students, it is difficult for the learning process to include the meeting of a maturing and a mature intellect. Too frequently students must be content to listen to lectures and pursue readings aimed at some abstracted image of a student.

Educational counseling as individualized teaching can represent a method by which this more personalized learning can be preserved even in a large institution. It is particularly necessary to freshman students, to whom new intellectual spheres are being opened, usually at a time when they have taken a big step away from their family and community roots. This is likely to be a time when a great many new assumptions and new ways of dealing with important ideas need to be digested. Educational counselors, because they have no commitment to covering a specific subject matter, can provide the students with an opportunity to digest and integrate the intellectual experiences they have been having. Far from being a chore to be assigned to the least successful faculty member, such a demanding responsibility is best undertaken by persons of broad intellectual interests and foundations who, at the same time, have strong pedagogical commitments.

This time, when students are making big strides toward greater independence from family and are trying to search out models who can represent innovations of the adult role to which to aspire, is a time when there should be opportunities for close relationships with faculty members. The very characteristics of the large university throw obstacles in the way of such an experience. Educational counseling is one of the important media for achieving it. It seems probable that the most effective pattern for doing this would be for counselors to plan small group meetings with the students assigned to them for counseling to provide an opportunity for the groups of new students coming from different parts of the state and country to exchange with each other and with a person of fully developed intellectual maturity the impacts of their initial university experiences.

CHAPTER 12 / *Project Methods and Independent Study*

If one goal of education is to help students develop the ability to continue learning after their formal education is complete, it seems reasonable that they should have supervised experience in learning independently—experience in which the instructor helps students learn how to formulate problems, find answers, and evaluate their progress themselves. One might expect the values of independent study to be greatest for students of high ability with a good deal of background in the area to be covered, since such students should be less likely to be overwhelmed by difficulties encountered. While this expectation contains some truth, motivation and work habits are also important. In this chapter we will consider two forms of independent study: individual projects undertaken as part of a course and small-group independent study; we will also consider team learning in large courses.

The Project Method

Independent study programs frequently involve the execution of projects in which a student, or group of students, undertakes to gather and integrate data relevant to some more or less important problem.

The results of research on the effectiveness of the project method are not particularly encouraging. One of the first "independent study" experiments was that of Seashore (1928). His course consisted primarily of guided individual study with written reports on eight projects, each of which took about a month to complete. Final examination scores, however, were no different for these students than for students taught by the usual lecture-discussion method (Scheidemann, 1929). Similar results were reported by Barnard (1936) for a "group study" method. In a study in a college botany course, Novak (1958) found that students in conventional classes learned more facts than did those taught by the project method. The project method was particularly ineffective for students in the middle third of the group in intelligence. Similarly Goldstein (1956) reports that students taught pharmacology by a project method did not learn more than those taught in a standard laboratory.

Unfortunately, criteria such as those used in the studies just noted are probably not sufficient for measuring achievement of the purported objectives of project instruction. Presumably the real superiority of the project method should be revealed in measures of motivation and resourcefulness. One morsel of support comes from Thistlethwaite's (1960) finding that National Merit Scholars checked requirement of a term paper or laboratory project as one characteristic of their most stimulating course.

Research on Independent Study

With the support of the Fund for Advancement of Education, a number of colleges experimented with large programs of independent study. As with other comparisons of teaching methods, few large differences were found between achievement of students working independently and those taught in conventional classes. Moreover, the expected gains in independence also often failed to materialize. Students taught by independent study did not always develop greater ability or motivation for learning independently. Nevertheless, a number of encouraging results emerged.

Small Group Independent Study

One of the most comprehensive research programs on independent study was carried out by Antioch College (Churchill, 1957; Churchill and Baskin, 1958). The Antioch experiment involved courses in humanities, social science, and science. Periods of independent study were varied, and a serious attempt was made not only to measure cognitive and affective achievement, but also to evaluate the effect of independent study upon "learning resourcefulness." As in most experiments on teaching methods, the predominant results were "no significant difference." An exception to this may be found in various indexes of student satisfaction in which several significant differences favored lecture-discussion over independent study and especially over independent small groups.

Much more favorable results on independent study were obtained in the experiments carried out at the University of Colorado by Gruber and Weitman (1960). In a course in freshman English in which the group met only about 90 percent of the regularly scheduled hours and had little formal training on grammar, the self-directed study group was significantly superior to control groups on a test of grammar. In a course in physical optics groups of students who attended class without the instructor but were free to consult him learned fewer facts and simple applications, but were superior to students in conventional classes in difficult applications and learning new material. Moreover, the areas of superiority were maintained in a retest three months later when the difference in factual knowledge had disappeared. In educational psychology an experimental class of five or six students without the instructor was equal to a conventional three-lecture-a-week class in mastery of content, and tended to be superior on measures of curiosity.

Variations in Amount of Classroom Time ═══════

Independent study experiments have varied greatly in the amount of assistance given students and in the patterning of instructional vs. independent periods. For example, merely excusing students from attending class is one method of stimulating independent study. The results of such a procedure are not uniform but suggest that classroom experience is not essential for learning. However, different kinds of learning may take place out of class than in class.

The experiment reported by McKeachie, Forrin, Lin, and Teevan (1960) involved a fairly high degree of student-instructor contact. In this experiment students normally met with the instructor in small groups weekly or biweekly, but students were free to consult the instructor whenever they wished to. The results of the experiment suggest that the "tutorial" students did not learn as much from the textbook as students taught in conventional lecture periods and discussion sections, but did develop stronger motivation both for course work and for continued learning after the course. This was indicated not only by responses to a questionnaire administered at the end of the course, but also by the number of advanced psychology courses later elected.

The results of the studies in a child development course by Parsons (1957) and Parsons, Ketcham, and Beach (1958) were, in a sense, more favorable to independent study. In the latter experiment four teaching methods were compared—lecture, instructor-led discussions, autonomous groups that did not come to class, and individual independent study in which each student was sent home with the syllabus, returning for the final examination. In both experiments, students working independently made the best scores on the final examination, which measured retention of factual material in the textbook. The instructor-led discussion groups were the lowest in performance on the final examination. There were no significant differences between groups on a measure of attitudes toward working with children. The authors explain their results in terms of the independent group's freedom from distraction by interesting examples, possible applications, or opposing points of view from those presented in the text.

Although the Parsons, Ketcham, and Beach results were favorable to independent study, they are not very satisfying to the advocate of this method, for they lead to the conclusion that if students know that they are going to be tested on the factual content of a particular book, it is more advantageous for them to read that book than to participate in other educational activities. In fact even better results might be obtained if the desired facts could be identified by giving the student test questions in advance as in PSI (see Chapter 21). But knowledge of specific facts is not the typical major objective of an independent study program. What instructors are hoping for is greater integration, increased purposefulness, and more intense motivation for further study. That independent study can achieve these ends is indicated by the Colorado and Michigan experiments. But the paucity of positive results suggests that we need more research on methods of selecting and training students for independent study, arranging the independent study experience, and measuring outcomes. Note that the Colorado and Penn State results came in courses in which a good deal of contact with the instructor was retained.

Time in Class

The independent study experiments demonstrate that education is not simply a function of time spent in a class with a teacher. Well-planned activities outside teacher-controlled classrooms can be at least as educational as conventional classes. But merely reducing time in class is not independent study. Generally speaking, the more time spent on learning, the greater the learning. Wakely, Marr, Plath, and Wilkins (1960) compared performance in a traditional four-hour-a-week lecture class with that in a class meeting only once a week to clear up questions on the textbook. In this experiment the traditional classes proved to be superior.

Similarly Paul (1932) found fifty-five-minute class periods to be superior to thirty-minute periods, as measured by student achievement. Shortening class periods, reducing the number of classes, cutting the length of the academic term may be advisable as part of a planned educational change, but they should not be undertaken with the blithe assumption that the same educational outcomes will be achieved.

SUPPLEMENTARY READING

For a British perspective read Donald Bligh, G. J. Ebrahim, D. Jacques, and D. W. Piper, _Teaching students_ (Devon, England: Exeter University Teaching Services, 1975).

CHAPTER 13 // *Reading and Programmed Learning*

While professors like to think that students learn from professors, it seems likely that students often learn more efficiently from reading than from listening.

Reading and Textbooks

For the past three decades the demise of the textbook has been eagerly predicted by advocates of each of the new panaceas for the problems of education.* First television, then teaching machines, then the computer—each was expected to revolutionize education and free students and teachers from their longtime reliance upon textbooks. Even the major book publishers scurried to the arms of electronic manufacturers and set up new nontextbook divisions to keep up with the coming age of educational media.

But each of the new media has settled into its niche in the educational arsenal without dislodging the textbook. In fact, the greatest revolution in education has come not from teaching machines or computers, but from the greater availability of a wide variety of printed materials.

The introduction of open-stack libraries, paperback books, inexpensive reprint series, and the photo-copying machine has given the college teacher the opportunity to choose from sources varying in style, level, and point of view. Many teachers are substituting paperback books, reprints, and collections of journal articles for the textbook as the sources of the basic information needed by students. The students thus have an opportunity to organize the material in a way meaningful for them. But in most undergraduate courses there is little hope that bits and pieces

---

* Much of the following section was included in a letter I wrote to the editor of *Change Magazine* published in May–June 1971. It was stimulated by an article predicting the demise of textbooks.

will be integrated by students into a meaningful whole despite the valiant efforts of instructors to give assistance. They know that learning is facilitated by organization and that, lacking organization, facts and concepts become so many nonsense syllables subject to interference, quickly forgotten and inaccessible. With inputs from field experience, discussion, paperbacks, reprints, and other sources, the student needs more than ever some frame of reference within which to assimilate the boomin', buzzin' confusion of points of view present in a modern course.

Ideally, the textbook can provide such a structure. That structure need not be dogmatic, but it need not be gutless. It need not be presented as irrevocable truth. Inevitably, certain parts of textbook information become dated. If teachers fail to recognize what is obsolete and insist on its memorization, the students' education is harmed rather than aided. Probably the main drawback of textbooks as teaching tools is their tendency to encourage encyclopedic learning of factual material rather than achievement of the facility to deal with the ideas that have a longer half-life in their application to the transfer-of-learning world. But dogmatic, out-of-date teachers can misuse any source. A good textbook can counter instructor dogmatism by presenting a more open framework. Structures should be presented as tentative, temporary, and incomplete. Textbooks should be up to date and frequently revised. That textbooks in the past have often been little more than a collection of topics is no reason to reject their potential usefulness in meeting important needs for the student learner today.

Modern education is focusing less on imparting facts and theories and more on development of student capacities for judgment, fact-gathering, analysis, and synthesis. Thus the encyclopedic textbook is an anachronism promoting the wrong kind of education. But the modern textbook can and should be aimed at the very goals that are now evolving. None of these desired capacities for critical thinking and usefulness for action can be developed without some grounding in essential facts and concepts. Without the structure provided by a good textbook, students, required to gather, judge, evaluate, analyze, and synthesize a diversity of sources and experiences by themselves, simply end in confusion and frustration.

Certainly, modern teachers should provide a variety of learning experiences for students. If individual differences are to be attended to in teaching, students need an opportunity to learn in laboratory settings, field experiences, discussion, lectures, or reading from diverse sources.

Textbooks are an important part of the teacher's compendium of tools, and the newer teaching methods and aids supplement rather than supplant the textbook. In fact a goodly part of higher education is education in how to read—how to read poems, how to read social science, how to read legal briefs, how to read the literature of our culture and our profession.

Research on Learning from Reading

An early study (Greene, 1928) found that students learned as well from reading material as from listening to the same material read aloud. The better students, moreover, profited more from reading than from listening. A number of other studies have compared printed materials with lectures, and the results—at least with difficult materials—favor print (Hartman, 1961). In fact Reder and Anderson (1982) found that students who studied textbook summaries scored better on achievement tests than those who read the entire text. The details in the text were distracting rather than supportive.

The eruption of research in cognitive psychology has pushed the frontiers of research into studies of meaningful prose passages. Most of the research to date has been on brief passages, but there are now a number of studies using material like textbook passages. Some of the theories resulting in these studies will be discussed in Chapter 24, but one or two studies with practical applications will be reviewed here.

The group of researchers at the Institute of Education, University of Göteborg, has carried out a number of studies applying concepts of cognitive psychology to the learning of chapters of textbooks and other meaningful, relatively complex reading. Their results, like those of Gates (1917) and other pioneers, indicate that questions can influence student learning. Marton and Säljö (1976b) found that questions designed to produce more thoughtful, integrative study were more effective than questions of fact. Nevertheless, study questions are not automatically a guarantee of better learning. Students sometimes tended to look only for answers to the questions while disregarding the other content of the chapter (Marton and Säljö, 1976a). Research by Rothkopf (1972) and other students of prose learning suggest that factual questions after reading may be more effective than factual questions before reading. Wilhite (1983) found that pre-questions focusing on material at the top of the organizational structure did facilitate learning, especially for the less able students. What instructors need are questions that get students to _think_ about the material.

Programmed Instruction

In the 1960s "programmed textbooks" began to appear. These are instructional books developed by utilizing the learning-in-small-steps sequences advocated by B. F. Skinner. Such books and booklets have sometimes been designed as adjuncts to normal teaching materials, but often were intended to replace textbooks.

The research with Skinnerian types of programs was not encouraging. Students do learn from the programs, but learning is generally slower than with conventional printed materials (but faster than lectures) (Smith, 1962). Reviews by Kulik, Cohen, and Ebeling (1980), Lange (1972), Nash, Muczyk, and Vettori (1971), and Schramm (1964) show programmed instruction to be superior to traditional instruction in about 40 percent of the over one hundred research studies reported, equally effective in about half the studies, and relatively seldom less effective.

One would expect strict control over the structure and pace of learning to be most helpful to students with poor study habits, those who read passively and tend to slide over important uncomprehended points, but little research has been done to determine what kinds of students gain from programs or what types of objectives can be most efficiently achieved. On the basis of the theoretical relationship between uncertainty and curiosity, it might be expected that most students would be bored by the practice of writing programs so that every question is answered correctly by almost every student. From Atkinson's theory it would be expected that students with a high need for achievement (those who work hardest in situations with 50-50 probabilities of success) would find the usual small-step program more boring than other students would. And this is what Moore, Smith, and Teevan (1965) discovered.

But even for students in general, a logical sequence of items may be less efficient for learning than a random sequence (Rosen, Frincke, and Stolurow, 1964). This makes sense in terms of the motivational theory that lack of change or surprises makes for boredom and also helps to explain why short programs, requiring half an hour or less, seem to be more effective and less boring than longer programs covering large blocks of material or an entire course (Beard, 1972).

The fervor of the 1960s proponents of teaching machines has now subsided, and research is beginning to clarify the uses of programmed materials (Lumsdaine, 1963). For a while it appeared that programmed materials might enable educators to shortcut the difficult problems of curriculum and course organization, but programs that teach unimportant concepts or untrue information are not of much help to education, and it is now recognized that the writing of a good program requires as much scholarship as the writing of a good textbook (Krumboltz, 1964). Unfortunately, programming is difficult work, and as yet scholars seem less willing to write programs than to write books. Thus, there are still only a very limited number of good programs for college use, although programmed texts are frequently used in military and industrial training and some of the educational computer programs essentially are programmed books.

SUPPLEMENTARY READING

Ference Marton, Dai Hounsell, and Noel Entwistle, eds., *The experience of learning* (Edinburgh: Scottish Academic Press, 1984).
T. M. Chang, H. F. Crombag, K. D. J. M. van der Drift, and J. M. Moonen, *Distance learning* (Boston: Kluwer-Nijhoff Publishing, 1983), Chapter 4.

CHAPTER 14 ∥ Computer Uses in Teaching and Learning

Computers can individualize instruction as printed programs do not. Computers can provide immediate, individualized feedback. Sequences of problems and instruction can be varied depending upon the student's previous performance. Diagnostic and coaching systems enable computers to adapt instruction to student needs.

Use in Instruction and Testing

Early attempts to use computers in instruction simply put conventional linear and branching programs into the computer so that the capacity of the computer was not really used to increase the complexity of the teaching. Feurzeig, Swets and others (1964) at Bolt, Beranek, and Newman, Inc., however, used computerized techniques to develop analytical thinking, such as that used in medical diagnosis. A similar program for simulating a laboratory in qualitative analysis was described by Hirsch and Moncreiff (1965). In these systems, students could ask questions as well as answer those posed by the computer. Students could also volunteer assertions or solutions whenever they wished. The computer responded in a meaningful way both to student questions and assertions It recognized inappropriate responses and remembered previous responses. The anthropomorphic terms "recognized" and "remembered" are not really inaccurate, for they describe the phenomenal experience of the student interacting with the computer. While it might be more objective to say that the program is written in terms of strings of conditional "if-then" probabilities, much of the motivational value of the computer lies in the student's attempt to test its humanlike qualities. Wood (1980) has developed a program to teach logical thinking. Students completing the program showed gains on the Watson-Glaser Critical Thinking Appraisal.

Bork (1975) and Pask (1976) have developed teaching "dialogues" or "conversations." Bork's dialogues are concerned with teaching content, concepts, and problem-solving skills in physics. Pask's "conversational domains" have been developed for physics and statistics. Both of these approaches involve extensive analysis of the conceptual structure of the material to be taught. Probably the major reason that Computer Assisted Instruction (CAI) has not spread more rapidly is the time-consuming, difficult work necessary to develop a system that uses the memory and adaptive capacity of the tutor.

In addition to using computers as instructional devices, teachers have used computers in testing. TIPS, which is discussed in Chapter 21, is one such system. One of the advantages of computerized testing is the ability to collect data on items over time so that a test can be constructed with reasonably good estimation of its difficulty and of the level of outcomes being assessed, so that a test is not primarily measuring low-level knowledge rather than application, analysis, or other more important goals.

"Camelot" is an individualized information system developed at Miami-Dade Community College that goes beyond TIPS by providing individualized feedback for students on multiple-choice tests, essay tests, or other assignments. Teachers can provide any statements of feedback appropriate for a given answer, a given type of student, or at a particular level of learning. Teachers can receive summaries of group or individual progress (Anandam, 1984).

CAI can relieve teachers of some time spent on drill (as can printed programmed instruction). Such drill can often be arranged in a game form on the computer. Repetition is important for developing the automatic responses one needs to function effectively in most domains of scholarship. Knowing technical terms in science or foreign language vocabulary is obviously valuable, and similar well-learned structures characterize expertise in most fields. A computer game can engage one in the kind of practice that might otherwise be drudgery.

Games differ in the degree to which the game is extrinsic or intrinsic to the learning goal. For example, one can teach addition by a game in which correct answers move an adventurer past hazards to a treasure or by a game in which the learners are adding up scores in a dart board game.

One promising direction for research is the approach used by Pask and associates (Pask and Scott, 1973), who carry R. C. Atkinson's (1972)

encouragement of response-sensitive paradigms to the point of a colloquy between the computer and the learner to determine the learner's
preferred learning strategy. Pask demonstrates that matching the structure of the learning program to the learning strategy (holist or serialist)
of the student results in more effective instruction than learner control
or an incompatible program. In general, the research on learner control
of CAI is inconclusive, leading Judd (1973) to conclude his review with
the suggestion that students may need specific training to exercise effective control of their own instruction.

Effective computerized instruction will demand the development
of more complex teaching strategies. CAI has not turned out to be the
revolutionary panacea some expected, but the impact is gradually
increasing.

A meta-analysis of evaluations of computer-based education in
higher education found that computers made small but significant contributions to achievement (Kulik, Kulik and Cohen, 1980b). The greatest
success has been with drill and practice programs.

The computer has the potential not only to help students automatize
basic skills but also to adapt to learners' learning strategies or styles and
to help students _learn_ about their learning strategies so that they can
become more efficient learners (Pask and Scott, 1973). For the moment
the hardware has outstripped the educational uses.

Although drill and practice programs are easiest to devise, there are
many other educational uses of computers, e.g.,

➔ monitoring, recording, and analyzing data in laboratories

➔ simulations of experiments, medical diagnoses, case study problems
   in social sciences

➔ instructional dialogs—Allan Collins at Bolt, Beranek, and Newman
   and Alfred Bork at the University of California, Irvine, have developed Socratic dialogs for computers

What Makes Computer-Based Education Fun?

Lepper and Malone (1985) have studied uses of computers in public
schools and have experimentally compared the motivational effects of
different components of computer games. Their analysis is important not

only for those devising computer-based instructional games but for consideration of the motivational elements in all instruction.

The first feature they identified is *challenge*. Computer games work because they provide difficulty levels that are variable depending upon the skill of the performer. The game becomes frustrating if one has no success; it becomes boring if one gets a perfect score routinely. Educational programs need to be flexible enough to provide increasing challenges as the learner becomes more adept.

In order to help students develop a sense of *self-competence* Lepper and Malone suggest that the instructional program, or game, should provide a good deal of early success, and the progression of difficulty should be such that the learner has a sense of accomplishment at each level of difficulty—a sense of progress—as new levels of difficulty are introduced.

Curiosity can be enhanced by highlighting incompleteness, inconsistency, or unexpected implications of the student's understanding.

Motivation is also enhanced if the learner has a sense of *personal control*—is perhaps given choices about when to proceed to more difficult problems or to a new set of materials.

Lepper and Malone's analysis of computer games highlighted one element not identified in conventional motivation theory. It was *fantasy*. From their research it becomes evident that one fascinating element in computer games is the chance to experience other roles—being a king, a knight, a professional baseball player, a foreign diplomat, or president of a large company. They suggest that such fantasies are more likely to be educational if the fantasy has some inherent connection with the educational objective and is not simply tacked on as a scorekeeping device.

The Cost-Effectiveness of CAI

Is computer-assisted instruction cost effective? Not so far, according to Lewis, Dalgaard, and Boyer (1984). Analyses of research on the teaching of economics have suggested that so far CAI probably has not been cost-effective. Nonetheless, with lower prices for hardware and improved programs CAI is likely to be a continuing feature of the educational environment.

SUPPLEMENTARY READING

Brian Simpson, who worked as Education Methods Advisor at the IBM Education Center in England, has written of the importance of the students driving the computer rather than the computer driving the students. He sees little likelihood that computers can simulate the ways in which teachers interact with students. For his views read B. Simpson, Heading for the ha-ha, _British Journal of Educational Technology_, 1983, _14_, 19–26.

Another useful discussion may be found in T. M. Chang et al., _Distance learning_ (Boston: Klower-Nijhoff Publishing, 1983), Chapter 6.

For a good description of computer-based instructional dialog, read A. B. Arons, Computer-based instructional dialogs, _Science_, 1984, _224_, 1051–1056.

Also see: Alfred Bork, _Learning with computers_ (Bedford, MA: Digital Press, 1981).

CHAPTER 15 // *Audiovisual Techniques*

Some college faculty members are anxious about technologically induced unemployment and resist innovations, so that critics of higher education often accuse them of academic featherbedding. Research suggests that there are valid as well as invalid reasons for faculty members' skepticism about the education- and cost-effectiveness of technology. Although many more glamorous aids are available, for most teachers the most valuable visual aids continue to be blackboards, slides, and overhead transparencies.

Much of higher education consists of verbal abstract material, such as Shakespeare, Weber, Freud, or the classics. But education also deals with physical realities, such as people, plants, animals, rocks, and stars. Here words may be poor substitutes for direct experience or for audio-visual representations.

Television

Before reviewing the research on teaching by television, consider two hypotheses that may help in anaylzing the research results.

Television is not a method of instruction in the sense that discussion and lecture are methods of instruction. Rather, it is a means of giving students a clear view of an instructional situation. Therefore one would expect that the relative effectiveness of teaching via television will vary depending upon the importance of being able to see clearly. For example, I would expect television to be effective when it is important for students to see demonstrations, visiting lecturers, or films, but to have little advantage when the communication is primarily verbal.

Early Research

The early research on the use of television in higher education was largely funded by the Ford Foundation's Fund for the Advancement of Education. Grants to Pennsylvania State University (Carpenter and Greenhill, 1955, 1958), Miami University (Macomber and Siegel, 1956, 1957a,b, 1960), and a number of other universities led to a large number of well-

158

controlled and well-evaluated studies of the effectiveness of television. Most of these studies involved semester-long comparisons of courses taught by television and live classes.

The results of this research may be used either to extol or damn television. Essentially they indicated that while there is little loss in student learning in courses taught by television as compared with courses taught conventionally, live classes tend to be superior (e.g., Sullivan, Andrews, Hollinghurst, Maddigan, and Noseworthy, 1976).

Most television students learned the information needed to pass examinations, and most did not object strongly to the televised classes, although they preferred live instruction.

Adapting a course for television by adding supplementary visual aids proved to be no more effective than televised lecture-blackboard presentations. In fact, both at Penn State (Carpenter and Greenhill 1955, 1958) and NYU (Adams et al., 1959), the "visual" productions tended to be less effective than "bare bones" television. This result should probably not be startling if we consider the Parsons, Ketcham, and Beach (1958) results with independent study. Just as discussion and lecture apparently interfered with learning the textbook, so here added visual materials may have distracted the students from the verbal content upon which the tests were based.

The Pennsylvania State research does provide some support for the idea that television's effectiveness is related to how good the students' view is. In one experiment students were given their choice, after three weeks of instruction, of whether to finish the course in television classrooms or in the original room. Depending upon the course, one-third to two-thirds of the students chose television. The most interesting aspect of this finding was that these students were predominantly those who had been assigned seats toward the back of the lecture hall.

If they could have had the same instructor, students generally preferred a small section to television or a large class. But they preferred television or a large class to a small class if they could be sure of an excellent instructor in the television or large class and had to take their chances in electing a small class. This is probably a realistic alternative.

Uses of Television

From the hypothesis that television would be of most value in courses depending upon visual presentation of information, it might be expected to be more effective in science and engineering courses than in social sciences and humanities courses. From the hypothesis that television would be of less value in classes where interaction between students and instructor is important, it might be expected to be relatively less effective in psychology, speech, and languages than in courses usually taught by lecture. If we simply look at the direction of the differences, about half the experiments in science classes favor television and half favor conventional instruction. In nonscience courses well over two-thirds of the differences favor conventional teaching.*

In summary, when used over an entire course, television instruction is generally inferior to classroom lectures in communicating information, developing critical thinking, changing attitudes, and arousing interest in a subject, but this inferiority is not great.

The preceding comments have been primarily concerned with television instruction on campus. The Open University in England and similar enterprises in other countries use television as part of a system of bringing education to people who would not otherwise have access to higher education. While there has not been much evaluative research, the television component seems to be appreciated by some learners who might not have responded to correspondence courses or other alternatives less expensive than television. Nevertheless, the number of students enrolling in broadcast television courses has generally been disappointing. Hoban (1968) suggests that this is a result of the serious limitations of television in giving students and teachers the sense of interpersonal interaction so central to higher-level education. He suggests, and the Open University type of courses have often adopted, small-group discussions following televised lessons.

Almost all research has dealt with television used as a major medium of instruction for a total course. While there is little research evidence, anecdotal accounts of the use of television as a teaching aid in conventional courses indicate that there are apparent advantages to its ability to magnify and to provide an unobtrusive means of observation. The continuing technological advances in television, videotape, videodisc, and computer-linked videodisc may give television potential usefulness for higher education.

---

* Note that the tests used in most studies are verbal. In any course where visual identification or discrimination is an important goal, a visual test item might be expected to be more valid. While many instructor goals primarily involve abstractions and verbal or symbolic concepts, tests may underrepresent goals involving learning to deal with objects and events.

Films

Motion picture films have been available for teaching for a good many years, but their impact upon college teaching has not been great. Nevertheless, well-made, educationally useful films are available, and it behooves college teachers to become familiar with the audiovisual resources available for their use.

The effectiveness of visual aids depends to a large extent upon the way they are used. Before showing a film, instructors should consider their objectives in showing the film and then plan how they can best utilize the film to attain these objectives. Before showing a film to a class, instructors should have seen the film, noting the points it illustrates and what misconceptions may be inferred from it. Occasionally it may be a dramatic procedure to dim the lights as soon as the students have arrived and begin the picture immediately. Usually, however, the film is of more value if the students know what to look for and how it has been related to the subject matter of the course.* A study guide may be distributed in the class meeting before the class meeting of the film, or the instructor may give a verbal introduction to the film. Sometimes verbal comments may be used to occupy periods when the film is of little interest. However, unless you are familiar with the film, your comments may run over into the next scene and be lost in a chorus of laughter.

As with all instruction a key variable in learning is student involvement—activity which encourages meaningful thought. Just as with readings, instructors may use films to provide background and stimulation for discussion. Thus, instructors may break a class into small buzz groups or lead a class discussion in which the students use the film material in analyzing and understanding the phenomena depicted. Another technique suggested by Susan Parman (1984) is the film essay. Alongside the film screen Parman shows on a side wall one or two questions about the film, using an overhead projector. Immediately after the film, students write short essays on the questions.

One of the biggest difficulties in using films is knowing which films to use. Previewing as many films as possible seems to be the usual solution, but critical reviews are available for most films.

---

* Experiments in the Armed Forces support this. See C. Hovland, A. Lumsdaine, and F. Sheffield, _Experiments in mass communication_ (Princeton: Princeton Unversity Press, 1949).

Research on Film Use in Teaching

The great mass of research on instructional films is relevant to our topic, even though most of it has not been concerned with college teaching. While it would be impossible for me to summarize all of the relevant studies, certain principles have emerged (for a more complete analysis, see Miller, 1957):

1. Students can learn from films and usually do learn at least as much as from a poor teacher (Vandermeer, 1950).

2. Repeating the film increases learning (McTavish, 1949).

3. Participation increases learning (Hovland, Lumsdaine, and Sheffield, 1949). In this study, active response with prompting and feedback was most effective on the most difficult material with the least motivated, least able students—a finding that probably has wide generality in teaching (also see Michael and Maccoby, 1953).

What Do You Do if the Projectionist Fails to Appear, the Film Breaks, or the Bulb Burns Out?

None of these catastrophes is common, but if you use films often, there will sometime come a day when you can't show the film as expected. One way of using the time productively is to summarize what you hoped to achieve by using the film. Other techniques are included in the section, "What to Do When You're Not Prepared" in Chapter 22.

Telephone and Radio

Cutler, McKeachie, and McNeil (1958) compared the effectiveness of teaching equal-sized groups in face-to-face groups or by telephone. Both groups showed significant learning and attitude change, and there was no significant difference in the two methods' effectiveness. Thus, if economy in instruction is desired, perhaps the expense of television cameras and receiving tubes is unnecessary. One of the few experiments comparing the effectiveness of radio and television, however, showed better learning and retention for television (Paul and Ogilvie, 1955). A number of colleges have used telephone to bring students into contact with well-known public figures, but no systematic evaluation has yet appeared.

Language Laboratories and Cassette Recorders

Cassette recorders are now convenient and relatively inexpensive tools available for teaching. The original and most common use of tape recorders was in language laboratories. Developed in the Army's intensive language training programs during World War II, language laboratories multiplied rapidly in the postwar years and boomed under the financial impetus of the National Defense Education Act of 1958. The core of the language laboratory is the tape recorder, which can present foreign language sounds and utterances with accuracy, fidelity, and endless patience.

With its emphasis upon the prepared recorded sequence of stimuli and frequent opportunites for student responses, the language laboratory has close kinship to the programmed-learning movement. Language laboratories are now an accepted part of the college scene, but experimental tests of their value are nonexistent, so far as I can ascertain. At other educational levels there is scanty evidence, some of which is favorable. For example, Allen (1960) reports higher achievement for high school students with language laboratory experience, and Banathy and Jordan report favorable experience at the Army Language School (1969). Bauer (1964) found that the success of the language laboratory depended upon the amount of supervision—a finding reminiscent of some of those in programmed learning and in independent study.

Other imaginative uses of tape recorders are in presentation of oral questions in programmed teaching, in dictation of comments about student papers, in lecture-poster or slide presentation (Johnston, 1969), in an automated taped lecture, programmed-question, filmstrip presentation (Postlethwait et al., 1969), and in recording lectures prepared by students as a technique for developing student motivation and active integration of material (Webb, 1965). So far as I can find, the only empirical study of the effectiveness of tape recording was a study of a thirty-minute lecture by Bligh (1970). In this study the lecture was given live, audiotaped, and transcribed by a secretary. A mulitple-choice test given immediately after students had heard or read the lecture revealed no difference in overall learning but a possibility that the tape was *superior* for the higher-level questions requiring synthesis and evaluation.

Photographs, Transparencies, and the Blackboard

In contrast to the dearth of evidence about the use of language labora-tories, research on other types of audiovisual aids has been encouraging. Carroll (1963) reports successful use of an audiovisual teaching machine to teach the Arabic writing system. Antioch College (1960) used acetate visuals projected with an overhead projector coupled with a language laboratory to achieve substantial savings of instructional time and im-prove instruction as measured by a test of reading ability. Similarly, Chance (1961) found that the use of overhead projected transparencies and overlays was significantly superior to conventional instruction (using the blackboard) in teaching descriptive geometry to freshman engineers.

One of the problems faced by the instructor with a large section is that of getting the students settled and quiet in order to begin the lecture. Louis Berman, while in charge of visual aids for a lecture section of 500 students at the University of Michigan, conceived of showing slides of review material, cartoons, and questions for the ten-minute period between classes. This directed the attention of arriving students to the front of the auditorium and eased the instructor's task of gaining attention.

The blackboard is the one audiovisual tool that is almost always readily available. It has no bulbs to burn out or mechanisms to break, and if you carry a spare piece of chalk, you can be quite sure that your visual aid will be usable even if the previous instructor threw the last piece of chalk at a student. Elaborate graphics merit pre-planning and preparation (probably the use of a transparency), but spontaneous use of the blackboard for key words, a running outline of the lecture, a record of student questions, or a quick linking of boxes and arrows to represent a set of relationships—this can get student attention, give them a point that can be referred to after the sound of your words has vanished, and provide a change of pace and breathing point for unpacking overloaded working memories. (It also gives you a chance to collect your thoughts if you're beginning to wander and wonder what to say next!)

Audiotutorial

The Audiotutorial method was developed by Postlethwait for use in a Purdue University biology course (Postlethwait, Novak, and Murray, 1969). It involves a combination of individual study of modules, including audiotapes, slides, and other media with a general assembly used for guest lecturers, films, and examinations. In addition, weekly small-group quiz sessions are held. Kulik and Jaksa (1977) found twenty-four studies, nine of which favored audiotutorial and two the conventional class. Thus the audiotutorial approach seems well worth instituting as a method in courses such as the sciences, where visual, auditory, or laboratory experience is needed in order to achieve course goals.

Media-Activated Learning Groups

The Technical University of Denmark has made effective use of a method described by Berman (1973, 1974). In media-activated learning groups a structural audiovisual program of transparencies and audiocassettes orients and directs activities of students who meet without the instructor. Such groups proved to be equal in achievement to lecture groups.

Audiovisual Aids: A Summary

The research to date indicates that television, films, and other media can be used to achieve educational objectives. The usefulness varies depending upon the objective, characteristics of the students, and the excellence of the materials. Research at present reveals no likelihood that they will eliminate the need for face-to-face interaction between professors and students. In fact no specific medium has proved to have great benefits for teaching and learning. Meta-analysis and reviews of research suggest that media deliver instruction, and their effectiveness depends upon the instruction delivered rather than upon the medium used (Kulik, Kulik, and Cohen 1980a; Clark, 1983). As Clark says, "(Media) do not influence student achievement any more than the truck that delivers our groceries causes changes in our nutrition." One of the most useful audiovisual devices continues to be the blackboard or its alternate, the overhead projector.

SUPPLEMENTARY READING

A good general reference on audiovisual methods is W. A. Wittich, and
C. F. Shuller, _Instructional technology: its nature and use,_ 6th ed. (Harper & Row, 1979).

A book going well beyond audiovisual methods is R. B. Kozma, L. W. Belle, and G. W. Williams, *Instructional techniques in higher education* (Englewood Cliffs, NJ: Educational Technology Publications, 1978).

Chang, et al. have a good chapter—"The Scope and Limitations of Audiovisual Teaching Media" in their book, *Distance learning* (Boston: Kluwer-Nyhoff Publishing, 1983).

CHAPTER 16 ‖ *Laboratory Teaching*

The laboratory method is now so widely accepted as necessary for scientific education that it may seem heretical to ask whether laboratory experience is an effective way to achieve educational objectives. Fortunately there is evidence that laboratory instruction can be educational. Whether it typically achieves its potential is another question.

Laboratory teaching assumes that first-hand experience in observation and manipulation of the materials of a science is superior to other methods of developing understanding and appreciation of research methods. Laboratory training is also frequently used to develop complex skills necessary for more advanced study or research and to develop familiarity with equipment, measures, and research tools.

From the standpoint of theory, the activity of the student, the sensorimotor nature of the experience, and the individualization of laboratory instruction should contribute positively to learning. However, information cannot usually be obtained by direct experience as rapidly as from abstractions presented orally or by printing. Films, demonstrations, or simulations may also shortcut some of the trial and error of the laboratory. Thus, one would not expect laboratory teaching to have an advantage over other teaching methods in amount of information learned. Rather, one might expect the differences to be revealed in retention, in ability to apply learning, or in actual skill in observation or manipulation of materials. Unfortunately, little research has attempted to test out these special types of outcomes. If these outcomes are unmeasured, a finding of no difference in effectiveness between laboratory and other methods of instruction is almost meaningless, since there is little reason to expect laboratory teaching to be effective in simple communication of information.

Research on Laboratory Teaching

In an experiment in a course, "Methods of Engineering," White (1945) found that students taught by a group laboratory method achieved more than those taught by a lecture-demonstration method. A study by Balcziak (1954), however, comparing, 1) demonstration, 2) individual laboratory, and 3) combined demonstration and laboratory in a college physical science course, found no significant differences between them as measured by tests of information, scientific attitude, or laboratory performance.

In experiments in physics and engineering, Kruglak (1952) and White (1945) found that students taught by individual or group laboratory methods achieved more than those taught by lecture-demonstration. In studies by Balcziak (1954), Dearden (1960), Trotter (1960), and Bradley (1963), however, laboratory teaching was compared with,1) lecture-demonstration, 2) combined demonstration and laboratory, 3) workbook, and 4) term paper. The comparisons were in physical science, general biology, and home economics courses. No significant differences were found between methods as measured by tests of information, practical application, scientific attitude, or laboratory performance. Earlier experiments found no significant loss resulting from reduction in laboratory time or from assignment of one cadaver to four students rather than two (Downing, 1913; Hurd, 1929; Jackson, 1929; Noll, 1930).

While reviews of research on laboratory teaching find that laboratory courses are effective in improving skills in handling apparatus or visual-motor skills, laboratories generally are not very effective in teaching scientific method or problem solving (Shulman and Tamir, 1973; Bligh et al., 1980).

The foregoing studies point to the conclusion that time spent in the laboratory could be reduced without educational loss. However, the results of research on methods of teaching in the laboratory indicate that the effectiveness of the laboratory depends on the manner in which the work is taught. Bainter (1955) found that a problem-solving method was superior to traditional laboratory manual methods in teaching students to apply principles of physics in interpreting phenomena. Lahti (1956) also found a problem-solving method to be superior to more conventional procedures in developing students' abilities to design an experiment. However, all of these studies point to the importance of developing understanding, rather than teaching problem solutions by going through a routine series of steps. Whether the laboratory is superior to the lecture-demonstration in developing understanding and problem-solving skills probably depends upon the extent to which understanding of concepts and general problem-solving procedures are emphasized as opposed to "cookbook" methods.

SUPPLEMENTARY READING

A good, brief review of work on laboratory teaching may be found in
Donald Bligh, G. J. Ebrahim, D. Jacques, and D. W. Piper, *Teaching
Students* (Devon, England: Exeter University Teaching Services,
1975), pp. 174–175.

CHAPTER 17 / Instructional Games, Simulations, and the Case Method

For some students and some teachers, education and games are simply at opposite ends of a continuum—they find it hard to conceive of games as educational. Yet in the past decade an increasing number of teachers have been finding games to be an important part of their educational resources. It may well be that within the next decade educational games will replace many of the noneducational game shows now on television.

Games and Simulations

An educational game involves students in some sort of competition or achievement in relationship to a goal, a game that both teaches and is fun. Many games are simulations; for example, they attempt to model some real-life problem situation. Thus there are business games, international relations games, and many others. Whatever the topic, the planner of the game needs to specify the teaching objectives to be served by the game and then plan the game to highlight features that contribute to those objectives.

The chief advantage of games and simulations is that students are active participants rather than passive observers. Students must make decisions, solve problems, and react to the results of their decisions. Lepper and Malone (1985) have studied the motivational elements in computer games. A summary of their findings can be found in Chapter 14, Computer Uses in Teaching and Learning.

Dekkers and Donatti (1981) conducted a meta-analysis of ninety-three studies of simulation and concluded that simulation was not more effective than conventional methods for achieving cognitive objectives but did have a favorable effect upon student attitudes and motivation.

Games typically create a high level of student involvement and thus can be a worthwhile adjunct to many courses. Following is a description of a game used in Russian History.*

Simulation in a Survey Course in Russian History

Game: Parties and Constituencies in Russian Revolution.

Instructor: Bill Rosenberg, Associate Professor of History.

Enrollment: About 100 students.

Game Time: 1½ hours (up to 2 hours).

Preparation: Four or five students volunteered to work out this game as their course project; two or three took a leadership role. The instructor consulted with them in planning; he suggested readings and consultation with an instructor who had worked on gaming and simulation.

The students prepared a twelve-page document on four parties and four constituencies that took part in the Russian Revolution. This program told each group what its orientation was (for example, what their methods tended to be). The program was given to students to read in advance of the day of the simulation.

Purpose of the Game: To look at the electoral processes, in terms of 1) where groups of people stood, and 2) how they related to each other politically.

Structure of the Game: There were, historically, two elections: in the middle of 1917 and at the end of 1917. One of these elections took place in the game situation after parties and constituencies had been playing their parts for an hour. The game then went on for another half hour or more.

Students volunteered for four "party groups" and four "constituency groups." A few were assigned to groups or chose not to participate. Each group consulted the program and met in caucus to decide on its actions. They could do about anything they wished: attempt to form alliances, appeal to another group for support, influence others, and even lie. Delegates were sent from caucuses to different groups and returned for further strategy discussions.

---

* Many of the games used at the University of Michigan were developed in workshops directed by Barbara Steinwachs and the staff of the Gaming Service of the University Extension Service.

After an hour, an election was held and tallied on the blackboard. The game continued for about half an hour after the election.

Physical Setting: The game took place in the usual large lecture hall, but smaller groups spilled out into the hallway and beyond the room. The usual lecture time of one hour was extended to two hours that day.

Evaluation: The instructor felt that the simulation was remarkably effective as a recreation of what actually took place in 1917. For example, the Bolsheviks were clear about what they wanted and went directly to the point of gaining power, while the Liberals were meeting in the hall and came in to ask at an advanced stage of the play whether the game had actually begun.

Evaluations of this session were elicited from students, who were uniformly positive. There were some suggestions that the instructions could have been clearer and more time might have been taken to explain in advance.

The educational use of the game might have been strengthened by planning for more student discussion afterwards. About twenty minutes or so were spent in discussion after the game in the lecture room, and there was some discussion in section meetings. However, more planning for postgame discussion might have strengthened this game as a teaching technique.

There are now a number of well-designed games that have been used in enough situations to have the kinks worked out. Some use computers to implement the complex interaction of various decisions. One example is SIMSOC (Gamson, 1966), a sociology game in which students are citizens of a society in which they have economic and social roles; for example, some are members of political parties, and some have police powers. METRO is an urban planning game involving conflicts between politicians, landowners, planners, school personnel, and so on.

The Case Method

The case method is widely used in business and law courses and is frequently incorporated for one or more class sessions in other disciplines. Generally case method discussions produce good student involvement. Case methods, like games and simulations, are intended to develop student ability to solve problems using knowledge, concepts, and skills relevant to a course. The students are also expected to be motivated by the case to learn from readings, lectures, or other resources.

The teacher's role in the case method is primarily to facilitate discussion—questioning, listening, challenging, and encouraging analysis and problem solving, and proposing hypothetical situations to test the validity of generalizations.

Typically the case method involves a series of cases, but in some case method courses the cases are not well chosen to represent properly sequenced levels of difficulty. Often, in order to make cases realistic, so many details are included that beginning students lose the principles or points the case was intended to demonstrate. As in classic studies in discrimination learning in the laboratory, teachers attempting to help students learn complex discriminations and principles in problem solving need to choose initial cases in which the differences are clear and extreme before moving to more subtle, complex cases. Typically, one of the goals of the case method is to teach students to select important factors from a tangle of less important ones that may, nevertheless, form a context to be considered. One does not learn such skills by being in perpetual confusion, but rather by success in solving more and more difficult problems. For a more detailed exposition see Hunt (1951) and Maier (1971).

Watson (1975) compared classes taught by the case method with a class taught by the lecture method. Students in one of the two case study classes scored better in knowledge and understanding than the lecture class. The other case study class and the lecture class were roughly equal. Both case study classes were superior to the lecture in ability to apply concepts. In view of the continuing popularity of the case method, it is surprising that so little research has been done on its effectiveness.

Cases, simulations, and games involve getting, recalling, and using information in order to solve problems. As I shall show in Chapter 24, this involves the kind of restructuring that is likely to result in better retention, recall, and use of the information outside the classroom.

SUPPLEMENTARY READING

H. S. Guetzkow, _Simulation in social sciences: readings_ (Englewood Cliffs, NJ: Prentice-Hall, 1962).

M. McNair (ed.), _The case method at the Harvard Business School_ (New York: McGraw-Hill, 1954).

C. Argyris, Some limitations of the case method, _Academy of Management Review,_ 1980, 5, 291–298.

CHAPTER 18 | Role Playing and Microteaching

Role Playing

Role playing as a teaching device developed from the psychodramatists centered around Moreno and the group dynamicists. Briefly, role playing is the setting up of more or less unstructured situations in which students' behaviors are improvised to fit in with their conceptions of roles to which they have been assigned. Role playing is like a drama in which each participant is assigned a character to portray, but where no lines are learned. The individuals portraying specific roles improvise their responses to the situation.

The purposes of role playing as used in my classes are:

1. To give students practice in using what they've learned.

2. To illustrate principles from the course content.

3. To develop insight into human relations problems.

4. To provide a concrete basis for discussion.

5. To maintain or arouse interest.

6. To provide a channel in which feelings can be expressed under the guise of make-believe.

7. To develop increased awareness of one's own and others' feelings.

Role playing can be utilized in a variety of classes, ranging from complex simulations of political or international situations to language classes in which role playing is used for practice of the language. In language classes, for example, role playing can provide useful linguistic information on appropriate speech levels (how to respond to rude questions, how to be politely evasive, persuasive, firm, and so on), use of gestures, and cultural points such as distance between speakers. Students may write and/or act out more than one way of handling a situation. Sometimes teachers take part in the role playing as participants; sometimes they act as "coaches."

In using role playing instructors may begin by bringing to class a problem situation that does not have too direct a relationship to the students' own personal problems. The situation should be one that is familiar enough so that members can understand the roles and their potential responses to the problem. Ordinarily, role playing seems to work best when it arises rather spontaneously from a problem being discussed in class. This does not mean, however, that instructors cannot foresee appropriate uses of role playing. In fact, until they have had some experience with role playing, they will probably role play only those situations they have worked out rather explicitly before class. Nevertheless, instructors should be willing to change plans in accordance with the needs of the group.

Instructors should have in mind some objective for the role playing other than that of showing off a new trick. In introducing the first role-playing situation to the class the instructor should describe the situation quite completely, picturing the roles required and the objective of the role playing before asking for volunteers for the roles.

For example, the instructor in a psychology class might say,

> We've been learning about the differences between Skinnerian and Freudian approaches to treatment. Let's imagine that Freud has come back to life and that he and Skinner have just read an account in the morning paper of a baseball player who punched his manager. Skinner and Freud are having coffee with a student who asks them, "What should be done about this player who punched his manager? This is the third time he has been in trouble for fighting." Who wants to play the role of the student? Who will volunteer to be Skinner? Who will volunteer to be Freud? . . . O.K. Here are three chairs; we'll imagine that you're sitting around a table. Let's begin by the student asking her question.

The goal of this role-playing situation would be to get the class actively involved in comparing Skinner's and Freud's viewpoints. The situation can be far-fetched or realistic, so long as it is interesting and involving. You might, in fact, even get the class to help you develop the description of the situation to increase their involvement.

Here is another role-playing situation used in language courses:

> Students are shown a picture of an apartment building. Students
> work in pairs, writing their dialogues first.
>
> Grammar points: Modal verbs; *too, very.*
>
> Instructions: You are the man who lives in the apartment that is
> too noisy. Call up the mother of the children who are playing foot-
> ball in their apartment. Be polite. *or* You are the man who lives in
> the apartment that is too noisy. Call up the mother of the children
> who are playing football in their apartment. Be rude. Be angry.

General considerations in handling role playing are:

➤ If you wish to point out different responses or solutions to a given
problem, use two or more presentations of the same situation with
different participants or have participants switch roles. In such cases
more natural behavior and more convincing differences are obtained
by not permitting participants in the replay of the situation to see
the first presentation. This also prevents the feeling of the first group
that the second group is trying to show them up.

➤ Even if you know the class fairly well, it is usually preferable to get
volunteers for the roles rather than to choose participants, for volunteers are less likely to feel on the spot.

➤ For the usual class situation, it is better to direct discussion away
from the reactions of specific participants to the reactions of people
in general in such a situation. As the group gains a sense of security,
more attention can be paid to feelings of the actual participants,
provided you are aware of the possibility of mobilizing anxiety with
which you may not wish to deal. Situations involving morals or
subjects of high emotional significance, such as sex taboos, are apt
to be disturbing to some students. The situations that are most interesting and reveal the greatest differences in responses are those
involving some choice or conflict of motives. Often the students
themselves will suggest good situations for illustrating certain principles. In any case, situations that are unrelated to student experience are apt to fall flat. The teacher can to some extent control the
depth of emotions and attitudes aroused by the context of the situation. For example, the same situation might be set up as father and
son, dean and student, or boss and employee.

➤ To help the nonparticipating members of the class observe skillfully, assign individuals to watch for specific things. For example, one observer may be asked to particularly observe expressive movements of the participants; another may observe the pattern of interaction between the participants. The class itself may suggest points to look for and to discuss.

➤ Some role-playing situations may end themselves. Usually, however, the instructor will have to "cut" the action. Generally the beginner lets the role playing run too long. Three to six minutes is usually sufficient to spark discussion.

➤ Players feel less defensive if they are asked to discuss the situation before the rest of the class begins discussion.

➤ After discussing the situation, you may wish to replay the situation reversing the roles, changing one role, altering the situation, or playing a probable following scene.

In general, role playing seems to stimulate much interest and give students the feeling that they are actually making use of what they've learned. As in most other novel teaching techniques, the effectiveness of role playing depends to a large extent upon the confidence of the instructor in the procedure and the students' feeling (gained from the instructor's attitude) that it is going to be a successful and valuable aspect of the course. Like any other technique, it can be used to such an extent that it becomes repetitious, but if used to accomplish definite goals, and if students perceive their progress toward those goals, it can be an extremely rewarding technique.

Microteaching

Microteaching is a technique primarily used in teacher training, but is also potentially useful for training in public speaking, interviewing, leading groups, or other communication or interpersonal skills. Microteaching involves presenting a lesson, speech, and so on in a brief period; for example, five minutes. The microlesson focuses on the use of a particular skill, such as asking questions, establishing rapport, or eliciting student comments. The microlesson may be videotaped to facilitate review and further practice of the skill desired.

By means of microteaching students can learn specific skills that are elements in large units of performance such as teaching. As we suggested in Chapter 11, "One-on-One Teaching," skill development often continues best when learners can progress by achievable steps. Microteaching reduces the complexity and stress that would be associated with a full-scale experience, such as teaching a full class period or delivering a complete oration. Leith (1982) showed that microteaching practice resulted in significantly better teaching than conventional preparation through classroom sessions on classroom management, lesson planning, etc. But an interesting attribute-treatment interaction emerged. Introverts benefited much more from the microteaching. Two years later the microteaching experience still showed a favorable effect but by this time the extroverts were rated as being superior to the introverts.

Microteaching is a form of role playing, and research results indicate that it is effective in teacher training. But even though you are not in teacher education, you may wish to consider microteaching as a means of enhancing your own skill as a college teacher or you may find the emphasis upon specific skill and videotape feedback useful in teaching other skills.

SUPPLEMENTARY READING

For further discussion of the use of role playing in teaching, I recommend:

W. Coleman, Role-playing as an instructional aid, *Journal of Educational Psychology,* 1948, *39,* 427–435.

N. R. F. Maier and L. F. Zerfoss, MRP: A technique for training large groups of supervisors and its potential use in social research, *Human Relations,* 1952, *5,* 177–186.

B. S. Fuhrmann and A. F. Grasha, *A practical handbook for college teachers* (Boston: Little, Brown, 1983), pp. 158–160.

PART V
Teaching Large Classes

CHAPTER 19

Why Classes Should Be Small, but What to Do if You Must Teach a Large Class

As budgets drop, more and more college teachers have to deal with large numbers of students enrolled in a single course. Typically, budget cuts result in gradual shrinkage in the number of courses available and the number of sections or frequency of offerings of remaining courses. Class sizes creep upward.

In writing this book, I originally began with the topic, "Class Size." I concluded that section by stating that more meaningful research on class size must take into account the methods of teaching classes of differing sizes. I thought this was a pretty insightful statement, but now I think that it was naive, for size and method are almost inextricably intertwined. Thus the research on class size and that on lecture vs. discussion overlap. Large classes are most likely to use lecture methods and less likely to use discussion than small classes. Since discussion tends to be more effective than lecture for achieving changes in thinking and problem solving, we might expect large classes to be less effective than small classes.

Research on Class Size

The question of class size was probably the first problem of college teaching approached by research. Are small classes really more effective for teaching than large classes? The professor's answer has generally been "yes." But the refreshing empiricism of the 1920s looked hard at many "self-evident truths" about human behavior; among them was the assumption that class size had something to do with educational effectiveness.

Among the first investigators were Edmondson and Mulder (1924), who compared the performance of students enrolled in a 109-student

181

class with students enrolled in a 43-student class of the same course in education. Achievement of the two groups was approximately equal, with a slight edge for the small class on an essay and the mid-semester tests, and for the large class on quizzes and the final examination. Students reported a preference for small classes.

The Edmondson and Mulder results at Michigan encouraged the Committee of Research of the University of Minnesota to begin a classic series of studies of class size. In fifty-nine experiments which involved such widely varying subjects as psychology, physics, accounting, law, and education, the results of forty-six favored the large classes.

Support for small classes, however, came from studies in the teaching of French conducted by Cheydleur (1945) at the University of Wisconsin between 1919 and 1943. With hundreds of classes ranging in size from nine to thirty-three, Cheydleur found a consistent superiority on objective departmental examinations for the smaller classes. Mueller (1924) found similar results in an experiment comparing elementary psychology classes of twenty and forty students.

More recent experiments are also favorable to small classes. Nachman and Opochinsky (1958) found a small class to be superior to a large on surprise quizzes, but the two classes were not significantly different on the final examination for which students prepared. Differences were also revealed in the more subtle and persisting results of Feldhusen's (1963) study showing that a small class in educational psychology produced more change in attitudes toward teaching than a large class.

The Macomber and Siegel experiments at Miami University (1957a,b, 1960) are particularly important because their measures included, in addition to conventional achievement tests, measures of critical thinking and problem solving, scales measuring stereotypic attitudes, and tests of student attitudes toward instruction. Statistically significant differences favored the smaller classes (particularly for high ability students). When retention of knowledge was measured one to two years after completion of the courses, small differences favored the smaller classes in eight of the nine courses compared (Siegel, Adams, and Macomber, 1960).

Few instructors are satisfied with the achievement of knowledge if it is not remembered, if the students are unable to use it in solving problems where the knowledge is relevant, or if the students fail to relate the knowledge to relevant attitudes. If one takes these more basic outcomes of retention, problem solving, and attitude differentiation as criteria of learning, the weight of the evidence clearly favors small classes.

Class Size: Theory

How can we account for these results?

Let us briefly return to theory. Insofar as information communication is a one-way process, size of group should be limited only by the audibility of the lecturer's voice. In fact, as Hudelson suggests, a large class may have sufficient motivational value for instructors to cause them to spend more time in preparation of their lectures, resulting, I would hope, in better teaching and in greater student achievement.

But usually we have goals going beyond communication of knowledge. If educators are to make wise decisions about when and where small classes are most important, we need to analyze more carefully the changes in educationally relevant variables associated with changes in size. One lead comes from social psychologists Thomas and Fink (1963), who have reviewed research on face-to-face groups—not only classroom groups, but laboratory, business, and other groups also. They suggest that two types of input increase with increasing group size—_resource input_ (skills, knowledge, and so on) and _demand input_ (needs). It is clear that the larger the number of group members, the greater is the likelihood that some members will have resources of knowledge, intelligence, or other skills needed for the educational purposes of the group. It seems likely, however, that there is a limited amount of relevant knowledge and skills, so that beyond some point additional students contribute little that is not already part of the group's resources. A group's utilization of resources is constrained by the simple facts that, 1) in a large group a smaller proportion of group members can participate orally, and 2) the larger the group, the less likely it is that a given person will feel free to volunteer a contribution. Because active thinking is so important to learning and retention of learning, constraints upon oral participation are likely not only to induce passivity but also to be educationally harmful.

Determining When Small
Classes Are Needed

In order to apply these general propositions to teaching, educators need to ask the following questions:

**In what teaching situations is the amount of information in the group important?** One might, for example, hypothesize that in most courses in which knowledge is the primary goal, the relevant information is contained in books and the instructor's mind, and the amount added by students is likely to be inconsequential; thus class size should be unimportant for this goal. On the other hand, if application is an important goal, varied knowledge of application situations contributed by students may well be significant; thus, if Thomas and Fink's principles are valid, there may be groups too small, as well as too large, to be maximally effective for this goal.

What kinds of students benefit most from small sections? Both Ward (1956) and Macomber and Siegel report results suggesting that the ablest students are most favorably affected by being taught in small classes. Siegel and Siegel (1964) report that personal contact with the instructor was particularly important for acquisition of concepts by three types of students: 1) those with low motivation, 2) those that are unsophisticated in the subject-matter area, and 3) those that are predisposed to learn facts rather than to apply or synthesize.

Educational Goals, Class Size, and Teaching Methods

In most courses there are several levels of goals—knowledge, critical thinking, attitudes toward learning, and so on. The teacher's task is to find methods that will achieve an optimal balance of all of these. If different methods are effective for different objectives, teachers need to be able to use an optimal combination of these methods. Unfortunately, most teaching research has studied the effect of one method vs. another when both are repeated day after day for a semester; thus, few data exist on the relative effectiveness of differing combinations or degrees of flexibility in teaching methods.

While many teaching methods could be used in large groups, it is probable that more time is devoted to lecturing than in smaller classes. The large class often reduces the teacher's sense of freedom in choosing teaching methods, assigning papers, or testing. Assuming that teachers have some repertoire of relevant skills, anything that handcuffs them is likely to be educationally damaging, and this may be the major way in which large classes are likely to sabotage education.

What goals are most likely to be sacrificed in large classes? As Table 19–1 indicates, large lectures are not generally inferior to smaller lecture classes when traditional achievement tests are used as a criterion. When other objectives are measured, large lectures are on shakier ground. Goals of higher level thinking, application, motivation, and attitudinal change are most likely to be achieved in small classes. Moreover, both students and faculty members feel that teaching is more effective in small classes.

Probably of more significance than class size per se is its relation to the teaching method used. For example, one would expect class size to be of minimal relevance in television teaching, of slight importance in lecturing, and of much importance for discussion.

Class Size: Conclusions

It is commonplace to suggest that the effect of class size depends upon the method used, and it is probably true that the size of the group is less critical for success of lecture, for example, than for that of discussion (Attiyeh and Lumsden, 1972). Moreover, class size interacts with student characteristics; that is, small classes are educationally more important for some students than for others. But most important, analysis of research suggests that the importance of size depends upon educational goals. In general, large classes are simply not as effective as small classes for retention of knowledge, critical thinking, and attitude change.

Multi-Section Courses

Unfortunately, there are seldom enough funds to teach all courses in small groups. As a compromise solution, I have scheduled large courses for two hours of lecture (in large sections) and two hours of discussion (in small sections). The assumption here is that lectures are valuable for certain purposes, such as communicating information, and that the effectiveness of the lecture method is not greatly affected by class size. Furthermore, large-group class meetings are economical for test administration, guest lecturers, and some films. By teaching the students in large sections part of the time, it becomes economically feasible to keep the discussion sections small enough to permit wide student participation. Thus, rather than offering 5 sections of 45 students each, you might consider the possible advantages of a 225-student lecture section and 9 sections of 20 to 30 students.

TABLE 19–1 / *Class Size*

Reference	Course	Criteria		
		Factual Exam	Higher Level Retention and Thinking	Attitude, Motivation
Nachman & Opochinsky (1958)	Psychology	*S		
Mueller (1924)	Psychology	S		
Elliott (1951)	Psychology			S
De Cecco (1964)	Psychology	S	L	S
Feldhusen (1963)	Educational Psychology			S
Casey & Weaver (1956)	Human Development			*S
Macomber & Siegel (1957a,b, 1960)	Psychology, Marketing		*S	*S
Siegel, Adams, & Macomber (1960)	Psychology, Marketing		*S (8 out of 9)	
Hudelson (1928)	Psychology, Physics, Accounting, Law, Education	L (46 exp.) S (13 exp.) *L (6 exp.) *S (2 exp.)		
Attiyeh & Lumsden (1972)	Economics	*S L = S		
Edmondson & Mulder (1924)	Education	L		
Cheydleur (1945)	French	S (1240 classes)		

L = Large Class Superior
S = Small Class Superior
* = Difference significant at .05 level or better. All other results are the actual direction of
the difference in the experiment.

Coordinating Multi-Section Courses

In any multi-section course taught by several different instructors the problem of coordination inevitably arises. In some courses this problem is resolved by enforced uniformity of course content, sequence of topics, testing, grading, and even anecdotes. Such a procedure has the advantage that students who later elect more advanced courses can be presumed to have a certain uniform amount of background experience. It also is efficient in that only one final examination must be constructed, only one course outline devised, and students can transfer from section to section with no difficulty in catching up.

The disadvantage of this approach is that such uniformity often makes for dull, uninteresting teaching. If the teaching assistants are unenthusiastic about the course outline, they are likely to communicate this attitude to the students. If the course can be jointly planned, this may make for greater acceptance, but may also take a great deal of time.

A second approach to this problem is to set up completely autonomous sections, with all the instructors organizing and conducting their sections as they wish. While this means that Psychology 1 from Professor Smith may be quite different from Psychology 1 from Professor Jones, proponents of this solution point out that transfer students who are accepted for advanced work are likely to differ even more from local students than local students differ from section to section under this plan, and that the difference in student learning between instructors is relatively small when compared with the total range of differences between students at the end of a course.

In the general psychology course at the University of Michigan we developed a plan that is in many ways a compromise between these two positions. We worked out together a set of objectives we all strove to accomplish. Half of the final examination was based on these objectives and given to all sections. In addition we agreed that the average grade given by each instructor would fall within a limited range. This grading restriction is not a minor matter, for one of the most common sources of friction in multi-section courses is the complaint from students that they got "C's" in Mr. Jones' section, but if they'd been in Mr. Smith's they would have made "A's" for the same work.

Whether or not variation between sections is permitted, a frequent sore spot in multi-section courses is the tendency for students to leave or avoid sections taught by certain instructors and to crowd into others. Some instructors intentionally depict their sections as being more difficult in order to drive away less motivated students. If this produces large disparities in the numbers of students taught by "popular" and "unpopular" instructors, the cohesiveness of the instructional staff is likely to be threatened. On the other hand, from the standpoints of both student learning and instructor satisfaction, it would seem wise to give students some opportunity to select the section they feel will be most valuable (or pleasant) for them.

Conflict may be minimized and education enhanced if certain sections are specifically labeled as being for a particular purpose. For example, certain sections may be labeled Honors sections or for graduate students; certain sections may be labeled as placing greater emphasis upon theory; certain other sections may be taught entirely by discussion and so labeled. One of the advantages of a multi-section course is the opportunity it provides for establishing homogeneous groupings, stimulating the superior student, and taking advantage of students' backgrounds.

Some Tips for Teaching Large Classes

Often one assumes that a large class simply requires skills in lecturing and writing objective tests. These are important, but one can do more. Large classes need not constrain you as much as you might expect.

Student Anonymity

The major problem of teaching a large class is that students not only feel anonymous, they usually *are* anonymous. And as social psychological research has shown, people who are anonymous feel less personal responsibility—a consequence not only damaging to morale and order, but also unlikely to facilitate learning. Moreover the sense of distance from the instructor, the loss of interpersonal bonds with the instructor and with other students—these diminish motivation for learning.

What can we do? The fact that with increasing class size it becomes less and less possible to know students as individuals is likely to make us feel that it is not worth trying to do anything. I think this is a mistake. In my experience the students appreciate whatever efforts you make even if they do not take advantage of them. Here are some things I've tried:

1. Announce that you'll meet any students who are free for coffee after class. (You won't be swamped.)

2. Pass out invitations to ten students to join you for coffee and to get acquainted after class.

3. Pass out brief student observation forms to 10 students at the beginning of class and ask them to meet you to discuss their observations.

4. Circulate among early arriving students to get acquainted before class starts.

5. Circulate among lab or discussion sections.

6. Use a seating chart so that you can call students by name when they participate.

7. Move out into the aisles during your lecture to solicit comments.

8. Teach one discussion or lab section yourself.

9. If you can't use regularly scheduled discussion sections, set up an occasional afternoon or evening session for more informal discussion of an interesting question or for review before an examination.

Getting Student Participation in Large Classes

While sectioning is preferable to the large class without sections, most teachers will at some time be faced with the necessity of teaching an unsectioned large class. In this situation my first advice is to try "learning cells" or student-led discussions, to be described in Chapter 20. If this is impractical, you can still get the advantages of student participation if you plan for it. Some techniques such as buzz groups will be discussed in Chapter 22; problem posting and the two-column method of large discussions were described in Chapters 3 and 4. The technique of role playing, discussed in Chapter 18, can be used for multiple role playing, with all students involved as role players. Maier (1971) gives examples of the use of such techniques.

Lumsden (1976) gives each student in his section a large square card with the letters A, B, C, and D printed so that one of the letters is visible at the top when each edge of the card is held up. For example, if A is first on the top side, B will be visible at the top when the card is rotated 90 degrees. Lumsden interjects multiple-choice questions into his lecture either orally, on the blackboard, or by use of a transparency, and then asks students to answer all at once by raising their cards. This enables him to get student participation and feedback on whether his points are understood.

Encouraging Student Writing in Large Classes

One of the most important losses of large classes is student writing. Because grading essays is so time-consuming, most faculty members reduce, or eliminate, writing assignments in a large class. Take heart! You can get some of the educational advantages of writing, and at the same time improve attention to the lecture, without being submerged by papers to grade.

The secret is the *"minute paper."* The minute paper is, as its title indicates, a paper literally written in a minute (or it can be a two-minute or three-minute paper). Announce at the beginning of the class period that you will interrupt your lecture midway through the period in order that the students may write a one-minute paper on a topic derived from the lecture.

At an appropriate point in the lecture, announce the paper and the topic or question you want students to address—or let students choose a topic. When the minute is up, you may either collect the papers or break the class into pairs or subgroups to review and discuss one another's papers.

If you wish, you can evaluate and comment on the papers as you would any other student papers. If the class is exceptionally large, you may announce that you'll read and return only a sample of the papers. Students can be motivated to think and write without the threat of grades, and this technique not only gets students thinking actively during the lecture but gives you feedback about what students are learning from the lecture.

Giving Tests in Large Classes

In classes of 200 or more, unwary instructors are likely to run into problems they would never dream of in teaching classes with an enrollment of 20 to 30. Most of these problems are administrative. For example, course planning almost inevitably becomes more rigid in a large class because almost anything involving the participation of the students requires more preparation time.

Perhaps you're used to making up your tests the day before you administer them. With a large class this is almost impossible. Essay and short-answer tests that take relatively little time to construct take a long time to score for 200 students; so you may spend long hours trying to devise thought-provoking objective questions for a part of the test. But once you've made up the questions your troubles are not over, for secretaries require a good deal of time to run off several hundred copies of a test. Thus, spur-of-the-moment tests are almost an impossibility, and by virtue of the necessity of planning ahead for tests, other aspects of the course also become more rigid.

As I indicated in Chapter 8, essay examinations are superior to typical objective examinations in their effect on student study and learning. Thus you are likely to regret the loss of the opportunity to give essay tests in a large group. But this loss is not inevitable. To some extent it can be compensated for by greater care in the construction of objective test items. But it is also possible to use essay items without increasing your load beyond reason. In a 500-student lecture course I regularly included an essay item on the final examination with the stipulation that I would read it only if it would affect the student's letter grade for the course. Since the majority of the students were fairly clearly established as A, B, C, or D students on the basis of other work and the objective part of the final examination, the number of essays I needed to read was not excessive. My subjective impression was that knowledge of the inclusion of an essay item did affect the students' preparation for the exam.

Outside Reading

The testing problem is just one of several factors structuring the conduct of large classes. Another is the assignment of readings in the library. With a small group you can assign library work with little difficulty, perhaps only making sure that the materials needed are available and, if necessary, reserved for the class. With a class of several hundred students a library assignment without previous planning can be disastrous. The library's single copy of a book or journal is obviously inadequate, and will probably be stolen within a few hours by some student who wants to assure time enough to study the assignment thoroughly. The librarians are then faced by hordes of desperate students begging for the book. Thus a library assignment must be conceived far enough in advance (usually several months) that enough copies of the book can be obtained, and the librarian can prepare for the fray.

Handling Diversity

The biggest problem in big classes (and in many small ones) is student diversity. Students differ in interests, motives, ability, and subject matter background. There is no magic way of coping; so most teachers try to ignore diversity and aim for the middle or top group in ability and motivation. But we can do better.

The first step is to get better information about diversity. Use a pretest and questionnaire or paper to check out student background and interests. Some students will already know most of what you were planning to teach. For them it might be more profitable to do an independent project than to attend lecture.

A second step in preparing lectures and assignments is to think of some things that will appeal to different groups you have identified. In a lecture you may need to review the textbook for students with little background as well as pointing up new findings and issues that will intrigue the abler students.

Probably the most effective tool you have is small group peer teaching techniques discussed in the next chapter.

Teaching Large Classes: Conclusion

Large classes are probably generally less effective than small ones. In any case, it is clear that many of the teaching problems are different. I have touched on only a few of the most salient ones. If you become involved in a large course, you'll also bump into such problems as whether or not to encourage individual contacts between yourself and students, how to use assistants effectively, and how to amplify your voice, gestures, facial expressions, and writing in order to communicate to the back rows. This is a challenge, but teaching stays interesting because of challenges!

SUPPLEMENTARY READING

Kenneth E. Eble, *The craft of teaching* (San Francisco: Jossey-Bass, 1976), Chapter 13.

CHAPTER 20 | *How to Have Smaller Classes Despite a Shortage of Faculty*

One of the recurring criticisms of higher education is that it hasn't increased its productivity at the same rate as industry. Surprisingly one even hears such statements from administrators who ought to know better. By productivity such critics typically mean that colleges should turn out more students using fewer teachers—as if colleges were factories producing shoes, automobiles, or soap. I once began to try to help a group of legislators develop a more sophisticated understanding by asking if a legislator's productivity should be measured by the number of bills introduced or if a doctor's productivity should be measured by the number of patients seen, regardless of the number who died. Obviously the product of education is learning, not credit hours.

But aren't professors simply featherbedding when they resist larger classes, television, computers, and other technological aids? "After all, there's no significant difference in effectiveness between these and the traditional classes," says the critic.

I have already shown that the "no significant difference" findings actually turn out quite consistently to favor live, small-class discussions if one is concerned about the longer term goals of higher education such as ability to apply knowledge, solve problems, or learn new material. Thus, more "efficient" methods allow professors to teach more students but with a *loss of learning* for the individual students.

The bottleneck in educational efficiency is that learning to think requires thinking and communicating the thinking through talking, writing, or doing, so that others can react to it. Unfortunately a professor can read only one paper at a time, can listen to only one student's comments at a time, and can respond with only one voice.

The problem is not one of communicating knowledge from professors to students more efficiently. Printed materials have done this very well for years, and for most educational purposes are still superior to any of the modern alternatives. The problem is rather one of interaction between the learner and teacher. For better education we need more rather than fewer teachers.

In fact, however, faculty-student ratios are getting worse rather than better. Faculties are shrinking. Is there any hope of improving education without increased cost?

The answer lies in broadening the definition of teacher to include students who teach one another. Highly trained faculty are essential for higher education, but not every question or comment needs to be answered by a full professor. Students can learn from one another.

Using Students as Teachers

Graduate students have been used as group leaders, laboratory supervisors, or tutors for many years, but little evidence has been gathered on their effectiveness.* The one published research study on this topic, conducted at Miami University by Macomber and Siegel (1960), indicated that graduate student teaching assistants leading small sections were at least as effective as professors teaching large lectures, and perhaps more effective. An unpublished study by Lamphear and McConnell found poorer performance of classes taught by graduate students. A more recent trend has been an increasing use of undergraduates as teachers of other undergraduates. The use of undergraduates as teachers is often expected to have two favorable outcomes: stimulating additional learning by the students who teach and facilitating learning by those being taught.

The research evidence supports the value of learning by teaching. For example, Nelson (1970) found favorable effects on the Graduate Record Examination performance of students who served as proctor-mentors in PSI (Keller Plan) courses.

The Pyramid Plan

Probably the most convincing demonstration of the effectiveness of undergraduate student-led discussions for the students taught was the "Pyramid Plan" at Pennsylvania State University (Carpenter, 1959; Davage, 1958, 1959). In this project, a faculty member, graduate students, and

---

* This section is based on W. J. McKeachie and J. Kulik, Effective college teaching. In F. Kerlinger, ed. *Review of research in education,* Vol. 3 (Itaska, IL: F. E. Peacock Publisher, 1975), pp. 166–174.

seniors planned the activities. The seniors, assisted by juniors, led small-group discussions. These small discussion sections led by more advanced undergraduate students supplemented the regular course activities. Compared with supplementary instructor-led lectures, film presentations, demonstrations, or no supplement at all, the small groups led by juniors and seniors read more, were more likely to go on to major in the subject, accepted more responsibility for their own learning (in psychology), showed a more intellectual (less vocational) attitude toward college, and performed better on tests of scientific thinking, persistence in critical thinking, and resourcefulness in problem solving. A favorable effect of the experience upon the junior and senior group leaders was also reported. Trowbridge (1969) similarly found favorable results with small groups led by advanced undergraduates as a supplement to lecture, reading, and projects. The experimental class was superior to a conventional lecture-discussion class, both on a standardized test of achievement and on change in self-concept.

Research on Peer Teaching

Even more daring is the use of students enrolled in a course as leaders for their own discussions. In experiments in educational psychology and general psychology, Gruber and Weitman (1962) found that students taught in small discussion groups without a teacher not only did at least as well on a final examination as students who heard the teacher lecture, but they were also superior in curiosity (as measured by question-asking behavior) and in interest in educational psychology. The discussion students reported a larger number of readings during the term, whereas the lecture students reported more attempts at applying their learning. In an experiment in a physical optics course, the lecture students were superior to student-led discussion students on a test of facts and simple problems, but inferior on a test containing complex problems and learning new material. The superiority of student-led discussions was particularly marked for students below the median in ability. Romig (1972) and Beach (1960, 1968) report similar results in English and psychology classes.

Webb and Grib (1967) report six studies in which student-led discussions were compared with instructor-led discussions or lectures. In two of the six studies, significant differences in achievement tests favored the student-led discussions. Both students and instructors reported that the student-led discussions increased student motivation; and students who had been exposed to student-led discussions tended to favor them over instructor-led discussions as supplements to lectures.

Webb and Grib (1967) note that students report that the sense of freedom to ask questions and express their own opinions is a major advantage of the student-led discussions. This may explain Gruber and Weitman's finding that the poorer students benefited most from student-led discussions. It makes theoretical sense that this opportunity to expose individual conceptions and misconceptions and compare ideas with those of others should contribute to learning if the group contains sufficient resources of knowledge and higher level thinking. The student-led group would most likely not be effective in areas in which students simply reinforced each other's biases.

Student-Taught Minicourses

Wortman and Hillis (1976) describe an unusual use of undergraduate teaching assistants. They recruited undergraduate volunteers to assist in a large introductory course. A key duty of each assistant was to prepare a two-week "minicourse" on some topic related to the course. The introductory students then had the choice of any one of the minicourses during the two-week minicourse period. Both the introductory students and the undergraduate assistants were enthusiastic about the value of the minicourses in their learning.

"Pay to Be a Tutor, Not to Be Tutored" =================================

Annis (1983) comparing learning under five conditions:

1. Students read a textbook passage.

2. Students read the passage and were taught by a peer.

3. Students did not read the passage but were taught by a peer.

4. Students read the passage and prepared to teach it to other students.

5. Students read the passage and taught it to another student.

The results demonstrated that teaching resulted in better learning than being taught. These results fit well with contemporary theories of learning and memory. Preparing to teach and teaching involve active thought about the material, analysis and selection of main ideas, and processing the concepts into one's own thoughts and words. A similar study by Bargh and Schul (1980) also found positive results, with the largest part of the gain in retention being attributable to deeper studying of material when preparing to teach.

Structuring Student-Led Discussions

In using students as teachers of discussion groups you are likely to have better success if you prepare and supervise the student-led discussion groups.

The ETSI Method

At Colorado State University, Kitchener and Hurst (1974) developed a highly structured approach based on W. F. Hill's work (1969), the Education Through Student Interaction (ETSI), to render student-led discussion groups more effective. A student manual (Kitchener and Hurst, 1972) guides the students through three phases of the discussion: In the *Overview,* the student is asked to define essential terms and state the main theme of the assignment or the lecture to be discussed. The *Discussion* includes the following four steps: analysis of the content, critique, integration, and application. The last phase is an *Evaluation* of the group discussion with respect to the content (task orientation and understanding material) and the process (responsible participation, climate of relationship, communication of feelings).

For the first two phases, students must do the necessary preparation before the session by completing a study guide, which in fact constitutes their "admission ticket" to the group discussion. The evaluation takes place after every session. For each session, three students are designated as discussion guides; the first is responsible for the overview, the second and third for the discussion and evaluation phases.

Groups using the ETSI structure performed better on subsequent tests of content mastery and evaluated the discussion groups more positively than two control groups that discussed course content without a specific procedure. ETSI groups, furthermore, were more effective when they had undergone workshop training on the ETSI method prior to the group sessions and when a specially trained student facilitator participated in the discussion (Arbes and Kitchener, 1974).

A number of other investigations (Churchill and John, 1958; Diamond, 1972; Vattano et al., 1973; Wrigley, 1973; Hockenberry-Boeding and Vattano, 1975) have also concluded that learning groups led by undergraduates represent a valuable alternative or supplement to large lecture courses.

Team Learning

Michaelsen et al (1982) also describes a team learning method designed to induce greater student involvement in large classes. In this method the groups are formed so that each group of 6 to 7 students contains a variety of skills and backgrounds. Thus in a physical chemistry course both chemistry and engineering majors were included in each group. The instructor gathers background information by show of hands or written questionnaire. In using the team learning method you may provide training materials, but you will probably still want student assistants to sit in with the groups occasionally to monitor and assist group processes.

In Michaelsen's team learning approach, individual study is followed by testing, group discussion of the test, then group examination, group activities (a case, role playing, etc.), and finally a lecture by the instructor.

This sequence has a number of desirable features.

1. Primary responsibility for studying the assignment rests with the individual student.

2. The individual and group tests provide feedback to the instructor about where the students are having difficulty.

3. Students teach other students—an exceptionally effective learning device.

Learning in Pairs: The Learning Cell ═══════════

While instructors sometimes assume that the ideal learning situation would be one where students might work individually at their own pace, with their own equipment, with individual help, the common practice in laboratory instruction of having students work in pairs has good educational justification as well as the economic one of saving equipment. At the Third International Conference on Improving University Teaching, both Fukuda of Japan and Elton of England reported that in computerized instruction students learned more effectively when two students shared a computer terminal rather than each having a separate terminal. This fits with other research and experience showing that working and studying in pairs can facilitate student learning.

One of the best-developed systems for helping pairs of students to learn more effectively is the Learning Cell, developed by Marcel Goldschmid of the Swiss Federal Institute of Technology in Lausanne.

The "learning cell" or student dyad refers to a cooperative form of learning in pairs, in which students alternate asking and answering questions on commonly read materials (Goldschmid, 1971). As with PSI, the learning cell must be highly structured for success (i.e., effective learning) to occur:

➤ To prepare for the learning cell, students read an assignment and write questions dealing with the major points raised in the reading proper or other related materials.

➤ At the beginning of each class meeting, students are randomly assigned to pairs and one partner (A) begins by asking the first question.

➤ After having answered and perhaps having been corrected or given additional information, B puts his first question to A, and so on.

➤ During this time, the instructor goes from dyad to dyad, giving feedback, asking and answering questions.

A variation of this procedure has each student read (or prepare) different materials. In this case, A "teaches" B the essentials of his or her readings, then asks B prepared questions, whereupon they switch roles.

The effectiveness of the learning cell was first explored in a large (250 students) psychology course (Goldschmid, 1970) where four learning options were compared: seminar, discussion, independent study (essay), and learning cell. Students in the learning-cell option performed significantly better on an unannounced examination and rated their ongoing learning experience significantly higher.

A more extensive "field test" in a number of other disciplines at the university (Goldschmid and Shore, 1974) demonstrated the learning cell's effectiveness regardless of the size of the class, its level, or the nature of the subject matter.

A third, more experimental, investigation served to evaluate the learning cell across three age groups (Schirmerhorn, Goldschmid, and Shore, 1975). Fifth- and ninth-grade pupils as well as university students studied probability at their respective intellectual levels for two class periods using the learning cell. All age groups showed significant learning after reading and formulating questions and after the discussions between partners (Goldschmid, 1975).

Learning cells work better for some students than others. Leith (1974a,b) found that introverts did about as well studying alone as in learning cells; extroverts did better in learning cells, but only if their partners were also extroverts. A learning cell composed of an extrovert paired with an introvert was no more effective than individual learning. In summary, learning cells increase learning for some students and do not hurt the learning of any students.

Why do learning cells work? One reason might be that the learning cell has both motivational and cognitive assets (see Chapters 24 and 25). Motivationally it has the advantage of interaction with a peer—an opportunity for mutual support and stimulation. Cognitively it provides an opportunity for elaboration—putting material into one's own words—and for stimulating students to look for main points and for monitoring their own learning.

Learning cells can also be used for discussion in large classes. In my large lecture class I form pairs for learning cells or for brief discussions simply by asking students at my extreme left in each row to yell out, "Odd," with the next yelling "Even" and so on across the rows until everyone is an "Odd" or an "Even." Then the "Odd" becomes the first questioner for the learning cell with the next "Even" as a partner.

Students Teaching Students: Conclusions

I shall discuss another method in which students teach students, the Keller Plan, in Chapter 21. In this chapter I have shown that well-planned use of students as teachers of one another is very effective educationally. There are at least two theoretical reasons why this may be so:

1. If students are to learn—to form new ways of organizing ideas in their minds—it is important that misunderstanding, emotional biases, and barriers to change be revealed and dealt with. Students

are more likely to talk in small groups than large; students are more likely to ask other students questions about their difficulties or failure to understand than to reveal these problems with a faculty member present.

2. Remembering and using learning depends upon restructuring and relating it to other meaningful experience. Students teaching other students must actively organize and reorganize their own learning in order to explain it. Thus they themselves learn from teaching.

SUPPLEMENTARY READING

One interesting use of students as observers in panel discussions is reported by Meyer M. Cahn, Teaching through student models. In P. Runkel, R. Harrison, and M. Runkel, eds., _The changing college classroom_ (San Francisco: Jossey-Bass, 1972), pp. 36–51.

Wm. Fawcett Hill's book _Learning through discussion: A guide for leaders and members of discussion groups_ (Beverly Hills, CA: Sage Publications, 1977) describes ETSI in more detail. This and other methods are described in Charles A. Goldschmid and Everett K. Wilson, _Passing on sociology: The teaching of a discipline_ (Belmont, CA: Wadsworth, 1980).

Team Learning and other group methods are discussed in Clark Bouton and Russell Garth. _Learning in groups,_ New Directions for Teaching and Learning 14. (San Francisco: Jossey-Bass, 1983).

CHAPTER 21
PSI, TIPS,
Modular Instruction,
and Guided Design

This chapter deals with a number of methods for segmenting and structuring courses. They probably had more impact upon college teaching in the 1970s than any other innovations, but in the 1980s their use seems to be diminishing despite demonstrated value.

The Keller Plan or Personalized System of Instruction (PSI)

The most influential recent plan for individualizing college instruction in large courses was described by psychologist Fred Keller in his 1968 paper "Goodbye, Teacher . . .".* The method, first used in 1964 by Keller and his colleagues at the University of Brasilia, is most often referred to as the Keller Plan or the Personalized System of Instruction (PSI), a term that seems somewhat misleading since the method is less personalized than most other methods of teaching. The method has been used in hundreds of courses and many evaluations of its effectiveness have been carried out.

Basic Features of the Keller Plan

Like some other systems of individualized instruction, the Keller Plan involves a sequence of units of material, frequent readiness testing, and individual pacing. Its distinctive features are heavy emphasis on instructor-prepared written materials to supplement textbooks and extensive use of tutors for individual assistance and evaluation of students. In 1968, Keller described the five features that distinguish the Keller Plan from conventional teaching procedures; it is individually paced, mastery oriented, and student tutored; it uses printed study guides for communication of information; it includes a few lectures to stimulate and motivate students.

---

* This section is adapted from W. J. McKeachie and J. Kulik, Effective college teaching. In F. Kerlinger (ed.), *Review of research in education*, Vol. 3 (Itaska, IL: F. E. Peacock Publisher, 1975), pp. 166–174.

Students beginning a Keller course find that the course work is divided into topics or units. In a simple case, the content of the units may correspond to chapters of the course text. At the start of a course, the students receive a printed study guide to direct their work on the first unit. Although study guides vary, a typical one introduces the unit, states objectives, suggests study procedures, and lists study questions. Students may work anywhere to achieve the objectives.

Before moving on to the second unit in the sequence, the students must demonstrate their mastery of the first unit by perfect or near-perfect performance on a short examination. They are examined on the unit only when they feel adequately prepared; they are not penalized for failure to pass a first, a second, or later examinations on the unit. When the students demonstrate mastery of the first unit, they are given the study guide for the next unit. They thus move through the course at their own pace. A student may meet all course requirements before the term is half done or may require more than a term to complete the course.

The staff for implementing the Keller Plan includes the instructor and undergraduate tutors. The instructor selects and organizes material used in the course, usually writes study guides, constructs examinations for the course, and gives fewer lectures and demonstrations than in a conventional course (perhaps six in the course of a semester). These lectures are not compulsory, and examinations are not based on them. The tutors evaluate readiness tests as satisfactory or unsatisfactory. Since they have been chosen for mastery of the course content, the tutors can prescribe remedial steps for students who encounter difficulties with the course material. The tutors also offer support and encouragement for beginning students. For further details see Keller and Sherman (1974).

Content Learning in PSI Courses

In the first courses offered by the Keller Plan, it appeared to teachers that students seemed to learn course materials remarkably well. About 50 percent of the students received A's as final grades. Grades in Keller courses, it should be noted, are assigned on a different basis than grades in lecture courses. Anywhere from 50 percent to 100 percent of the student's grade in a Keller course comes from a number of repeatable examinations passed on short units of content. Differences in grade distributions may therefore reflect either the differences in grading method or differences in amount of content learned. There is complete confounding.

Studies comparing examination scores of students in Keller and lecture courses offer more promise, but the ideal experimental design is easier to imagine than to achieve. A number of methodological precautions must be taken. Comparison groups must be equivalent, the performance of each subject in the two comparison groups must be taken into account, and students must not be "taught the test" to different degrees in the two groups. Of several studies made, at least three seem relatively free of difficulties in design and analysis, and in each of these the performance of the Keller section was superior to that of the conventional section.

In McMichael and Corey's (1969) study a final examination in which items did not overlap with unit tests was administered to students in an experimental section and three control sections of a course in introductory psychology. Sections were very large (about 200 per section), and students registered for these sections without prior knowledge of the teaching method to be used in the section. Withdrawal rates for the four sections were nearly equal. The experimental group's performance exceeded that of each of the control groups.

Other good studies are those of Witters and Kent (1972) and Morris and Kimbrell (1972), in both of which the Keller sections clearly did better than lecture sections on hourly and final exams. Neither of these studies is plagued by problems of initial differences between experimental and control groups or overlap of items on unit tests and other examinations. There were apparently no withdrawals from courses described by Witters and Kent, and the withdrawal problem was handled by the appropriate statistics in the study reported by Morris and Kimbrell. Kulik, Kulik, and Smith (1976) found nine studies of retention of PSI content, and in all nine, PSI results were superior to lecture. Five studies compared PSI and conventional student performance in subsequent courses. In all five, PSI students were superior.

The only cloud dampening enthusiasm about these results is a methodological problem troubling almost all studies comparing teaching methods. Typically the evaluation of achievement is based on the only content common to two methods—in most cases, a textbook. Ideally, what instructors would like is a sample of all learning achieved by either method. If one method covers a great range of material, of which only a small part overlaps with another method, and the other method teaches very little except the content overlapping with the first method, an achievement test on the overlapping content is not an adequate basis for a comparison of the relative educational effectiveness of the two methods. In the experiments cited, students in the lecture groups may have learned much not covered in the criterion tests; those in the Keller Plan may have had tutors who took them beyond the prescribed materials. The ideal evaluation would sample from this entire domain. Moreover, the ideal evaluation would also attempt to sample systematically from the higher levels of cognitive objectives of the Bloom (1956) taxonomy. (As an aside, it is worth noting that the high proportion of A's often assigned in Keller Plan courses is not justified by superior achievement. Even when Keller Plan courses are superior to conventional courses, the average level of achievement in the Keller Plan course is at the level of a B grade in the conventional course.)

PSI Summary

A review of evaluative research on the Keller Plan establishes the following points:

1. PSI is an attractive teaching method to most students. In published reports, students rate the Keller Plan more favorably than teaching by lecture.

2. Self-pacing and interaction with tutors seem to be the features of the Keller courses most favored by students. Frequent testing with immediate feedback is, however, the feature supported by research (Henderson and Wen, 1976; Kulik, Kulik, and Smith, 1976).

3. Content learning as measured by final examinations is good in Keller courses. Moreover, superior performance is found in courses following the PSI course.

4. Courses initiating the use of PSI often drop it, sometimes for non-educational reasons. For one account of the sociology and politics of PSI use, see Friedman et al. (1976).

TIPS

TIPS, an acronym for Teaching Information Processing System, was developed by Allan C. Kelley, an economist (Kelley, 1968, 1970). In TIPS students are given "surveys" eight to ten times a term. These surveys consist of nine to fifteen multiple choice questions intended to measure student achievement, but they are not used for grading. Rather, a student receives a "Student Report" shortly after completing the survey. The report provides a set of assignments for the ensuing period based on the student's mastery of previous material as assessed by the survey.

In addition to this feedback to students, students provide feedback to the teaching assistants and professor via regular reports. A computer is typically used to provide the prompt feedback, but computers are not essential for the system.

Modular Methods

Modular methods of teaching essentially involve analysis of course content and division into relatively independent units or modules. Typically, modules are intended to be self-instructional and often include tasks involving field work or audiovisual media. The Keller Plan (PSI) is one example of a modular approach, and modules are often used as well with computer-assisted instruction (CAI), contract plans, or other methods.

Leith (1974b) has suggested that the structure of a course may have either a linear, network, or spiral structure. A *linear* structure is one in which each unit of a course depends upon and builds upon the previous one. Mathematics courses, for example, are often linear. In *network* or *spiral* courses many starting points are possible, leading to relationships that become part of larger and more detailed structures. In a *spiral* structure there are, presumably, certain natural relatively complete structures or loops that can provide the base for the next loop of a spiral of greater breadth and comprehensiveness.

A fixed sequence, such as that of the Keller Plan, is thus appropriate for content structured in a linear (or skyscraper?) fashion. When dealing with content structured in a network or spiral, instructors might offer students a choice of starting points and sequences. It is here that modularization is helpful. You may offer each student, or group of students, a choice of modules. (Leith forms teams of five or six students.) Each module consists of a problem, a group task with specific individual assignments, and a report to be made. In carrying out the instructions and organizing their efforts team members should engage the material much more actively and thoughtfully than if they were simply to read the material individually. Leith uses this approach with self- and group-evaluation to achieve the goal of developing skill in self-evaluation.

One of the better known modularized approaches, Audiotutorial, was discussed in Chapter 15.

Guided Design

"Guided Design" is a method of course organization and teaching developed by Charles Wales, Professor of Engineering at West Virginia University, to teach engineering students problem solving and decision making. The method proved to be so successful that it has been used to teach problem solving and decision making in hundreds of courses in the humanities and social sciences as well as in the natural sciences and engineering.

Guided design courses involve textbook and problem solving assignments out of class and small group decision making in class. The class time is spent on a sequence of open-ended problem-solving projects (perhaps 3–5 projects in a term). In one of Wales' classes, they were:

1. Developing Better Housing in a Rain Forest
2. Making University Campus Buildings Accessible
3. Providing Water and Power to a Mountain Cabin

Each project involves use of subject matter from the text and is guided by printed material prepared by the teacher. The first printed instruction describes the situation and specifies the students' roles (e.g., Peace Corps workers). Students are asked first to identify the problem and set a goal for their work. After completing this step they are given a printed sheet showing how other groups have responded. Students are not asked to agree with other groups but to consider the other viewpoints. Similar feedback and directions are given at each step of the problem-solving process; e.g.,

1. Situation
2. Goal
3. Gathering information
   What information is needed?
   Where can it be obtained?
   Who will get what?
4. Possible solutions
   List 3 or more ways to attain the goal

5. Constraints
   List limiting factors
6. Choose a solution
   Test solutions for positive and negative consequences before choosing
7. Analysis
   Identify important factors to be considered in working out the details of the solution
8. Synthesis
   Produce a detailed solution
9. Evaluation
   How can the solution be evaluated?
10. Recommend a course of action

Students who took this course showed better achievement in advanced courses and were less likely to drop out of engineering than comparable previous students.

SUPPLEMENTARY READING

J. G. Creager and D. L. Murray (eds.), *The use of modules in college biology teaching* (Washington, DC: Commission on Undergraduate Education in the Biological Sciences, 1971). This brief book includes general as well as biologically oriented articles.

R. B. Johnson and S. R. Johnson, *Assuring learning with self-instructional packages or, up the up staircase, a how-to-do workbook* (Chapel Hill, NC: Self-instructional Packages, Inc., 1971).

C. E. Wales and R. A. Stager, *Guided design* (Morgantown, WV: Center for Guided Design, West Virginia University, 1977).

C. E. Wales and A. Nardi, *Teaching decision-making with guided design, Idea Paper No. 9* (Kansas State University: Center for Faculty Evaluation and Development, November, 1982).

CHAPTER 22

Large Classes: Morale, Discipline, and Order

The things under consideration here are mainly practical problems of the social psychology of the classroom.* No single set of recommendations will work for any particular instructor or for any particular classroom situation. What is considered good discipline will vary from instructor to instructor and from one situation to another. What I recommend is based on the philosophy stated in the introduction of this book—basically respect for students.

Order in the Classroom

I now turn to some specific considerations. The first of these concerns order in the classroom. A certain degree of quiet and attention seems to be almost essential to the effective running of the educational enterprise. How can this end be achieved? There seem to be two ways to go about it. The first is to insist upon strict attention, set up stringent rules on the point, and enforce them. This is not, however, a method I recommend in spite of its rather common adoption. One difficulty with such a method is that order, when it is achieved in this fashion, is dictated to the students. It has a way of putting the instructor into perpetual conflict with the students. The general upshot appears to be that, in such a classroom, the students try, in the numerous ways at their disposal, to beat the game. Whether or not this involves basic needs for revolt against authority, it seems that any interest that they may have initially had in cooperating with the instructor in an attempt to accomplish certain purposes is at least partly supplanted by a feeling of revolt. Furthermore, this policing technique contradicts two basic considerations. As I have already indicated, education, pursued in this manner, is a noncooperative enterprise. Students get to play a much less active part in the classroom than they might. Their enthusiasm is dampened; their tendency to

---

* Much of this chapter is derived from Gregory Kimble's advice to young faculty members.

ask questions is reduced; even if they are cooperative, their behavior seems to be directed less toward a real understanding of materials than toward an effort to parrot the wisdom of the instructor. Their learning thus becomes learning by rote, which minimizes understanding and thus defeats part of the purpose of being in the class in the first place. This rather common disciplinary procedure is also one of the major contributors to the perpetuated adolescence of the college students. Instructors who use this method set themselves up as parent figures. By doing this, they may elicit the submissive, unthinking obedience that is sometimes characteristic of children's behavior toward their parents.

Having to some extent discredited the austere schoolmaster method of handling a class, I turn now to the positive side of my argument. I want to suggest a method that will give you almost as good order in the classroom without sacrificing education itself. To accomplish this, three procedures that parallel the basic considerations just discussed seem to be useful:

1. Give the students the notion that the accomplishment of course objectives is partly their problem.

2. Give the students the notion that they have certain responsibilities and, at the same time, certain rights. More of this later.

3. Give the students the notion that you are willing to entertain reasonable suggestions, objections, and questions in connection with course materials.

Unfortunately these ideas are new to many students and cannot be accomplished in a single day. They are ideas that mean the students will have to learn what may be a new adjustment to the classroom situation. If you use these ideas, you will have to be willing to put up with a certain amount of disorder in the class for a short time. They mean that you sometimes suppress your own needs for aggression and prestige and maintain a constant awareness of student needs.

I try consistently to use this method in classes where enrollment may run as high as 500. The class is permitted to operate on an informal basis. Questions and comments from the floor are allowed. (In a class this size, questions from the floor should be repeated for the benefit of the class as a whole before they are answered. Avoid the entirely informal discussion with a single student.) The result of this informality may be an initial unruliness in the class. It does not, however, interfere to any important extent with a well-planned lecture, and it disappears after five or six lectures. The students placed in an informally run class of this sort seem to be in a situation analogous to that of the boys in the Lewin, Lippitt, and White investigation (1939) who shifted from the autocratic to the democratic group atmosphere, and their behavior is much the same. There is the initial outburst of horseplay (and occasionally aggression) and finally the settling down to a more cooperative, objective, and efficient level of performance.

Whether I am correct in recommending the democratic as opposed to the authoritarian group atmosphere in a _particular_ class is a question of fact; it can be decided by experimentation.

I want to consider now some typical problems of discipline and order and attempt a few concrete suggestions of methods of handling these problems.

Questions and Answers in a Large Class

The lecture section is sometimes not regarded as the place for questions and discussions from the floor. Instructors often try to have the questions handled by an assistant in a quiz or discussion section. Potentially this solution is a good one; actually, it often leaves much to be desired for two reasons:

1. Handling a discussion section is sometimes more difficult than giving a lecture. A more reasonable arrangement than the one that is commonly used might be to have the assistants give the lecture and the instructors handle the quiz sections. The difficulties in discussion sections are apt to be that the assistants are not well enough acquainted with the materials the lecturers have covered and have difficulty keeping the discussion going. This can be surmounted if the assistants attend the lectures, participate in lecture planning, and receive help and supervision in planning the discussion, but the discussion-leader role should be one of developing skills in application and problem solving rather than interpreting the lecture. If senior professors have any advantages over teaching assistants, it presumably lies in their knowledge of the field. Thus, to the extent feasible, questions of fact and interpretation are best answered in the lecture itself.

2. Whatever its potential usefulness, the discussion section does not provide for the prompt answering of questions that arise in connection with specific lecture materials.

In most classes (even large ones) I believe that it is possible to answer such questions. If you also believe this and want to try to handle such questions, keep some of the following relevant considerations in mind.

The students must know that such questions are permitted. This is usually not difficult because certain students try to ask questions in almost any class. If you find yourself with a particularly inhibited group, questions written out and passed to the front of the room may handle the situation or you may ask students to write out questions and then ask for them orally. In any event it is important to repeat the question before answering it.

One of the problems in large-group question answering and discussion is that a student's question may, in a group where several hands are raised, refer to something that was covered several questions back. By writing all questions on the board before beginning to answer them, you may save time and confusion since some groupings and relationships are apparent. Also grouping questions enables you to better apportion your time to those that are most significant or troublesome.

Experience in teaching a particular class will give you an understanding of the sort of questions that are apt to be asked on particular topics. Thus, you can be ready for the typical questions. Occasionally, however, you will be asked an atypical question; and it can happen that, for some of them, you will not know the answer. In this event, about the only course open to you is to admit that you do not know, promise to look up the answer and report on it at a later class meeting. If you use this method, *try to find the answer*. I do not recommend the technique of telling students to look up the answer for themselves. The students usually will not take the trouble, and they are apt to discover that this is simply a way of hiding your own ignorance. So far as finding the answers is concerned, remember that your colleagues are a good source, probably more useful than text materials.

Irrelevant questions may sometimes prevent important points from coming out. One way of handling such questions is to write the question on the board to answer later. By writing it down you indicate that you've heard the question and remove the necessity for the student to keep thinking about it. Frequently the question will have been answered by the end of the hour.

A somewhat different situation arises in the case of the student who flatly disagrees with you. Such disagreements are apt to be presented with at least the suggestion that anyone's opinion is as good as anyone else's. In such cases, factual evidence for your point of view would appear to be in order. In cases where the question is a controversial one, you may have to admit the possibility that the student is right. If this is necessary, you can turn the situation to your advantage, by showing the kind of experimental test of the question that is implied. My own discipline, psychology, is vulnerable in this connection. Students come to the psychology class (and sometimes leave it) with the notion that everyone is a psychologist. A part of the purpose of the elementary course is to demonstrate that this is the case, but that there are still characteristics of rational scientific thought that make some hypotheses more tenable than others. But the task is not an easy one. The reason for this seems to be that since everyone has experiences and observes behavior, they demand of the psychologist something they demand of no other scientist— namely, that the psychological account of emotion, perception, or what not, corresponds to their own naive experience of them. This is to be contrasted with the position of the physicist. Physics also presents the students with an account of the nature of a part of the world. The tables and chairs of the physicist are not solid objects, but are actually made up of minute whirling particles. It is a tribute to the maturity of physics that this nonsense view of the world can be made reasonable. And it will presumably sometime come about that psychology will be able to describe its subject matter in this way. For some students, it may be useful to point out this sort of thing. For many it will not. While psychology is particularly vulnerable on this point, I have the notion that instructors in other disciplines face some of the same problems. Certainly in the arts and literature there is something of the "I know what I like" syndrome.

If I were asked how to summarize my ideas about handling questions, disagreement, and discussion in the classroom, I might put my argument this way: There are two stock formulas that seem to go a long way toward handling these problems. One is "This is the evidence." The other is, "You may be right."

In summary, my general advice is to encourage rather than discourage questioning. For more detailed consideration of large group discussion techniques, see Chapter 4.

Interference with the Course Routine by Other "Interests"

Here I refer to the students who knit, sleep, read comic books, draw pictures, gossip, or do any of the other things that students are apt to do instead of taking notes. As a general rule, the desirable way in which to eliminate these practices is by making it important to the students to listen to your lectures. This can be accomplished in one of two ways. Probably the most satisfactory from your point of view would be to discover ways of making your presentation interesting enough to command the attention of the student.

If you are convinced that you are already doing everything that you can in this connection, it may be worthwhile to look at your examination procedures. If you do not include lecture materials on your examinations, some students will feel that there is very little to be gained in listening to you or in making notes on anything you say. This can be true of the most interesting lecturer. Since a large part of the students' motivation is directed toward passing examinations, you can make use of this in getting a class to pay attention and at the same time probably improve your teaching. There is nothing wrong, as I see it, in telling the students that certain materials of the lecture will probably appear on an examination.

Preparing for a Class Period

Disciplinary problems sometimes are a reflection of student dissatisfaction with your teaching. The time college teachers spend in specific preparation for their classes varies from none at all to many hours. Those who are low on the scale usually rationalize that the most effective illustrations and problems are those that arise spontaneously from the class. This may be true, but instructors who make effective use of them are usually those who have thought through their goals and procedures so well that they no longer have to worry about whether or not the class is going to fall apart.

Thus, I do advocate preparation for each class and suggest that the following steps be included:

1. Consideration of specific goals for the day in the light of overall course goals.

2. Review of previous work and especially of the previous day's discussion.

3. Review of the day's assignment.

4. Reading background materials related to the day's lesson.

5. Looking at work ahead and future assignments. As in most matters, students like to know where they stand in relation to assignments. They appreciate a schedule of future assignments passed out early in the semester. In courses without laboratories, students are conventionally expected to do two hours work outside class for each hour in class. In a freshman or sophomore course, the average students seem to be able to master up to a hundred pages a week for a three-hour course. This figure, of course, will vary depending upon the difficulty of the reading, the accessibility of the books, and the amount of written or committee work required.

6. Choosing the teaching methods or techniques to be used in terms of the goals to be attained and remembering that it pays to "throw a change of pace" now and then.

7. Working out an estimated budget of time for each activity in the class period, remembering that it is to be a guide, not a straitjacket, and allowing time for a summary and lead-in to the next day's work.

What to Do when You're Not Prepared

Unless you are exceptional, there will be some classes where you arrive without preparation, despite your dedication to good teaching. This can provide an exciting learning experience for you, but it can also be educational for the class. Here are some techniques to use when your car has broken down, you were called before the President for an unexpected honor, or you simply overslept.

1. Use the technique of Problem Posting described in Chapter 3.

2. Ask students to spend the first five minutes reviewing the assignment and previous lecture notes before writing down the one question each would most like to have you discuss. Collect the questions. Answer one or more yourself, then throw one out to the class, and while a student is answering, do a quick sort of the questions to group them more logically.

3. Split the class into buzz groups (see Chapter 4) and ask each buzz group to come up with one question to be discussed. Ask the first

group for its question, discuss it, and ask if any other group had a question related to the first. Answer that and go on in a similar fashion.

4. Ask the class to spend the first ten minutes reviewing a particular part of the assignment so that they have it clearly in mind. While they are reviewing it, think of a discussion problem involving the material they are reviewing. Then break the class into buzz groups to discuss the problem. Use the remainder of the time to get reports from the discussion groups or start a second cycle by asking each group to discuss the advantages or disadvantages of two of the groups' solutions to the problem.

5. Admit that you're unprepared and ask the class how the time can best be spent. (Don't spend so much time discussing what to do that there's no time left to do it.)

Saving Time: Visiting Lecturers

There are inevitably times when you will be over committed—too busy to prepare a decent lecture and too rushed to think of an alternative. The preceding section deals with last minute situations. But sometimes pressures can be anticipated. Scheduling a film, a guest lecturer, or giving students a class day off to work on projects are techniques for prevention of being overwhelmed. If they are used frequently, students may suspect your commitment to their education. Properly planned they can provide a welcome change of pace and can enhance learning.

How do you find an appropriate visiting lecturer? Oftentimes students themselves will know someone with special expertise and experience in an area being discussed. A first person account has impact much beyond that of pages of print. Letting a student, or group of students, host the guest, helping prepare the guest for the class, and the class for the guest, encourages a sense of responsibility for learning that is important for effective education.

For maximum success the students need to be prepared for the visitor and some effort should be made to get the class to formulate the questions the expert will attempt to answer. If the visitor is to lecture, he or she should be warned to allow some of the class period for questions so that students can follow up with the questions formulated before and during the visit. Then part of the following class period should be allotted to discussion of the visitor's contributions. Often it is more fun both for the visitor and the class if class members are selected to form a panel to interview the visitor rather than for the visitor simply to lecture.

When possible, I encourage students to join the guest and me for coffee after class. This gives the most interested students a chance for personal contact and the guest a chance to relax.

A guest need not spend an entire class period. Ten or fifteen minutes may be sufficient to achieve your objectives.

SUPPLEMENTARY READING

R. D. Mann et al., *The college classroom* (New York: Wiley, 1970).

PART VI

Perspectives on Teaching and the Teaching Environment

CHAPTER 23 / *Motivating Students*

If I were following a purely logical approach to the organization of this book, chapters on motivation and learning would certainly come early, for decisions about teaching techniques should be based upon the principles of learning. However I have found that most beginning teachers have too many immediate problems to worry very much about general questions of educational theory. It is only after you have mastered some of the day-to-day problems that you are able to sit back and wonder why some things work and others don't. The next three chapters deal with psychological material relevant to these broader concerns.

Motivation

Instructors know that student learning and memory are closely tied to *motivation*. Students will learn what they want to learn and will have great difficulty in learning material in which they're not interested. Students are not poor learners; nor are they unmotivated. They are learning all the time—new dance steps, the status hierarchy on campus, football strategy, and other more or less complex things—but the sort of learning for which students are motivated is not always that which contributes to attaining the goals of our courses. Too often teachers think of learning only in terms of formal instruction. It might be more realistic for teachers to think of themselves as individuals who facilitate certain kinds of learning. They can neither learn for their students nor stop them from learning.

A primary problem, then, is motivating students toward course goals. Usually the learning psychologist stops with this point, but to be useful the principle of motivation needs to be accompanied with information about dependable motives of college students. Teachers know, for example, that many of their students are taught by their parents to want to do well in school. Thus we can count on some motivation for *achievement,* but there are other motives that are also important.

Curiosity

Psychology has a good deal more to contribute on the subject of motivation for learning than it did a few years ago. A decade or two ago psychologists would have talked about reward and punishment and would have asked you to look at the rewards for learning in the classroom. This is still worth considering. Rewards and punishments often influence learning. But the revolution in research and theory lies in new evidence that people are naturally curious. They seek new experiences; they enjoy learning new things; they find satisfaction in solving puzzles, perfecting skills, and developing competence.

Thus, one of the major tasks in teaching is not how to scare students into doing their homework, but rather how to nurture their curiosity and to use curiosity as a motive for learning.

Fortunately, I can do more than point to curiosity as an important motive for learning. A good deal of research suggests that people seek and enjoy stimuli that are different from those they are used to—but that these stimuli must not be too different. When stimuli are totally incongruous or very strange, students develop anxiety instead of curiosity.

How does this generalization apply to learning in college? It is tempting to answer this question in vague phrases like "varied teaching methods," "posing new, but soluble problems," or "setting realistic standards of achievement." But it is possible to go beyond this. One hint comes from studies by Berlyne (1954a and b). He found that asking students questions, rather than presenting statements of fact, not only improved learning, but also increased interest in learning more about the topic. Questions were particularly effective in arousing curiosity about things that were already familiar. The most successful questions were those that were most unexpected. This agrees with the finding that National Merit Scholars describe the classes that influenced their choice of field as ones where they didn't know what to expect next (Thistlethwaite, 1960). The interplay between familiar and novel may be very significant in the development of curiosity.

How do instructors bring students into contact with novelty? Meaningful laboratory experience may be one answer. For example, outstanding scientists report that their motivation for science resulted from early participation in research. This has implications for other disciplines. Perhaps instructors offer too few opportunities for students to experience the thrill of discovery.

Complexity can also arouse curiosity. Chapter 13, "Reading and Programmed Learning," reviewed evidence that study questions requiring thought produce greater learning from reading. This is not only because of greater meaningfulness, but also because questions requiring "deep processing" make studying more interesting (Svensson, 1976).

Competence

One of the reasons curiosity is important is that it is a motive intrinsic to learning, and thus continued learning is not dependent upon a teacher to reward learning.

Another intrinsic motive for learning is competence or self-efficacy. Human beings receive pleasure from doing things well. To the degree that teachers can help students develop a sense of standards that will enable them to see that they are developing increasing skill, teachers can also contribute to the goal of continued learning after the class has been completed. Bandura (1977) has developed in some depth a theory of self-efficacy. This theory suggests that while teachers are important sources of information about self-efficacy, students will interpret the same information in differing ways depending upon the context of the information and their previous experience. Thus, seeing the teacher or other students perform a task will not help students who see themselves as so different that another's success bears no relationship to their own chances to perform the task. Even their own success may be misinterpreted as luck. For such students teachers need to link success with the perception that the success was due to the student's own ability and effort. Success alone is not enough. For students who lack a sense of efficacy teachers must not only provide situations where success occurs, but also give students opportunities to undertake the task on their own to prove that they have themselves mastered it without special help.

Conflicting Motives

Most students want to be liked. This motive may work against instructors as well as for them. The teacher's friendly approval can be an important reward for learning, but the "average raiser" is not always well liked. Thus, in some colleges, students who want acceptance by their classmates may avoid any conspicuous display of academic achievement. Many students suffer from conflict between the need to get good grades and the need to be well liked. One of the symptoms of this conflict is the ostentatious neglect of study by some bright students and their apparent surprise when they get good grades. This ploy is so well known that its techniques have been analyzed carefully by Stephen Potter in his scholarly volume, *One-upmanship* (1955).

Many students have conflicting motives. One common conflict is between independence and dependence. This means that students are likely to resent the teacher who directs their activities too closely, but they also are likely to be anxious when given independence; so that teachers have the neat trick of finding ways of simultaneously satisfying both needs. As a result of this conflict some students disagree with their teachers not on rational grounds but simply as a way of expressing emotions. Similarly, student apathy in a required course may be irrational expression of resentment about being required to do anything.

Achievement Motivation

Atkinson's theory of achievement motivation suggested that students with high achievement motivation would be more highly motivated in situations in which they perceived their chances of success as about fifty-fifty. Laboratory research supported the hypothesis. Atkinson and O'Connor (1963) then hypothesized that grouping by ability would be particularly effective for students with strong desires to achieve, since the homogeneous class should provide an achievement situation in which the students' judgments of their own success as compared to their peers should be more likely to be intermediate. The Atkinson and O'Connor results showed that the high-achievement motive students not only made greater academic gains in homogeneous classes, but also reported greater interest in school work.

The Atkinson and O'Connor results are relevant not only for the problem of ability grouping, but also for the general problem of motivation for learning. From Berlyne we have the suggestion that motivation is highest in situations of moderate novelty; from Atkinson we learn that for students with basic motivation for success, motivation is highest when chances of success are moderate. Both of these findings point to the value of pacing learning so that each step offers some newness and only a moderate risk of failure—a motivational principle also found by Lepper and Malone (1985) in their analysis of motivational elements in computer games (see Chapter 14, Computer Uses in Teaching and Learning).

One of the first steps in teaching may be to stimulate doubt about what has previously been taken for granted. I've never really studied the teaching role of the "devil's advocate," but this may be an important way to stimulate motivation.

Grades as Incentives

Let us consider the case of the most important motivational device—grades. Whatever students' motivations for being in college, grades are important to them. If students are really interested in learning, grades represent an expert's appraisal of their success; if they're interested in getting into professional school, good grades are the key that unlock graduate school doors; if they want to play basketball, grades are necessary for maintaining eligibility. Most students are motivated to get at least passing grades, and much as instructors resent record keeping, the grades for which they are responsible are a powerful motivational tool (as we saw in Chapter 9).

Many teachers are a little embarrassed by this, regarding grades as one of the necessary evils of teaching. They try to discount grades in discussion of the organization of the course and try to arrive at grades in such a way that they can avoid trouble with disappointed students. But they frequently fail to use grades to bring about the sort of learning they desire.

Because grades are important to them, many students will learn whatever is necessary to get the grades they desire. If instructors base grades on memorization of details, students will memorize the text. If they believe grades are based upon their ability to integrate and apply principles, they'll attempt to do this.

As far as speed of learning goes, it probably doesn't matter what motives instructors use, but this doesn't mean that the type of motivation used is unimportant. A good deal of evidence has accumulated to suggest that negative (fear) and positive (hope) motives affect behavior differently. Teachers usually use mixtures of positive and negative motives. When students are motivated by the threat of low grades, they may work hard, but only if this is the only way to avoid undesirable consequences. If there are ways out of the situation, they'll take them. The result frequently is that students do the least they can get away with or spend their time devising elaborate methods of cheating.

Negative motives are not as effective outside the learning situation as are positive motives, because fear is a more effective motivational device if the threatened danger is close than if it is distant. Students who are afraid are likely to want to avoid being reminded of the possibility of failure. Hence they may avoid study until the pressures are so great that they simply have no alternative. Thus, teachers who motivate their students by fear of bad grades need to use frequent tests if their threats are to be effective.

The striking difference in behavior between students motivated by fear and students motivated by hope is illustrated in their behavior during examinations. A study by Atkinson and Litwin (1960) showed that male students who were high in anxiety about tests were among the first to leave the examination room and tended to do more poorly on the examination than in their work during the course. Students with positive motivation to succeed tended to stay in the examination room longer. Note that this illustrates the tendency of the fearful person to avoid the situation that arouses anxiety.

Attributions

Such students can be helped. Heckhausen (1974) showed that students who fear failure improved in performance when they were helped to attribute failure to lack of effort rather than to lack of ability and to set reasonable standards for themselves. But many students work hard and still do poorly. Is there hope for them? Yes. I currently teach a course "Learning to Learn," that has both cognitive and motivational goals. Motivationally I aim at teaching students that, in addition to effort, learning strategies can account for success and failure. A study by Anderson and Jennings (1980) showed that attributing failure to ineffective strategies improved motivation for success.

To sum up my argument thus far, motivation is important in learning. Curiosity and competence motivation are important motives for learning. We can use student motivation for success, approval, and so on to produce learning. Grades are important incentives for many kinds of motivation. Thus it's important to make sure that grades are not separate from the kind of learning desired. Using grades chiefly as a threat may produce avoidance rather than interest.

The Teacher as Model

One of the major sources of stimulation of motivation is the teacher. Your own enthusiasm and values have much to do with your students' interest in the subject matter. Probably nonverbal as well as verbal methods are used to communicate such attitudes; that is, facial expression, animation, and vocal intensity may be as important as the words you use.

SUPPLEMENTARY READING

T. W. Malone and M. R. Lepper. Making learning fun: A taxonomy of intrinsic motivations for learning. In R. E. Snow and M. J. Farr (eds.), *Aptitude, learning, and instruction: III. Conative and affective process analysis* (Hillsdale, NJ: Erlbaum, forthcoming). Malone and Lepper carried out an elegant study of what makes computer games so motivating, and here they provide a list of ways teachers can design educational experiences that are intrinsically motivating.

CHAPTER 24

Learning and Cognition in the College Classroom

A teacher's job isn't done when he or she interests the class, for the amount students learn depends upon the amount taught, and this is not so simple as it may at first appear. It may well be that the *more* instructors teach the *less* their students learn! Several years ago some of our teaching assistants were arguing furiously over how to teach about the nervous system. One group argued that since students wouldn't remember all of the details, they might better omit them and teach only the basic essentials which we want everyone to learn. Another group argued that students would forget much of what they learned. "But," they said, "if they're going to forget a large percentage, we need to teach much more than we expect them to remember. Otherwise they'll forget even the important things."

To a psychologist such an argument is simply an invitation to an experiment, and consequently the combatants agreed that they'd try out their ideas in their own classes and compare the results on the final exam questions covering the nervous system. The outcome was clear. The students whose instructor had omitted details were clearly superior to those whose instructor had given them the whole story. This result would not have been surprising to David Katz (1950), the German-Swedish psychologist who devised a number of unique experiments demonstrating that, beyond a certain point, adding to the elements in an intellectual task causes confusion and inefficiency. Katz called this phenomenon "mental dazzle."

Organization

Fortunately, teaching is an area where you can have your cake and eat it too, for it is possible to teach more and have it remembered better. The magic formula is *organization*. As Katona (1940) demonstrated in a series of experiments on organization and memory, people can learn and re-

228

member much more when their learning fits into an organization. If I give you a series of numbers chosen at random, like 73810547, and ask you what the fourth number was, you probably have difficulty remembering, but if I give the numbers 12345678, you can remember immediately what the fourth number was. Teaching that helps students find a framework within which to fit new facts is likely to be more effective than teaching that simply communicates masses of material in which the student can see no organization.

The successful teacher is one whose students see meaningful problems. The ideal class would begin with a problem so meaningful that the students are always just a step ahead of the teacher in approaching a solution. If students can develop their own ways of structuring the material, it is likely to be recalled and used better than if the structure is provided by the teacher. My own research suggests that students often dislike and do not necessarily learn well from teachers who are highly organized—you can have too much organization as well as too little. The important thing is that students find some way of structuring the material. Students with more background and ability can do this even in relatively unstructured situations, but in courses where the material is new to the students it is probably important that the teacher provide ways of organizing the material. There is an old maxim, "Tell them what you're going to tell them. Tell them. Tell them what you've told them." Like many old maxims, this one is not true—or at least is oversimplified. Giving a summary in advance sometimes helps, but it is detrimental for some students (for example, extroverts; Leith, 1974a), and its effectiveness depends not only upon the type of organization provided, but also upon the succeeding content and the previous background of the students. Questions are likely to be better than statements, and questions requiring thinking are generally better than those simply calling attention to main points.

Variability and Verbalization

How can instructors help students develop principles and concepts they can apply much more broadly than answering a problem requiring only a memorized answer? I suppose all instructors have been disheartened by having a student answer a routine problem perfectly and then fail to use the same knowledge in solving another problem where it is relevant. There have been a number of educational attempts to solve this problem.

One of the early slogans was, "Learning by doing," a theory that if people learned something in the situation where the learning was to be used they wouldn't have the added step of learning when to apply it. This is perfectly reasonable and makes sense psychologically. The only problem is that the number of situations in which one must use knowledge is infinite. If each human being had to learn everything by doing it, civilization would still be in the Stone Age.

Our whole civilization is based on the fact that people can use *words* to shortcut the long process of learning by trial and error, but direct experience may be useful at certain stages of learning. If we are to learn to apply a principle in new situations, we need to develop it from experiencing specific instances in varying contexts. A number of experiments have demonstrated that repetitive drill is much less effective than varying problems which help to develop principles that can be applied to new situations (for example, Wolfle, 1935). Verbalization can help us identify the common elements in these situations and shorten the learning process. In fact research suggests that even such a complex skill as learning to solo an airplane can be learned in much shorter air time if the learner practices the skill mentally and verbally. *Shoot basket by imagery*

Among the most interesting research programs were the studies of learning by monkeys carried out by Harlow and his colleagues at Wisconsin. Harlow was studying discrimination learning in monkeys. The monkey was rewarded with food whenever he chose the correct one of two objects, such as a cube or sphere. Harlow's monkeys displayed the usual pattern of beginning with virtually chance responses and gradually becoming more consistently accurate. Harlow, however, did not stop with one problem as most learning experimenters have done. Rather, his monkeys were kept at work learning one problem after another, and the monkeys' learning curve gradually changed. With more and more experience the monkeys learned the problems more and more quickly until eventually they needed only one trial to learn which was the correct object. Harlow's monkeys had learned how to learn. They might have learned how to learn even more rapidly had Harlow been able to talk to them about the critical dimensions of their problem solving.

If these experiments are relevant to college teaching (and I think they are), instructors may be able to teach students how to solve problems in their fields by giving them a series of related problems to solve, so that they learn the critical dimensions and most likely approaches.

Feedback, Contiguity, and Active Learning =========

If instructors expect students to learn skills, the students have to practice, but practice doesn't make perfect. Practice works if learners *see the results* of their practice and gain information from the results about what to do.

A number of experiments suggest that active learning is usually more efficient than passive learning. One reason for this may be the improved opportunities for feedback in active learning. Discussion techniques may help develop critical thinking because students do the thinking, and there is an opportunity to check their thinking against each other. But one of the dangers of "student-centered" or "nondirective" discussions is that the results are not apparent. Students may make comments, express opinions, and participate actively, but this doesn't guarantee that their opinions are any more informed at the end of a semester than they were at the beginning. Of course not all feedback has to come from the instructor—students can learn much from other students or from books—but in order to learn, students need to test out their ideas in a situation in which they can get the results of the test and see examples of better thinking.

Nevertheless, instructors need to go a step beyond the principle that students learn what they practice with knowledge of results. It's not always easy to get students to practice critical thinking in the classroom. After all, why stick your neck out? The student who remains quiet in class avoids the risks of disagreement, criticism, and embarrassment. To develop critical thinking, students must learn to want to think.

This brings us back to motivation. Curiosity and competence are powerful motives, but a smile, a nod of encouragement, an excited, "Good. Let's follow that idea through"—these are also tools that teachers can use, not only to provide knowledge of results, but also to develop the motivation to continue intellectual activity.

To maintain motivation instructors need to pose problems that are within the range of their students' abilities. Studies of the development of achievement motivation in children indicate that parents develop this motivation by encouraging the child to do well and by setting standards that the child can achieve. Other parents who orient their children toward achievement fail because they set unreasonable goals. Both for the purposes of motivating students for critical thinking and for developing the ability to think critically, experience in solving problems within the students' ken is essential. This by no means implies that students should not experience failure or criticism, but it does mean that they should be faced with problems that will, as often as not, be soluble.

Cognition

Psychology has been undergoing a revolution in theory during the past two decades.* The older associationist-behaviorist approaches have been superseded by and incorporated into newer information-processing approaches, derived in part from computer analogies and in part from a long tradition of cognitive theories. These approaches, called cognitive psychology, seek to explain behavior in terms of mental processes. Methodological and theoretical advances have enabled psychologists to make precise tests of theories about the processes human beings use in learning, memory, problem solving, and decision making.

As compared with earliest research on human and animal learning, cognitive approaches place more emphasis upon meaningful human learning. They thus have more potential applicability to problems of education than earlier theories had.

Learning, Semantic Memory, and Retrieval

Until the past few years the basic construct of learning theory was "reinforcement." For many years psychologists believed that stimulus-response connections were stamped in by rewards or "reinforcements." Memory was the reactivation of these connections. Now theorists go beyond simple reinforcement analysis of learning and memory. Some think of memory as consisting of different types of storage. The fundamental units of storage are meaningful propositions, concepts, or images. Instead of a telephone switchboard metaphor of the mind, theorists now think of semantic learning as more like the building up of structures, networks, or maps. When we learn, we may add more details to the maps, or we may add more connections between points on the map, or we may even construct alternative maps that are more compact and useful for certain purposes, much as a map of the Interstate Highway system omits details, but is useful in planning long auto trips. But even these metaphors are inadequate; they imply a static storage. The current view

---

* The remaining section of the chapter is derived in large part from a paper I wrote as a partial summary and afterthoughts from a seminar held at the Exxon Educational Foundation in October, 1976.

is rather that memory refers to some properties of an information-processing system—a system involving nerve cells in activity—activities having to do with learning and retrieving meaningful relationships. Learning and remembering are active processes.

Donald Norman of the University of California at San Diego (1977) suggests differentiating three processes of complex learning:

1. Accretion.
2. Restructuring.
3. Fine tuning.

Accretion is adding knowledge to existing cognitive structures. _Restructuring_ implies reordering knowledge into new patterns or extending and making connections between existing patterns. _Fine tuning_ is the process involved in adapting a cognitive structure so that it can be used more efficiently and appropriately for particular purposes. Much higher education involves developing a more specialized form of a structure than most students already have. Often teachers fail to help students see the link to the general schema they already know.

Students differ not only in how they fit what instructors teach into their existing structures, but also in how readily they develop appropriate new structures. The task of the teacher differs depending upon which kind of learning is involved. _Accretion_ may be achieved simply by referral to a previously learned principle or use of a familiar example; _restructuring_ may require challenges to old structures and much activity on the part of the student in trying out new understanding.

Instead of thinking of learning and memory in terms of tighter and stronger associations between stimuli and responses, with the associations strengthened by reward, psychologists now think of storage as being influenced by attending to things and interacting with them in such a way that they are related to existing memory structure. We store memories in terms of their potential uses—their meanings. What we store is not just what was said, read, or observed at a particular time; rather what is stored depends also upon previous experience.

Collins and Quillian (1972), who have proposed one model of memory, give as an example the sentence: "The policeman held up his hand and the cars stopped." We accept this statement matter-of-factly and probably remember it as a policeman standing in an intersection directing traffic. Had an earthquake started parked cars rolling down a hill, the sentence becomes surprising.

In any case, the point here is that we store the sentence about the policeman not just in terms of the dictionary meanings of the words in the sentence, but also in terms of other things we know, such as that policemen often direct traffic, and that moving cars normally have drivers. We process and store meanings without thinking about the process consciously until something does not fit with our previous experience.

Because understanding and learning involve adding previously learned relationships of meanings, students differ in what and how they learn in a particular lecture or assignment. Often teachers have an inadequate comprehension of what students have learned and what is blocking understanding. If you can link what you teach to what students already know, they are more likely to understand and remember it.

Analysis of Cognitive Processes

Since students' previous knowledge determines how they will learn what we teach, an important part of effective teaching is to analyze students' existing structures of knowledge as well as the learning tasks we are asking them to perform. Effective teaching is as much diagnosis as presentation.

The kind of education involved in higher learning is more general purpose than that involved in teaching machines and previous computer assisted instruction. Higher learning needs to be more modifiable and more transferable to situations remote from the training situation. Thus the problem of task analysis is much more complex than that involved in the simpler types of training that were relevant for teaching machines or early computer programs.

If education is general, it should be possible to define general kinds of tasks cutting across situations. If educational psychologists can define intellectual factors in terms of the cognitive processes demanded, they probably have a good start at defining generalizable task characteristics. They can then analyze learning tasks such as studying a textbook or listening to a lecture, both with respect to the cognitive processes involved and the structure of the content.

Even a relatively simple analysis of an educational task may be useful. For example one might ask, "Why does a student fail an essay question on an exam?"

1. The student does not understand the question.

2. The student has not learned the material.

3. The student lacks specific cues for retrieval.

4. The student lacks an appropriate strategy for retrieving the material.

5. The student lacks words needed for an answer.

6. The student lacks a conception of the required solution; for example, when asked to "explain," she lacks an adequate conception of what is involved in an adequate explanation.

7. The student cannot hold the required material in active memory while writing the answer.

The thought that one could forget part of an answer while beginning to write it may seem preposterous. Yet when long-term memory is unorganized, a heavy load is placed on short-term memory during the task of writing an appropriate answer. For example, Cole et al. (1971) found that nonliterate African children seemed deficient on free-recall tests, but when they were led by special techniques to respond in meaningful _categories,_ recall was similar to that of American children. Some college students may have similar difficulties in organizing course material into meaningful categories.

The point of such an analysis of an essay test is that rather than simply telling a student to study a particular chapter more thoroughly, instructors can look for common threads of difficulties exemplified in several questions; they can even design tests laying bare different possible sources of difficulty, so that remedial action can be taken.

Can Learners Be Helped by Cognitive Psychology?

I teach a freshman introductory course in cognitive psychology called "Learning to Learn." In this course I try to teach students more effective strategies for learning. I not only try to help students learn these strategies or methods of getting meaning from their reading and classes, but I also try to help them understand the theoretical reasons why these strategies work. By giving them an awareness of the processes they use in learning I hope to enable them to develop more personal control over their education.

Most of you who read this book will not be teaching such a course, but you still can have great impact upon your students' later learning. All too often we make assignments, lecture, discuss, and give tests on the blissful assumption that it is obvious why what we are doing facilitates learning. Cognitive psychology reminds us that as students learn a subject matter they also learn something about the skills involved in learning that subject matter. I would suggest that we help students become more effective at learning if we are explicit about the reasons we engage them in discussion, require a term paper, or carry out other activities.

In lectures we all too often present the products of our thinking without revealing the process by which we arrive at our conclusions. If our goal is to help students develop as learners and thinkers, more of our lectures should model the processes we use in arriving at conclusions, and we should identify the directions we have followed in order that students can understand the model we represent.

Not all teachers need to be cognitive psychologists, but all teachers have some implicit or explicit theories about how one learns and thinks in one's own discipline. Helping students become aware of these theories is an important aspect of teaching.

Can Teachers Be Helped by Cognitive Psychology?

Teachers should not expect to make big improvements in education. Norman (1977) suggested that good lecturers and good textbook writers today are probably close to the best that is achievable; similarly, good students probably learn about as efficiently as they can. But many teachers and learners are probably not very efficient. When preparing a course, teachers may simply update a set of lecture notes; when told to learn something, students may simply repeat and rehearse materials—using methods not very effective for learning, remembering, and using meanings. Analyses of the processes students use in reading an assignment, answering a question, or in other aspects of education may be useful in locating difficulties and suggesting more effective learning and teaching strategies.

Granted that teachers lack much of the research needed to apply cognitive theory to higher education today, are there any suggestions that might be helpful to them right now?*

---

* A useful paper on this topic is George Leith, "Implications of cognitive psychology for the improvement of teaching and learning in the universities." In B. Massey (ed.), *Proceedings of the Third International Conference, Improving University Teaching* (College Park, MD: University of Maryland, 1977).

past experience
expectation
learning strategies

I do not think psychologists can any longer simply say, "Reward correct responses." But I think some general statements may be helpful as you analyze the problems of teaching:

1. Human beings are learning organisms—seeking, organizing, coding, storing, and retrieving information all their lives; building on cognitive structures to continue learning throughout life (certainly not losing capacity to learn); continually seeking meaning.

2. Human beings can remember images; they can remember transcriptions of the exact words that were used in a lecture or textbook; or they can remember _meanings,_ depending upon the demands of the situation. What meaning a student gets depends not only upon the student's past experience, and expectations, but also upon the student's learning strategies.

Marton and Säljö (1976b) differentiate among students in terms of depth of processing, a concept current in cognitive psychology (for example, Craik and Lockhart, 1972). The difference between deep-level processing and surface-level processing is in some ways comparable to the difference between literal interpretations of the Bible and the interpretations of scholars using formal criticism.

Probably the easiest way to communicate Marton and Säljö's distinction is to quote an actual example from their study. Their students read chapters from Coombs, _The World Educational Crisis: A Systems Analysis_ (1971, Swedish edition). They were then asked, "What is meant by the output of an educational system?" Answers going from surface to deep processing were the following:

➡ Level 1: (Surface) What Comes Out of the Educational System.

"Something to do with . . . well . . . you know, the result of." "The product . . . I think."

➡ Level 2: Those Who Leave the Educational System with a Completed Education.

"It's the trained work-force that the educational system produces. It's, well, for example . . . well, simply the trained work-force."

➡ Level 3: (Deep) The Effects of Education on Society and on Individuals Produced by Knowledge and Attitudes Acquired Through Schooling.

"Mm, it's the knowledge that . . . and values . . . yes, the knowledge and values that students have acquired. That is, whatever it is that influences them and makes them read this or that and do this or that."

Surface-level processors tend to study as if learning were something that happens to the learner; deep-level processors act much more as if learning is something the learner *does*. (Dahlgren and Marton, 1976.)

3. Instructors teach students not only the *knowledge* of history, biology, or psychology, but also structures, modes of thought, and strategies for learning (Olson, 1976). The important thing taught is form, not content. Different means may produce the same knowledge but not the same broader understanding for different learners or different uses. Comparisons of college teaching methods typically find no significant differences in tests of knowledge. There are, however, differences between teaching methods in retention, application, transfer, and other outcomes (McKeachie and Kulik, 1975).

Greeno (1976) suggests that general cognitive structures not only are taught along with content, but are also prerequisites to understanding content. Students who have no general structures for understanding science may be as lost in a biological science course as an American attempting to use our conventional narrative structures to understand an Indian folk-tale using a different kind of narrative structure. Thus, teachers have to consider structures not only as results of instruction, but also as prerequisites for instruction. In addition, teachers must find ways of getting from the structures in students' minds to the desired structures. It may be that sometimes inadequate, and even incorrect, simple concepts or analogies are the quickest way to bridge the gap. Summaries and reviews also help (Leith, 1971).

At the very least, the cognitive approach indicates that teachers need to be aware of several kinds of outcomes—not just *how much* was learned, but also *what kinds of learning* took place.

4. Intellectual ability—skills in learning, problem solving, and decision making are strongly influenced by prior knowledge. This means that persons who are excellent problem solvers in a familiar domain may seem completely unintelligent when asked to solve problems in domains in which they lack experience.

5. Learning something in the classroom may have different consequences from learning it from peers, from books, or learning it from one's own experience.

This does not mean that all learning should be experiential. Written language is very powerful.

6. In addition to the differentiated effectiveness of different methods for different outcomes, methods are differentially effective for different learners.

Egan and Greeno (1973) found that some learners learned most readily by the formula, or algorithmic, method, while others learned more effectively by the meaning method. The optimal method of training involved a combination of methods. For learners who did well with algorithms, additional training on the meaning of the variables after the normal training resulted in good performance on both criterion measures, while for the meaning group, additional drill on problem solving brought their performance on routine problems up to that of the other group. Thus, adaptation of instruction to individual differences in cognitive abilities or styles can result in greater effectiveness.

7. Because of interactions among student characteristics, teacher characteristics, goals, subject matter, and methods (Cronbach and Snow, 1977), flexibility and variability of approaches is more likely to be effective than a single method. Any given method is likely to be effective for some students and ineffective for others.

Perhaps one of the problems is that many students are unable to identify their own most effective style. Pask and Scott (1973) taught elementary concepts of probability theory by a system in which the computer carried on a tutorial conversation with the student in order to learn the student's idiosyncratic method of problem solving. Adaptive teaching systems are designed to present material at increasing levels of difficulty as students become more proficient. Pask and Scott argue that such systems will not be effective if students use different problem solving strategies.

Pask and Scott studied two strategy classes—serialist and holist. Students using a serialist strategy break problems into subproblems, taking one step at a time. They assimilate data from specific relations of low order. Students using a holist strategy solve problems *in toto*; they assimilate data widely from high-order relations without certainty about particulars. Holist students tended to come from philosophy, history, and the social sciences; serialists were more likely to come from natural science and mathematics.

Pask and Scott developed a test to identify serialist vs. holist disposition of students and developed teaching heuristics to match the serialist and holist strategies. When students were matched with the appropriate teaching treatment, they learned and retained material well; those who were mismatched learned very little. Unfortunately, students given their choice of treatments did not consistently choose the method optimal for their own strategy.

8. In addition to teaching students to identify their own most effective learning strategies, can instructors teach students to be able to use a larger repertoire of strategies? If this were achieved, instead of adapting teaching methods to students, students could adopt the learning strategy most effective for whatever teaching method they encountered.

9. Testing practices influence students' learning strategies. The classic study in this area antedates information-processing approaches by three decades (McCluskey, 1934). It was concerned with the practical problem of the relative advantages of essay vs. objective tests. One group of students expected to be tested by an objective test; another group expected to be tested by an essay test. Each group was tested with both objective and essay questions. The groups made equivalent scores on the objective test, but the group preparing for an essay test did better than the objective test group on the essay questions. The results suggest that the strategy used by students preparing for an essay test is superior to that used when studying for an objective test.

In a more recent study Marton and Säljö (1976b) showed that students' depth of processing of a given chapter was influenced by the type of questions asked following the reading of an earlier chapter. Rote memory questions such as, "According to the author the shortage of teachers depends on three factors. Which three?" produced surface-level processing, while deep-level processing was induced by questions such as, "Explain the meaning of the following quotation—'Too many poor teachers will drive good ones out of the market.'"

Does a course using essay tests have different effects on students' later approaches to similar subject matter than a similar course using objective tests? Does the type of questions used produce an effect lasting beyond the particular course? My guess is that the breadth of effect of essay testing may well depend upon the sort of comments or questions written by the instructor on the test. Comments may help students learn new strategies or skills for learning and _using_ a particular subject matter—and perhaps several types of courses taught in this way may produce effects generalizing across subject matters.

How do you teach such general skills or strategies? So far as I know there are no systematic rules; yet I suspect that good teachers do it intuitively. Probably helpful comments not only indicate errors and inadequacies, but also ask questions or make suggestions steering students to a more sophisticated, or deeper, approach. Johnson (1975) has shown that creativity of answers is influenced by marginal comments. Probably most teachers have some implicit models of how they can influence student learning and such models probably contain much truth. If psychologists can help teachers become more explicit, there should be a better chance for the model to improve with experience.

10. The cognitive structure of each student is different from that of the teacher. Thus, the paradox arises that the teacher must learn from students the students' structures if the teacher is to be effective in helping students learn from the teacher.

11. Talking, writing, doing, interacting, and teaching others are important means for learners to restructure their learning.

If teachers are to make bridges between: a) structures in the subject matter, curriculum, or course design, b) structures in the teacher, and c) structures in learners, they need to carry on discussions in which students have an opportunity to externalize their problems and progress. Since such interaction becomes increasingly difficult as class size increases, teachers need to provide at least some opportunities for small-group discussion, dialogue, writing, explaining, or doing something to which the teacher, other students, and the learner, herself, can respond (for example, Leith, 1974b).

12. In the classroom at least five kinds of learning are going on. The figural aspect is:

a. _The subject matter content,_ but inseparably linked with content are

b. _Learning relationships_ or _cognitive structures_

c. _Learning strategies_ (effective or ineffective) are also being learned and practiced

d. _Motives_ for learning are being strengthened or weakened. And in the background of these cognitive aspects of teaching-learning is

e. *The interpersonal level* of emotional relationships of students to teachers.

Psychologists know little about how to integrate these levels in such ways as to optimize education, but it is clearly a dynamic, ongoing process involving much adaptation on the part of both teacher and students.

13. Increases in effectiveness of education may come as much, or more, from helping students understand their own learning processes as from varying your teaching (Norman, 1977).

SUPPLEMENTARY READING

Richard E. Mayer, *Thinking and problem solving: An introduction to human cognition and learning* (Glenview IL: Scott-Foresman, 1974).

W. J. McKeachie (ed.), *Learning, cognition, and college teaching* (San Francisco: Jossey-Bass, 1980).

John D. Bransford and Barry S. Stein, *The ideal problem solver* (New York: W. H. Freeman, 1984).

Ference Marton, Dai Hounsell, and Noel Entwistle (eds.), *The experience of learning* (Edinburgh: Scottish Academic Press, 1984).

Bransford, J. D., *Human cognition: Learning, understanding, and remembering* (Belmont, CA: Wadsworth, 1979).

CHAPTER 25 / *Personalizing Education*

For almost one hundred years the image of the ideal education has been Mark Hopkins on one end of the log and James Garfield on the other. Whether or not such a faculty-to-student ratio is optimal might be questioned, but whatever the case, it is clear that most faculty members have to work with larger groups in which personalization of education depends upon sensitivity to individual differences among students. But there is an infinite variety of differences among students. What sorts of differences are most important to teachers as they strive to make the learning experience most valuable for each class member?*

It is not enough to know that certain variables affect learning generally. Intelligence, for example, has an obvious influence upon student learning, but knowing student differences in intelligence is not important to a teacher unless highly intelligent students need to be taught in some way different from students of less intelligence. Of concern here are interactions, that is, characteristics differentiating students for whom different kinds of teacher behavior are differentially effective.

Basically, this chapter questions the assumption that the ideal educational situation is one in which all students have personal attention from their instructors. Rather, my thesis is that the goal is to educate all students to the best of their and our capacities. Personal attention is one means to that goal, but not an end in itself. Different students need different things. Some may need individual personal attention from instructors, but some don't. For some students at some times really personalized education may involve opportunities for independent study, for work in student-led groups, or for other types of learning involving *less* rather than *more* individual contact with faculty members. Moreover college teachers should keep in mind that their students are survivors of

---

* Parts of this chapter are based on my chapter in W. J. Minter, ed., *The individual and the system* (Boulder, CO: Western Interstate Commission for Higher Education, 1967). Footnotes have been omitted.

twelve years or more of formal education. They have been selected and trained for certain kinds of academic achievement. While they differ in many ways, they are not nearly as diverse as people in general. They have well-practiced ways of learning and coping with different kinds of instruction. We may not produce major changes in their achievement, but we can do some things if we have some ideas about what differences are worth paying attention to.

Now, what can research to date tell us?

Student Characteristics

Intelligence and Prior Knowledge Intelligent students do better than less intelligent students in most educational situations. But it does make a difference how students of differing intelligence are taught. Remmers (1933), in three experiments comparing varying combinations of lecture and recitation, found fairly consistent results favoring a greater proportion of recitation for abler students and a greater proportion of lecture for the less able students. Ward's study (1956) indicated that the ablest students, more than other students, are favorably influenced by small classes. Calvin, Hoffman, and Harden (1957) found in three experiments that *less* intelligent students consistently did better in group problem-solving situations conducted in an authoritarian manner than in groups conducted in a permissive manner. The same difference did not occur for bright students. Hansen, Kelley, and Weisbrod (1970) found that TIPS, a system involving frequent testing, was most effective for less able students. All of these probably indicate that less structured methods, such as discussion, are more appropriate for bright students than for less able students.

Siegel and Siegel (1964) found that low-ability students performed better on a test of conceptual acquisition if they had been previously tested with an emphasis on factual rather than conceptual learning. High-ability students were affected by the difference in methods based on their previous knowledge; high-ability students with high previous knowledge benefited from emphasis on conceptual learning, while the unsophisticated high-ability student, like the low-ability student, performed better on conceptual acquisition if previous emphasis had been on factual learning.

These results fit well with the wisdom of college faculties who have generally urged smaller classes, greater use of discussion, and a higher conceptual level in honors classes. Bright students will generally be able to handle a greater information-processing load than less able students; that is, the able students can figure out things better for themselves and provide their own organization. The less able students are more likely to benefit from attempts to simplify and organize the material for the students, organization that may be detrimental for the better students (see Snow, 1976). Siegel and Siegel, however, inject a cautionary note—being bright is not enough. The naive bright student is perhaps more like the less able student than is sometimes recognized by college honors committees, a point also illustrated in the research of Mayer, Stichl, and Greeno (1975).

The importance of prior knowledge is also indicated by the study of Stinard and Dolphin (1981). Using self-paced mastery examination modules in an anatomy and physiology course, they found that the self-paced testing helped students with less science preparation. As compared with comparable students in a conventional course, these students used the self-paced tests as guides and stimuli for increased study time.

Comparing students in conventionally taught classes with those in which students were given major responsibility for the course, Patton (1955) found that the degree to which students accepted responsibility in the latter classes was positively correlated with gain in ability to apply psychology and interest in psychology. What sort of student accepted responsibility in such a course? Patton found that the students who liked his experimental class and assumed responsibility were likely to be independent of traditional authority figures and high in need for achievement.

Similarly, in the Oberlin studies (McCollough and Van Atta, 1958) students who were less rigid and less in need of social support profited more in measured achievement from independent study than those students who were not as independent.

Domino, using the Achievement via Independence and Achievement via Conformity scales of the California Psychological Inventory, found in two studies (1968, 1971) that independent students did better with teacher styles stressing independence, while students high in Achievement via Conformity did better with more structure.

Despite the variety of measures used, the studies cited in this section show some consistency in finding that a certain type of student, characterized as independent, flexible, or high in need for achievement, is happy and achieves well in classroom situations that give students opportunity for self-direction.

Social Motivation Our studies at Michigan have shown that need for affiliation is an important determinant of student reactions to differing styles of teaching. Students who are high in need for affiliation do better work in classes where the teacher takes a personal interest in them; conversely, those who are low in need for affiliation tend to do relatively poorly in these classes (McKeachie, et al., 1966).

Beach (1960) studied the personality variable of sociability as a predictor of achievement in lecture and small-group teaching methods. In the lecture section the nonsociable students (as measured by the Guilford Inventory of Factors STDCR) achieved significantly more than the sociable students; in the small-group sections the results were reversed.

These studies reinforce the point I made earlier. Personal contact with the instructor is valuable for some students, but not for all. Those likely to be favorably affected are those with low motivation and those high in sociability or need for affiliation. There are many students who fall in these groups, but also many who are not positively affected and may even achieve less when personal contact with the instructor is increased.

Anxiety What is the effect of anxiety upon learning? How can you best teach anxious students?

The answers to these questions turn out to be less obvious than one would expect. Generally, psychologists assume that anxiety is detrimental to learning. The research evidence suggests that the relationship is more complex, depending equally on the level of anxiety, the difficulty of the material, and the ability of the student. Generally speaking, anxious students do less well under high levels of stress, but what is stressful may differ for different students.

Since anxiety is generally believed to be increased by uncertainty, the anxious person should work most effectively in a highly structured situation. This hypothesis is partially supported by the research of D. E. P. Smith and his co-workers (1956), who found that anxious students who were permeable (sensitive to stimuli, impulsive, socially oriented, and low in ego strength) made optimal progress in a remedial reading course when taught by directive methods. Impermeable anxious students, however, were unaffected by differences in teaching methods. H. C. Smith (1955) found that students with high anxiety and low initial achievement gained more on achievement tests and were more highly satisfied in a "teamwork" class than in a conventional lecture. Dowaliby and Schumer (1973) found that anxious students did relatively better with directive teaching. Domino (1974) replicated this finding, but Peterson (1976) shows that the situation is more complicated. Highly anxious, high-ability students and nonanxious, low-ability students need structure; others do not.

Anxiety and testing The relationship between anxiety and performance on classroom examinations administered under varying conditions has been the subject of several experiments. To test whether the anxiety created by tests might be dissipated by permitting students to write comments on tests, half of the students in a University of Michigan experiment were given answer sheets with spaces for comments and half were given standard answer sheets. Measures of students' feelings about the tests failed to show any difference between the two groups, but the students who had the opportunity to write comments made higher scores on the test. These results held up in a series of experiments (McKeachie, Pollie, and Speisman, 1955). The findings suggested that student anxiety during classroom examinations builds up to such a point that it may interfere with memory and problem solving. Reducing the stress of the examination by permitting students to write comments resulted in improved performance.

This interpretation is supported by the work of Calvin, McGuigan, and Sullivan (1957), who found that students who were given a chance to write comments on an achievement test were superior to control students in their performance on the second half of the test, and that the students who made the greatest gain were the highly anxious students as measured by the Taylor Manifest Anxiety Scale. Similarly, W. F. Smith and Rockett (1958) found that instructions to write comments significantly interacted with anxiety, helping the performance of high-anxiety students but hurting the performance of students low in anxiety.

The experimental results on interaction of anxiety and teaching variables are tantalizing enough to stimulate further work, but they are not consistent enough to lead to any stable generalizations. It does look as if anxious students do better with greater structure and are helped by chances to express themselves. But differences in sex and in other personality variables, such as permeability, interacted with anxiety in the experiments above.

Introversion—extroversion Leith (1974a) has carried out and reviewed a number of studies on differential effects of various educational situations on introverts and extroverts. For example, as I noted in my discussion of the "learning cell," extroverts learn better when studying with another extrovert than when working alone. Leith also found that extroverts learned better by a discovery method, while introverts learned better by reception. Similarly, extroverts learned better with less feedback, while introverts learned better with more feedback.

Student Cognitive Stage

William Perry (1981) has suggested that individual differences in student responses to teaching may be conceptualized in terms of student stages of cognitive development. In any class students at differing stages are present but those at the lower stages are more common in freshman courses and those at the higher stages more common in senior courses.

Students at the lower stages are characterized by a dualistic view of knowledge. Things are either true or false, right or wrong. The teacher knows the truth; the student's job is to learn the truth. Students in the middle stages have learned that authorities differ. There seems to be no settled truth; everyone has a right to his or her own opinions. This stage is succeeded by the recognition that some opinions, some generalizations are better supported than others. The student's task is to learn the criteria needed for evaluating the validity of assertions in different subject matter fields. The final stages involve student commitment to values, beliefs, and goals with the recognition that despite the lack of complete certainty one must make decisions and act on one's values.

Perry suggests that the effective teacher must find a way to provide support and stretching for those at the lower levels while avoiding boredom for students at the higher levels. One practical suggestion is that a term paper may be challenging to the advanced students and at the same time stretch the less advanced students by letting them see that not all sources agree.

Sex   Our coeducational institutions may have a vested interest in the assumption that the best education for men is also best for women. In any case, until recently little research has dealt with the differences in learning styles of men and women.

Carrier (1957) investigated the manner in which individual differences in four personality variables affected performance in more and less stressful testing situations. He found that one of the most important variables determining reaction in his experiment was sex. Women were much more detrimentally affected than men by his stress situation.

In a later experiment (McKeachie, 1958) half of the students in a large class received a tranquilizing drug, meprobamate, while the other half received a placebo just before an examination. If students tend to be too anxious, such a drug should improve test scores. The results did not confirm this hypothesis. Students who had the drug reported experiencing less anxiety during the examination than did the placebo group, but they did not make better scores.

The really interesting result of the experiment was the interaction between the student's sex and the drug. Women benefited from the drug more than men. Thus sex once again turned out to be an important variable. The results make sense if a curvilinear relationship between anxiety and performance is assumed, with women too anxious and men less than optimally anxious. Thus, reduced anxiety should result in improved performance for women, but poorer performance for men.

We have found in our research at Michigan that instructors who assign more difficult work are particularly effective with women. Men do particularly well in a class in which the instructor compliments students when they have done well.

With the current interest in Women's Studies and changing images of "proper" sex roles, one would expect interest in research on the differences in college learning between men and women. The results cited above suggest that the methods most effective in teaching men have not necessarily been those most effective with women. At least at Michigan, women students in the past have tended to be somewhat more concerned about achievement, more willing to do what the instructor demands, and more responsive to personal interest from instructors. Nevertheless, a good deal more research is needed before we can talk confidently about what personalization of education means for both men and women. Earlier results may not be generalizable to the current generation of women.

Student-discipline interactions The characteristic learning problems differ somewhat from discipline to discipline, and the general student characteristics I have discussed in this chapter may be far less important in individualizing instruction than student characteristics related to hang-ups in particular disciplines. Research is needed to identify these, but I would guess, for example, that religious background might be a very important characteristic of both student and teacher in certain courses in philosophy and behavioral science. The combination of a fundamentalist student with an instructor who is still rebelling against his own religious training may result in the sort of conflict that interferes with, rather than facilitates, learning. Similarly, in mathematics a relevant characteristic may be the student's attitude toward mathematics, previous success in it, and for women, perhaps the degree to which mathematics is seen as a masculine activity.

Instructor Characteristics

Even less is known about instructor characteristics affecting personalization than about student characteristics. We do know that faculty members who are attentive to individual students are more likely to be effective teachers than those less attentive to students (McKeachie et al., 1966; Wilson, 1975).

The instructor has a major effect on personalization through influence on group norms in the classroom and college. Some student groups stifle individuality, chop down creative contributors, and are insensitive to members' needs. How do you create groups in which individual students can feel respected, free, and motivated to make the maximum contributions of which they are capable? One relevant factor is almost certainly the degree to which the course is structured along competitive or cooperative lines. As Haines and McKeachie (1967) showed, students in classes stressing competition for grades show more tension, self-doubt, and anxiety than those in classes structured for cooperative achievement.

Faculty members find it is easier to accept the possibility that students may have personal barriers to learning than to recognize that as teachers they often defend against real changes in themselves. If we accept Roger Heyns' definition of college as a community of learners, every teacher-student interaction carries potential for learning by both teacher and student. One of the barriers to student learning is that many professors see themselves as handing down learning from a celestial throne. We know very little about professors' views of themselves and their roles and the effect of different role concepts upon personalization of instruction.

Educational Strategy

If the "Mark Hopkins on the end of a log" ideal is impossible in these days of soaring enrollments, is there any real hope of individualization? I believe there is. Too often teachers have carried the academic lockstep into each individual course, meeting classes faithfully three times every week, giving the same assignments to every student, treating each student exactly the same in the interest of fairness. But even large universities and large classes can provide for individuality. Couldn't instructors in a large class, for example, permit some students to gain information from reading in the library rather than from attending lectures? Might not some students be encouraged to do laboratory work, while others gain direct experiences in field settings? Could instructors provide small group discussions for some and computer consoles for others? Could short blocks of course time be used for diverse activities? At present no one knows much about which students best achieve which goals with which experiences, but I would bet that the mere presence of several alternatives would result in educational gain.

Students themselves have opinions about how they can best learn. Although these opinions are not always accurate, giving students some opportunity to determine their own conditions of learning, to suffer the consequences of bad choices, and to learn from these consequences may be an important way in which education can be personalized.

This, however, should not be taken to mean that effective learning is always pleasant and satisfying. When teachers really touch students deeply, the students may face a painful reorganization of their definitions of themselves and of their relationships to others. Their methods of thinking, their conceptions of the universe, even their values, may be challenged by the mode of thinking of a discipline taught in a way that reaches them as people. They have the choice of incorporating the learning and reorganizing themselves or compartmentalizing the content in such a way that it has minimal effect upon them. In the struggle between compartmentalization and reorganization, teachers and the other students can be important allies of growth if they are able to respond to feedback from the affected students about the problems they are having in incorporating the learning.

One implication of the research on interactions of student characteristics and teacher characteristics in affecting learning might be to feed all the data into a computer to assign students to the classes of those teachers who best fit their needs. But this seems to me an unlikely and possibly undesirable consequence. Not only is the information too unreliable to guide decisions for individuals, but also it may well be better to teach students to learn from a variety of teachers than to restrict them to teachers to whom they can adjust most easily.

Similarly, teachers might be trained to identify and teach effectively those students who are not normally "turned on" by their style of teaching. Sensitive teachers can respond to feedback from students, modifying their tactics from week to week and day to day as they observe their effects. Teaching should be a two-way process in which both students and teachers learn from one another; as long as teaching conditions facilitate two-way interaction, the good sense of teachers and students can be substantially relied upon.

The studies I have cited are really only the first toddling steps necessary for understanding how to personalize education. They give instructors some clues about what kind of differences in students to look for, as well as some leads about what kinds of procedures may be helpful to them. But such categorization is only a beginning. While it is an improvement over the attitude that students are all about the same, categorization of students may be a disservice if it leads teachers to forget that students are living, growing, changing individuals and need different things from teachers at different times. My colleague, Richard Mann, points out that students whose motivation is low, who mistrust the teacher, and who seem rigid and anxious early in a term may, after some resolution of their relationships with the teacher, have an enormous inrush of energy and now be much more flexible and creative. Mann's own research has been directed toward understanding the development of student-teacher relationships over a term, and this is at the heart of the problem of personalizing education.

Mann suggests that particular teachers can be characterized not so much as having a hard time with a particular type of student as having trouble with a particular type of feeling—such as dependence, depression, hostility, or even affection. While certain students may be the articulators of this feeling, it may be more important for the teacher to note that the feeling characterizes the whole group at this time than to note the particular students who lead in expressing the feeling. It may be just as important to teach teachers how to cope with these feelings, or to wait them out, as to teach them how to deal with particular students. Mann suggests that difficulties with particular students often are the result of responses to the mood of the entire class, which are so defensive or inappropriate as to permanently alienate those students who feel this mood most strongly. A teacher may, for example, become so angry or punitive in response to a rebellious class that the most rebellious students simply are "turned off" from then on. (See Mann et al., 1970)

As classes become larger, the opportunity for two-way communication and moment-to-moment shifting of educational strategy is reduced, and teachers are more and more likely to misperceive student needs and feelings. Knowledge of the student characteristics I have discussed can be helpful in formulating an initial educational strategy, but real educational success depends upon continual reevaluation and modification of your teaching plans as you observe student responses. As financial pressures increase, there is danger that instructors will abandon all pretense of two-way interaction and subvert teaching into one-way communication of information. If this occurs, there will be an increasing pressure to "technicalize" the communicator's role. Just as teachers have turned student counseling over to professional counselors, they may turn large lecture and television teaching over to "master teachers" or actors. But for effective education, colleges need to preserve student-teacher interaction as the central aspect of higher education and to preserve opportunities for teachers to get satisfaction from teaching.

SUPPLEMENTARY READING

Samuel Messick et al., _Individuality in learning_ (San Francisco: Jossey-Bass, 1976).

Lee Cronbach and Richard Snow, _Aptitudes and instructional methods_ (New York: Irvington, 1977).

CHAPTER 26 / *Ethical Standards in Teaching*

As part of the code of ethics for psychologists, the American Psychological Association has published a code of ethics for teachers of psychology. Those portions relevant for all college teachers follow:*

"The teacher should encourage students in their quest for knowledge, giving them every assistance in the free exploration of ideas. Teaching frequently and legitimately involves a presentation of disquieting facts and controversial theories, and it is in the examination of perplexing issues that students most need the guidance of a good teacher. Disturbing concepts should not be withheld from students simply because some individuals may be distressed by them. When issues are relevant, they should be given full and objective discussion so that students can make intelligent decisions with regard to them. However, presentation of ideas likely to be difficult for some students to accept should be governed by tact and respect for the worth of the individual."

"Differing approaches to one's discipline should be presented to students in such a way as to encourage them to study the relevant facts and draw their own conclusions. Free expression of both criticism and support of the various approaches is to be encouraged as essential to the development of individual students and the field. In dealing with an area of specialization other than his or her own, a teacher should make it clear that he or she is not speaking as a specialist. In attempting to make an understandable and interesting presentation of subject matter to students, an instructor should not sacrifice adequacy of treatment to considerations of popular appeal."

"A teacher should respect students' right to privacy and not require students to give information which they may wish to withhold; neither

* Reprinted by permission of the American Psychological Assocation.

should the teacher reveal information which a student has given with the reasonable assumption that it will be held in confidence."

"A teacher should require of students only activities which are designed to contribute to the student in the area of instruction. Other activities not related to course objectives and not having secondary values should be made available to students on a voluntary basis. Exploitation of students to obtain research data or assistance with the teacher's own work is unethical."

"Faculty members advising students electing their own field as a major field of study with the intent of entering the profession should be sure that students understand opportunities and requirements in the field, e.g., that few positions are open to those with only a bachelor's degree, that there is considerable screening of candidates at the graduate level, that the doctorate is required for many positions (and that academic positions are scarce in the 1980s)."

"A teacher who becomes aware of an adjustment problem in a student who might profit by counseling or psychotherapy should assist the student to find such help if it is available. When a student requests assistance, and counseling facilities are not available, the nonclinically trained instructor may offer help as an immediate expedient. In doing so he or she should indicate to the student that he or she is acting not as a trained counselor or clinical psychologist but simply as a teacher interested in the student's welfare. Teachers should not enter into counseling relationships with students for a fee."

Interestingly enough the APA statement, which was one of the earliest codes of ethics dealing with academic behavior, does not deal with one of the most salient current issues—sexual harassment. Sexual harassment as defined in my university is:

Unwelcome sexual advances, requests for sexual favors, and other verbal or physical conduct of a sexual nature constitute sexual harassment when—

1. submission to such conduct is made either explicitly or implicitly a term or condition of an individual's employment or education;

2. submission to or rejection of such conduct by an individual is used as the basis for academic or employment decisions affecting that individual;

3. such conduct has the purpose or effect of substantially interfering with an individual's academic or professional performance or creating an intimidating, hostile or offensive employment, education, or living environment.

Sexual harassment is illegal under both Michigan and U.S. law.

SUPPLEMENTARY READING

Many other disciplines have ethical codes. I suggest that you review the code of your own discipline. Most of us aren't even aware of the code until we, or some colleagues, are accused of a violation.

In the area of sexual harassment, a good book, despite its title, is by Billie Wright Dzich and Linda Winer: *The Lecherous Professor* (Boston: Beacon Press, 1984).

CHAPTER 27

How to Win Friends and Influence Janitors

The beginning instructor's teaching may be greatly facilitated or hampered by relationships with other personnel of the college or university. You will occasionally wish to recommend or assign readings in library references. Sometimes instructors make such assignments without informing the librarian. The unhappy librarians are then deluged with students demanding a book that has already been taken out for two weeks or that is not even listed in the catalog. After a few such experiences, the librarian may not greet requests for special favors with great enthusiasm. Thus, one of the essentials of pre-course planning is giving the library a list of books in which reading will be required, perhaps with a description of the nature and time of use, and making sure that students are given the correct authors and titles.

Often, too, instructors ask the library to order many copies of books they plan to use. The next year they decide to use different sources, and the library is left with twenty copies of a book of which only one or two copies have ever been used. Usually librarians are happy to advise an instructor how many copies of a supplementary book should be ordered in terms of the number of students and the extent of the readings required.

Similar problems may arise in scheduling movies and audiovisual aids. It should be obvious that instructors cannot expect films and projectionists to be available the day they decide to fill in class time with a movie. As I pointed out previously, effective use of visual aids requires planning. Moreover, if you have scheduled a movie, it is not conducive to good relations with projectionists to tell the operator when he or she appears loaded with projector and screen that you have decided not to use the film.

Relationships with janitors are also important. Instructors sometimes complain of lack of chalk, messy rooms, or broken seats but fail to recognize their own responsibilities in building maintenance. You can

hardly blame janitors for getting discouraged when they enter a classroom to find the floor littered with bits of paper, chalk, and cigarette
ashes, the blackboard smeared with scrawling, and the room in general
disorder.

In beginning work in a different college, you may find that the rules,
traditions, and usual channels to go through for a particular service are
not the same as you are accustomed to. If you ask with humility for
information rather than attempt to order conformity to your expectations, you will have a much easier time in learning the ropes.

Important problems also arise in relationships with administrators,
colleagues, and the student body. For example, the records and deadlines
required by the registrar's office and other administrative offices often
seem unimportant to instructors, and they are apt to feel that a slight
delay is of no consequence. However, an office that processes hundreds
or thousands of records must have scheduling as rigorous as that of a
factory production line. Laxness on the part of a few instructors may ruin
a beautiful schedule.

Instructors also sometimes fail to remember that their courses may
have relevance for the courses of their colleagues. If the faculty members
who teach courses following yours know what you are doing, they can
shape their own courses accordingly. Because they have an interest in
the course, they are usually pleased if they are consulted when any drastic
changes are to be made. Certainly the department chair should be kept
informed.

It should be evident that students, too, have an interest in your
teaching. One of your first obligations is to make sure that the course
description in the college catalog is adequate. The academic counselors
should have a more detailed description of the course if they are to coun-
sel students wisely.

Periodic student evaluation of teaching and courses is helpful to
most instructors. I have found that it is helpful simply to have students
write "Things I like," "Criticisms," and "Suggestions." Often it is helpful
to get evaluations not only from students taking the course, but also from
students who took the course at an earlier date.

Most college instructors are asked at some time to sponsor a student
group, to give an informal talk at a student meeting, or to meet with a
student committee. My only words of advice here are, "Act naturally."
Don't try to knock yourself out trying to prove that you're a human being,

and don't fear that the proper barriers between students and faculty will be breached.

There is one exception to my advice to act naturally—when college regulations prohibit certain activities that are condoned in your own circle of society. The most common issue is that of student drinking or use of drugs. Whether you approve or disapprove of the college's regulations, I see no great gain in achieving popularity as a faculty member who winks at violations.

SUPPLEMENTARY READING

Kenneth E. Eble, _The craft of teaching_ (San Francisco: Jossey-Bass, 1976), chapter 6, pp. 163–172.

CHAPTER 28
Doing and Evaluating Research on Teaching

Determining which of two teaching methods is more effective looks like a simple matter. Presumably all that is necessary is to teach something by both methods and then compare the results. This is essentially the research design of many of the studies that are widely quoted to show the effectiveness of PSI, television, discussion, independent study, or other methods. Unfortunately, there are some hidden traps that enthusiasts for one method or another are likely to overlook.

The Methodological Problems

Suppose, for example, that a group of students is given an opportunity to take a class taught by some method quite unusual in their college. The very fact that the method is different gives it excitement. Sometimes the reaction may be one of enthusiasm; in other cases it may be one of outraged hostility. The latter reaction seems to be particularly likely when students taught by a new method know that they are competing on examinations with students taught by the tried and true traditional methods. In any case it is difficult to know how much of student improvement (or loss) in learning may be accounted for by the emotional reaction to a new and different method and how much can be expected when the new method is routine. This "Hawthorne effect" influences not only students but also professors. How many new curricula, new courses, or new teaching methods have flowered briefly and then faded as the innovators' enthusiasm waned or as new staff members replaced the originators? Unfortunately, relatively few studies have made comparisons over a period longer than one semester. Students who have experienced a semester of instruction by a new method (except television) are generally more likely to choose a section by this method than are students without previous experience. This difference in motivation, as well as added skill in the requisites of "Studentship" in a new method, might result in greater advantages for a new method after two or more semesters of trial than after a single semester.

A second methodological problem is establishing a suitable control group. In some experiments a single instructor uses both teaching methods. Here the obvious problem is that it is difficult to determine how much the instructor's own personality and skills have influenced the outcome. It is impossible to know whether or not other teachers would obtain similar results. The obvious remedy for this defect is to persuade several professors to use both methods. Leaving aside the salesmanship necessary to institute such a research design, the effort involved in trying to teach by two methods, keeping strictly to each, is tremendous. As a result, the methods either tend to coalesce or, in an overzealous attempt to avoid this, the experimenter institutes artificial and additional constraints to accentuate the differences.

Another problem in establishing controls is that the conditions of the experiment may introduce special factors that interfere with normal results. For example, the experiment may require extensive testing, the presence of observers in the class, or other interferences with normal classroom routine. A class in which a "live" professor is talking to television cameras is probably not a suitable comparison group for classes watching the lesson on television receivers.

A fourth problem is biased sampling. According to newspaper reports, studies of educational television have demonstrated that students taking the course at home learn as much as those on campus. The obvious problem is that people who sign up for a television course and come to campus to take the exam are probably somewhat different in motivation and background from typical college sophomores. As Greenhill points out (1959), efforts to equate such groups are never successful.

A fifth problem is in the statistical methods used to analyze the results of teaching-methods experiments. Ordinarily experimenters are concerned about avoiding the type of error involved in concluding that one method is more effective than another when in reality they do not differ significantly. However, they are less likely to be sensitive to another type of error that may be just as damaging—the error of concluding that there is no difference in effectiveness when two methods are not found to differ significantly. In addition to the logical fallacy involved in accepting failure to disprove the null hypothesis as proof of no difference, there is the problem of choice of methods of analysis. The chance of obtaining such results depends upon the type of statistical analysis used. With "weak" statistics, a difference is less likely to be detected than with "strong" statistics. The true effect of a variable may be clouded if no effort

262 Doing and Evaluating Research on Teaching

is made to remove other sources of variance. As I suggest later, the application of multivariate statistics, such as analysis of covariance, might, by taking out other sources of variance, reveal more clearly the true effects of varying methods. Further, when several tests of the same hypothesis are made with different groups, experimenters might well use combined tests of significance. For example, if ten groups come out in the same direction, it is extremely unlikely that the methods are not differentially effective even though no one difference would be statistically significant.

But even with better statistical methods, large, consistent effects are not likely. Education is a tremendously complex effort affected by many variables. No one thing, or group of variables, is likely to stand out clearly amidst the noise of the other variables not under study.

A sixth problem is the interaction among teaching methods, student characteristics, teacher characteristics, or other variables. What is effective for some students may not be for others.

The Criterion Problem

The major problem in experimental comparisons of teaching methods is the criterion problem. Stuit and Wilson's (1946) prediction studies in naval training showed that as the criterion was increasingly well defined, prediction of success improved. Undoubtedly one of the reasons for the many nonsignificant differences in studies of teaching is poor criterion measures.

The criterion problem is illustrated by the experiment of Parsons, Ketcham, and Beach (1958). In order to determine the effectiveness of various methods, they took the brave step of setting up some groups in which students didn't come to class at all. The groups who didn't come to class did *best of all* on the final examination. The catch is that the examination was based entirely upon the textbook. As Parsons and Ketcham point out, their results with the other groups suggest that as more and more new ideas and points of view are introduced, students become less likely to remember what the textbook says. This points to the problem of evaluation of effectiveness. If the instructor's goal is that students remember the textbook, a test on the textbook is appropriate; but one cannot conclude that a particular method is superior in achieving all goals, if only one outcome has been measured. Frequently comparisons of two teaching methods only assess learning of content common to both methods.

All too often, studies of teaching effectiveness have confused different goals of evaluation. Course examinations are typically intended to aid teachers in determining student grades. For this use fairness requires that the examination give each student an equal opportunity to obtain a good score. Thus the content of the examination is ordinarily that studied by all students. But when comparing two methods of teaching, you want to know what each group learned that the other did not. Thus a comparison of the lecture method with a discussion method based on a common final examination from a textbook does not really compare what the two groups of students learned in their different classes, but rather what they learned from reading the text. Many of the early experiments on PSI not only tested material covered in the PSI course, but also actually used on the criterion test items students in PSI had answered on previous quizzes. The point here is that the criterion measure should sample progress on *all* goals, not just a small sample chosen for a particular method. If separate scores for different goals can be assigned, the researcher and the audience are then free to assign their own values to those goals well achieved vs. those poorly achieved.

The difficulty in arriving at an overall index of teaching effectiveness is complicated by the probability that a teacher effective in achieving one course objective is not necessarily effective in achieving others. Bendig (1955), for example, found a significant interaction between instructors and tests in an introductory psychology course. Some instructors' students did particularly well on certain tests during the course, but not well on other tests. Cross (1958) and McKeachie (1959a) found that instructors whose students did well on an objective test in psychology were ineffective when their students' achievement was measured on an essay test designed to gauge understanding and integration of the materials. In studies of teaching it is thus important to specify objectives and to use measures of each objective. Measures of retention after the end of a course can often add to your confidence in reported differences.

Few professors complain that students are too highly motivated. Yet for purposes of research, the degree of student motivation for good grades may actually make it very difficult to evaluate the effectiveness of two teaching procedures. Because passing or excellent grades are so important to students, they may compensate for ineffective teaching by additional study in order to pass the course examination at the level to which they aspire. Thus, the results of ineffective procedures may be masked or even misinterpreted when course examinations are used as criterion measures. Nachman and Opochinsky (1958) provided a neat demonstration of this when they found differences between a small and large class on surprise quizzes, but no difference on a final examination. When significant differences in achievement are found in an experiment, the difference may simply reflect the degree to which students in differing classes were able to find out what the examination was to be and the degree to which it would determine their course grade.

Because achievement measures have been so insensitive to differences in teaching methods, most experimenters stress the favorable student reactions to the new method they have introduced. Although the relationship between student satisfaction and learning is low, it can certainly be argued that, assuming equal learning between two methods, teachers would prefer to have students leave their classes with warm feelings about their experiences. Moreover, teachers would expect these feelings to be related to interest in learning more, and there is some evidence to support this (McKeachie and Solomon, 1958). However, when researchers use student satisfaction as a criterion, they should be aware of the fact that it is highly influenced by the role expectations students have of college teachers. Marked deviations from these expectations almost inevitably will be rated lower than more conventional teaching behavior. Laboratory studies of problem-solving groups reveal that authoritarian leaders are rated by group members as being more efficient than democratic leaders (Haythorn et al., 1956). This makes sense both in terms of members' expectations for leaders and also because a leader who plays an active role is almost inevitably going to make a more vivid impression on a group than a leader whose behavior is more subtle. In evaluating student reactions, therefore, researchers need to be conscious of these role expectancies and determine what is a proper base line against which to evaluate the reactions.

As an aside here, let me also point out that new methods are not usually tested except by a teacher who is enthusiastic about them. Consequently the comparison may be between student reactions to a new method and an enthusiastic teacher vs. an old method taught unenthusiastically.

The prospective researcher also needs to be warned that even a careful definition of desirable outcomes does not end the criterion problem. In many cases, laudable attempts to measure attitudinal or affective outcomes have led to the conclusion that neither of two teaching methods was superior to the other in achieving this or that goal, when there is no evidence that *any* teaching could affect the goal as measured by the tests used. At the very least, the experimenter needs to report some evidence that the measure is at least sufficiently sensitive to reveal significant changes from the beginning to the end of the semester. If there is no change on a variable over a semester, it is unlikely that two teaching methods will differ in the amount of the change they cause.

Finally, evaluation need not end with tests given to the students who are enrolled in the experimental classes. In a large university it is easy to assume that an experimental course is assimilated into the whirlpool of activity without even a ripple. Seldom, however, has this assumption been tested, and in smaller colleges or for large-scale innovations it is not a safe assumption. Researchers might gain much useful knowledge by looking outside their experimental classrooms to other effects of the experiment. Do students taught by one method rather than another make more use of their knowledge and skills in other courses they are electing? Is superior achievement in the experimental course won at the expense of achievement in other courses? What is the impact of the use of a particular teaching method upon other faculty members? How does the use of a new method change faculty perceptions of teaching and its value; how does it affect faculty-administration relationships? In short, what effects does a new method have upon the total culture of the college?*

SUPPLEMENTARY READING

Lee Cronbach and Richard Snow, *Aptitudes and instructional methods* (New York: Irvington, 1977).
Carolyn L. Ellner and Carol P. Barnes, *Studies of college teaching* (Lexington, MA: D.C. Heath, 1983).

---

* Morris Janowitz started my train of thought along this line.

CHAPTER 29 / *Improving Your Teaching*

Is there really any hope that teachers can improve—and continue to improve—their teaching?* Does successful teaching depend upon adopting a particular teaching method? Does it depend upon having a particular type of personality?

These are disquieting questions to those concerned about their teaching. Here are my answers: Teachers can improve; they don't need psychotherapy; and not everyone can use the same methods equally successfully.

Let's take an example. Bob, one of our graduate students, was a brilliant theoretician. In all of his academic work he was outstanding. There was no question that he knew psychology, but when he began to teach it, his students almost revolted. After the first four weeks of the semester, his students were asked to evaluate his teaching.

Here are some of their comments:

➤ "Mr. Smith has convinced me that he knows his material, but he is way over my head."

➤ "I have no idea what we are supposed to be getting either from textbooks or lectures."

➤ "Mr. Smith does right by his material, but not by his students."

Naturally Bob was concerned about these reactions. It would have been natural for him to say, "These students are just stupid. If the material is over their heads, it is their fault for not studying more. I'll simply tell them they'll have to work harder."

Fortunately, Bob thought instead, "What can I do about this?" He came to me with some anxiety and a willingness to make any changes that would produce better results.

---

* Material in this chapter is adapted from W. J. McKeachie, Improving your teaching, *Adult Leadership,* 1955, 3, 14–16.

There was no doubt that he was spending enough time in preparation. His lecture materials were carefully worked out to ensure complete coverage of the topic. However, it was obvious to him that he had to change the level of his lectures. How was he to know when he had reached the appropriate level?

In discussing this we decided that he needed more prompt and continuous feedback from the students if he was to keep the presentation on their level. Perhaps if the classroom atmosphere were less formal, if the students participated more, their discussion would provide clues to their understanding of the material.

"But," Bob said, "if I let the students talk, how can I cover the material? I'm crowded for time now. Still—I guess it doesn't do me much good to cover the material if the students don't get it. Maybe I shouldn't worry so much about covering everything."

Bob was particularly puzzled by the student's comment that he didn't know what he was to get from the course. "Why did he sign up if he doesn't know what he wants to get out of the course?" Bob asked. "I suppose this is a new field to the students, and I know it isn't what they expected, but what can I do?"

After some discussion we decided that he might work out study questions for the students to take home. He tried devising these questions to focus on major points in the assignments. He handed these questions out in advance. Frequently these questions came up again during the class period and often stirred up lively discussions. When student evaluations were collected six weeks later, Bob's students rated him a very good teacher.

The point of Bob's experience is not to suggest that everyone should use study questions. Rather, it is intended to indicate how improvement can result from getting feedback from the students themselves.

Student Feedback

This chapter is based upon the assumption that the purpose of education is to bring about changes in students. If instructors agree with this assumption, it is apparent that information from students is required to provide a basis for improved teaching. Student evaluation of instruction is a relatively direct method of obtaining this information and I discuss this in the next chapter. But there are other sources of feedback available to the instructor. What are they?

A venerable one is the classroom examination. Too often instructors simply check off errors automatically, with little thought of interpreting them to find out the general areas in which students did poorly and where they did well. Instructors thus lose a potentially valuable source of feedback. By asking a colleague to look over a few student papers you can get a check on whether or not your expectations are reasonable.

Another source of feedback, which is even more valuable because it is immediate, is the behavior of students in class. One of the most useful features of class discussion is that it reveals so well the misconceptions, biases, and emotional reactions of the students. Teachers who minimize student participation dam up one of their most useful channels of feedback.

Even in the lecture hall instructors can get many cues for improving their teaching. While few teachers can ignore students who are sleeping or reading newspapers, many of them fail to note restless shifting of position, blank stares, whispered asides, and other indications that the students are not with them.

In a lecture class a useful source of feedback is student notes. You can ask a sample of students to lend you their notes and get from them some sense of problems in communication.

As another source of feedback teachers can use individual conferences with students outside of class. While these students are often not typical of the entire class group, their problems sometimes indicate possible inadequacies in instruction that teachers can use as cues for improvement.

In multi-section courses I have asked each section to elect a representative to meet with me to tell me how the course is going. Because the representatives can say, "Some students say . . . ," the comments are usually quite candid.

More Sources of Feedback

My emphasis thus far upon feedback from students has undoubtedly raised some questions. Some readers may be saying, "Our job is to educate students, not to please them. Making students happy doesn't necessarily contribute to education."

This point is well taken. Research on teaching methods has not thus far shown a strong relationship between student satisfaction and student achievement. It seems obvious that students must give some interest and attention to their work in order to learn, and student reactions are therefore valuable, but it is probably fallacious to assume that what the students say they like is always what contributes most to their education. Hence, teachers should not rely upon the students as their only sources of help in teaching. Let's now turn to some other sources.

One of the most frequently neglected aids is the advice of colleagues. Sometimes teachers seem afraid to discuss their teaching methods with other teachers or to ask for advice in handling some teaching problem. Insecurity about teaching is so great that it is almost unheard of for a teacher to visit a colleague's class. Yet in our University of Michigan program for training college teachers, the trainees report that they gain much from discussing teaching problems with their colleagues, from observing other teachers, and from suggestions by observers of their classes. I suspect that all teachers dread having a colleague see them get tripped up on some simple question, but one of the things most difficult for the new instructor to learn is that other teachers get tripped up in the same way. Learning that one's problems are not unique is a wonderful remedy for the tenseness and anxiety that often characterize the new (and not so new) teacher.

New Ways in Teaching

Thus far we have been primarily concerned with the problem of spotting teaching weaknesses or of diagnosing difficulties. I have assumed that intelligent teachers who learn of their errors will be able to change their teaching techniques for the better. This, however, assumes that they know, or will be able to devise, other teaching techniques that will be more successful. Unfortunately, this is not always the case. There are teachers who think reading from lecture notes is the only teaching method possible for their subject matter. How then may you increase your working repertoire of teaching techniques?

First of all, of course, you may learn about techniques other teachers use. Talking about teaching, observing other teachers, and reading journals on college teaching are ways of becoming acquainted with the techniques other people are trying.

Have you tried PSI, buzz groups, role playing, nondirective discussion, directed discussion, field trips, or guest experts? These are some of the methods available to add variety to your teaching. But the problem then remains, "How can I put these into practice?"

As one of my trainees said, "I've read all about role playing. I'm convinced it would be useful in my class, but I'm scared to death to try it."

What are the barriers that keep teachers from trying new teaching techniques? One barrier is simply effort. Usually it is easier to teach a class as you've done in the past than to try something new. This barrier is probably not so hard to overcome if you have used the diagnostic information discussed earlier and are aware of weakness in your teaching.

A far more important barrier to change is fear of loss of status. To most instructors the status of the teacher is a cherished reward for years of study. To be an authority who dispenses crumbs of wisdom to the multitudes is a very satisfying role. Trying a new technique may involve a threat to your status. If the new method fails, the students are likely to feel that you don't know what you're doing. But even if it works, it may mean some change in your status. For example, permitting student participation means that more embarrassing questions are likely to be asked, that less emphasis will be placed on learning from the instructor, and that the instructor's leadership may be challenged by aggressive, intelligent students.

A third barrier is simply fear of failure. Teachers who try new techniques are not likely to be skilled in its use and are likely to imagine consequences far more catastrophic than any which are likely to occur. In using new techniques instructors may feel that they are losing control of the situation and that anything may happen.

Another barrier is fear of unfavorable reactions from colleagues. Even when a new teaching method is successful, experimenting instructors are likely to feel that other professors think they are deserting the tried and true academic traditions in order to curry student or administration favor.

How Do You Make the Change?

Overcoming these barriers depends first of all upon being sure of the reasons for trying a new technique. Unless you have thought through the goals, you may miss any evidences of success in the use of a new method. This is particularly important because these evidences of success are among the most important rewards you can get.

A second aid in overcoming barriers is to try new techniques in a group in which you are secure and from which you can expect cooperation. This may mean making the first trial in your best class. In some cases it may even be worthwhile to ask for volunteers to join a special section of the class that will experiment with a new learning method. Those who volunteer thus will not be shocked by changes in your behavior and usually will give the method a fair trial.

A third aid in putting new methods into practice is to gain group support. In the Michigan teacher-training program we encourage formation of friendships among the teacher trainees; we encourage them to talk about methods and discuss experiences in trying them out. This furnishes the instructors with emotional support, enables them to express their anxieties, and gives them the rewards of approval by friends for their trials of new methods. Such support can be found by almost all teachers. Almost always you can find others who enjoy teaching and who like to talk about it. Such an informal group can serve the same functions as our training group.

Faculty Development Programs

When I wrote the first edition of this book, the term "faculty development" had not even been conceived. Now almost every college and university has a faculty development program. This means that on many campuses you can get professional help in improving your teaching. Most faculty development centers offer workshops to assist you in developing additional skills. In addition they will consult with you about specific problems and offer technical or financial assistance for changes you wish to make. They will suggest sources of additional information. Each of the suggestions made in this chapter can be facilitated by the faculty development (or instructional development) center. Moreover there is no opprobrium attached to consulting such a center. Their customers are predominantly good teachers trying to be better. Try it. It's free!

Student-Teacher Relationships

In discussing methods of diagnosing teaching weaknesses and improving methods, I have purposely avoided what is probably the basic problem in improving teaching. That is: "How do we build a different pattern of relationship with our students?"

The obvious way to write this chapter would have been to exhort teachers to understand student needs and to like and respect their students. These are the foundations upon which successful teaching methods are laid. But most teachers already like their students and try to understand them. The trouble is not that they don't try to obtain these fundamentals, but rather that they aren't able to.

This chapter is intended to help you sneak around your own emotional blocks to different relationships with students. By focusing attention on teaching methods you can sometimes make discoveries about student needs that might have evaded you through years of worrying about them. By finding teaching methods that elicit increased student interest, you may gain that approval of students that will give you enough security to build new relationships. In any case, teachers who begin to improve their teaching will again discover that teaching is fun!

SUPPLEMENTARY READING

There are now a number of excellent books on teaching—each covering different facets.

Stanford C. Ericksen, *Motivation for learning: A guide for the teacher of the young adult* (Ann Arbor: University of Michigan Press, 1974).

Stanford C. Ericksen, *The essence of good teaching* (San Francisco: Jossey-Bass, 1984).

Barbara Fuhrman and Anthony Grasha, *A practical handbook for college teachers* (Boston: Little, Brown, 1983).

Margaret Morganroth Gullette (ed.), *The art and craft of teaching* (Cambridge, MA: Harvard-Danforth Center for Teaching and Learning, 1982).

Robert B. Kozma, Lawrence W. Belle, and George W. Williams, *Instructional techniques in higher education* (Englewood Cliffs, NJ: Educational Technology Publications, 1978).

Janet Donald and Arthur Sullivan (eds.), *Using research to improve university teaching* (San Francisco: Jossey-Bass, forthcoming).

While the title suggests usefulness only for faculty members teaching distance learning courses, the following book has good ideas for all teachers.

T. M. Chang, H. F. Crombag, K. D. J. M. van der Drift, and J. M. Moonen, *Distance learning: On the design of an open university* (Boston: Kluwer-Nijhoff Publishing, 1983).

CHAPTER 30 // Student Ratings of Faculty

In 1969 I was commissioned by the AAUP Committee C on College and University Teaching, Research, and Publication to write an article on student ratings of faculty for the *AAUP Bulletin*.* In the years since that article appeared, a great deal of research has been done, and colleges and universities have accumulated much experience with student ratings. The purpose of this chapter is to bring the reader up to date on the evidence with respect to the issues discussed earlier, as well as additional issues that have come to the fore more recently.

Validity: Do Student Ratings Measure Teaching Effectiveness?

There is now a good deal of evidence supporting a positive answer to our question, but it has also become evident that the question is overly simple. With respect to the general validity question, the cumulating evidence continues to support the conclusion that highly rated teachers tend to be those whose students achieve well. Such a statement is, however, better understood in the context of two more analytic questions.

1. How are different aspects of teaching effectiveness related to student ratings? Or put in other words, "What educational outcomes are related to student ratings of effectiveness?" Ratings may be differentially valid for different educational goals. There is ample evidence that we achieve some goals at the expense of others. Teachers effective in teaching a good deal of knowledge are not necessarily effective in teaching critical thinking. So one needs to make value judgments about the importance of differing goals of education.

2. What is the intended use of student ratings of teaching? For personnel decisions? For improving teaching? For facilitating student choice of courses and teachers? Ratings may be differentially valid for different uses.

---

* This chapter is an update of my article in *Academe*, October 1979.

For personnel decisions we want student ratings to be valid measures of teaching effectiveness. For improving teaching we want student ratings to be valid in terms of accurate diagnosis of problems and, perhaps, for prescription of solutions. For guiding student choices of courses we want student ratings to provide information valid for enabling students to choose more valuable educational experiences. Let us consider these purposes in turn.

**What Do We Mean
by Teaching Effectiveness?**

Obviously if we are to answer the question "Are student ratings valid measures of teaching effectiveness?" we need to define "teaching effectiveness." Simply put, we take teaching effectiveness to be the degree to which one has facilitated student achievement of educational goals. But assessing teaching effectiveness is not simple. Much of student achievement is determined by factors other than teaching; for example, student ability or previous experience. Moreover, student achievement in different courses is not comparable since there is no way of estimating how many units of mathematics achievement equal a given number of units of achievement in English.

One might expect that one could simply judge effectiveness in terms of how well students achieve course goals. But such "criterion referenced" measurement ultimately rests upon a judgment about what sort of achievement it is reasonable to expect, and what is reasonable to expect depends upon knowledge of what other teachers have done with similar classes. Thus, to validate a measure of teaching effectiveness, such as student ratings, we must have a number of teachers teaching the same course to comparable groups of students. Only in such a situation can we determine whether those teachers whose students learn the most are rated highest by their students. Let us now examine the evidence from such situations with respect to teaching effectiveness for different educational goals.

**Validity of Student Ratings
as a Measure of Teaching Effectiveness
on Achieving Cognitive Goals**

Most college professors who have thought about their goals describe both cognitive and motivational goals for their courses. We want students to make gains toward such cognitive goals as knowledge, skill in solving problems, and ability to evaluate. Typically we also want to achieve affective goals, such as increasing students' interest in the area studied, so that they will be motivated to continue learning after they leave college.

When we speak of student learning as the ultimate criterion of teaching effectiveness, we usually think of the cognitive outcomes. Usually we assume that these outcomes are measured by the final examination for the course. In fact, however, final examinations typically weigh knowledge much more heavily than application, problem solving, or other cognitive objectives. Moreover, since students are strongly motivated for grades, they will do the best they can to pass the examination regardless of the quality of teaching they have had. If the teacher has been confusing or unhelpful, students often will make up for deficiencies by extra studying. Thus performance of students on a final examination is not an ideal measure of teaching effectiveness. Nevertheless, this is the best we have in most of our validity studies.

In my 1969 article, the most persuasive evidence cited for the validity of student ratings of instruction was the research of Elliott (1949) who demonstrated that student ratings of instruction were related to teaching effectiveness in terms of student achievement in multi-section courses in chemistry.

A substantial amount of research on validity has been carried out since 1969. The results are mixed, but taken as a whole they confirm our earlier conclusion that teachers rated as effective by students are generally those teachers whose students achieve most.

The studies by Sullivan and Skanes (1974) and Centra (1977) are the only studies in which students were randomly assigned to instructors. Such random assignment is an important feature in designing validity studies since differences in mean student achievement between teachers may otherwise be the result of differences between the students rather than differences in teaching. Thus, the substantial positive relationships (.4 to .6) between mean student ratings and mean student achievement found in these two studies are particularly significant.

Of especial interest in the Centra study is the finding that global ratings of value of the course to the student tended to have higher validities than items assessing specific aspects of teaching. Ratings of the difficulty of the course, for example, had no significant relationship to student achievement. The Sullivan and Skanes study is also interesting in that greater validity was found for student ratings of regular faculty than for rating of teaching assistants. It may well be that when students feel that they have learned a good deal in a course they are more likely to attribute their success to their own efforts if their teacher was a teaching assistant and more likely to give the teacher some credit if the teacher is a professor.

Cohen (1981) carried out a meta-analysis of 41 validity studies of student ratings. The over-all correlation between course rating and mean student achievement was .47, a higher correlation than expected in view of numerous factors other than teaching that affect student learning.

One important educational goal is that of helping students develop the ability to evaluate their own learning. If we are at all successful, we would expect greater validity for student ratings in advanced courses than in elementary courses. Unfortunately, validity studies require multisection courses in order that the effectiveness of several teachers can be compared on common measures of student achievement. Such multisection courses are most commonly found at the elementary level so that we cannot compare the validities of student ratings in elementary courses with those in advanced courses.

The studies of the validity of student ratings are thus reasonably encouraging with respect to the goal of achievement on course examinations measuring cognitive goals. What of other educational outcomes?

Validity of Student Ratings as a Measure of Teaching Effectiveness in Achieving Attitudinal and Motivational Goals

One important goal of higher education is that of motivating students for continued learning—lifelong learning. In most courses one would not be happy if students mastered the content of the course but wanted never to learn anything more about that sort of material. The ultimate measure of achievement of this goal is later learning behavior, such as buying books or magazines related to the discipline, later reading habits, atten-·dance at lectures, workshops, or other opportunities for learning, election of further courses, etc. For end-of-the-course evidence it is hard to conceive of a measure with more face validity than answers to such items as: "This course is increasing my interest in learning more about this area."

With respect to the goal of motivating further student learning, a small study by McKeachie and Solomon (1958) found that students of highly rated introductory psychology teachers tended to elect more advanced courses in psychology. Sullivan and Skanes reported that students of highly rated psychology teachers were more likely to major in psychology: teachers who were effective in terms of student achievement also influenced course elections positively, even when the instructors did not receive high ratings.

In the attitudinal domain, Mann (1968) found that students in classes of highly rated teachers developed more sophisticated attitudes about economics than students of less highly rated instructors.

Other Data Relevant to Questions of Validity of Student Ratings as Measures of Teaching Effectiveness

One common criticism of student ratings is the plaint, "You can't really appreciate good teachers until you have been out of college a while. We hated 'Old So-and-So' when we were students, but now we know he really was a great teacher."

The evidence is that such cases are the exception rather than the rule. Drucker and Remmers (1951) and Centra (1974) found that alumni ratings of faculty correlate highly with those of current students. Aleamoni (1981) and Marsh (1984) report similar results in comparing current ratings with those by graduating seniors. Additional evidence supporting the validity of student ratings comes ironically from a series of studies widely believed to attack their validity. The Dr. Fox studies (Naftulin, Ware, and Donnelly, 1973) demonstrated that even professors, professionals, and administrators are unable to tell when a single lecture not directly in their field of expertise is not authentic.

The series of studies following this finding indicate that students, too, are not always good judges of whether teachers present more or less material than normal. This is not a surprising finding since the students haven't been through the course before. However, when content is equivalent, students tend to rate higher the teachers from whom they learn most.

Perry, Abrami, and Leventhal (1979) carried out a well-controlled study replicating the Dr. Fox research. Their results, however, did not replicate those reported in the original Dr. Fox studies. In only one of four situations were the results similar. In general students both learned more and rated instructors higher in sections with more content and in sections in which the instructor was more expressive. However, ratings were influenced more by the instructor's expressiveness than by achievement. This finding was confirmed by Meier and Feldhusen (1979) and fits with Frey et al.'s finding (1975) that student ratings of instructor skill are more highly related to student learning criteria than are student ratings on the "rapport" dimension. This does not mean that student ratings are invalid measures of "rapport." It simply means that "rapport" is not highly related to student achievement. In fact, the Dr. Fox studies provide further evidence that students rate teacher *behavior* validly, since the item showing the largest difference between their high-expressive and low-expressive conditions was "The lecturer was enthusiastic about the subject."

To sum up, students know when they are learning, but they do not know whether what they are learning is current, biased, or appropriate for course goals. They do rate lower an instructor who provides less content, but their ratings of effectiveness are probably less affected by amount of content than by other characteristics of teaching. These findings suggest that when student ratings are used as evidence of teaching in promotion decisions, peers should check term papers, examinations, syllabi, etc., to determine that the content is appropriate. (Although we do not know how reliable and valid such peer judgments are, one hopes that peers can provide useful data.)

Faculty critics of student ratings sometimes complain that students cannot evaluate academic competence. Such criticism seems oddly misdirected. Surely students should not be expected to be better judges of subject-matter competence than the department chairperson, who assigned the instructor to the course. One does not need to be an internationally famous researcher to teach an undergraduate course effectively; it seems that students have the right to assume that an instructor assigned to a course will have at least adequate subject-matter competence. If faculty members have doubts about an instructor's competence in the subject matter, it seems illogical for them to turn to students for such judgments. On the other hand, when there are questions about what instructors do in the classroom or how they affect students, the students themselves seem a plausible source of information.

Can Student Ratings Help Teachers Improve?

The ultimate test of the usefulness of student ratings as a measure for improving teaching is whether teaching becomes more effective as a result of the use of student ratings. Although some studies have reported no improvement, a few have reported positive results. The most impressive results are those reported by Overall and Marsh (1979). As compared with a control group, students of instructors receiving feedback from student ratings not only gave their instructors more favorable ratings at the end of the year, but also scored higher on an achievement test and on a measure of motivation for further learning and application of the material learned.

Failures of improvement after feedback from student ratings may be due to any of three factors:

1. The ratings may not provide new information.

2. Low ratings and critical comments may create anxiety, discouragement, and lack of enthusiasm for teaching—lowering rather than improving motivation for teaching.

3. Even when faculty members want to improve they may not know what to do.

Centra (1973) and Pambookian (1972) demonstrated that new information was important. Their research revealed that teachers whose self-ratings were higher than their students' ratings improved after receiving the student rating; teachers who were accurate or who underestimated the student ratings did not improve. Braunstein, Klein, and Pachla (1973) obtained similar results. Pambookian found that instructors in the middle range of ratings tended to benefit from feedback while the top and bottom teachers did not, suggesting that teachers receiving low ratings may become discouraged.

In a study at the University of Michigan (McKeachie et al. 1980), we attempted to meet the conditions governing improvement following feedback of ratings by giving counseling to provide encouragement and suggesting alternative teaching strategies. This proved to be superior to a printed report of the results. Centra also found that instructors were more likely to improve if they had information to help interpret their scores.

Can Students Use the Results of Student Ratings to Make Better Choices of Courses and Teachers?

So far as I can ascertain, no one has studied the validity of student ratings with respect to student uses. Not only do we not know whether they enable students to choose courses or instructors more wisely, we do not

even know whether the ratings provide valid descriptions of characteristics that make a difference for student choices—right or wrong. Coleman and McKeachie (1981) found that students who had the results of
student ratings were likely to choose a more demanding, more highly
rated, instructor over others with good, but lower ratings. Research by
Borgida and Nisbett (1977) indicated that ratings have less effect than
face-to-face comments. Whether or not the effect of student advice on
choice of courses enhances education is still a moot point.

General Thoughts About Validity

Even though the data are now strongly supportive of the validity of student ratings for certain goals, this does not mean that they are impervious
to influences by other factors. Validity studies are carried out within a
given course in which a group of teachers with comparable students and
comparable teaching conditions is working toward common goals. In
such circumstances, student ratings provide good evidence of teaching
effectiveness. But promotions committees and administrators want to use
student ratings to make judgments comparing individuals in different
courses and in different departments. Obviously, comparing the effectiveness of a mathematics teacher with that of a teacher of history is
comparing apples and oranges. Even though one may be able to evaluate
apples or oranges validly, one cannot as easily evaluate the relative worth
of an apple versus an orange.

In everyday life we do, nevertheless, make such judgments regularly,
deciding whether a new television set should be purchased rather than a
new hi-fi, whether the head lettuce is better than the romaine, and so
forth. And in academia, comparisons of two professors' research are
made without concern that the research may deal with different problems
in different fields. If I am deciding whether to hire one professor rather
than another, I make a judgment of relative merit. In our own grading of
students we may worry and vacillate, but we still are able to assign grades
to students who differ in terms of how well they do on objective tests,
how well they have written their term papers, or how well they have
participated in class discussion. So we *are* able to make judgments about
relative excellence even though the excellence may be achieved along
different dimensions.

Student ratings can provide information that may help make such
judgments, but we should remember that ratings by different groups of

students about different teachers do not necessarily provide valid comparisons between two teachers even though the ratings result in numbers that appear to be comparable. The evaluative judgments need to be made by peers or administrators using *evidence* from student ratings but not mechanically assigning certain values to certain numbers.

Moreover, when using student ratings to evaluate teaching, we should remember that students cannot judge all aspects of teaching effectiveness equally well. Student ratings are highly valid as indices of achievement of attitudinal and motivational goals of education. They are reasonably valid as indices of achievement of conventional cognitive goals. Judgments of the appropriateness of content, goals, and level of achievement are probably more competently made by peers.

What Factors Influence Student Ratings of Teaching?

We have now seen that student ratings can provide valid evidence with respect to important aspects of teaching effectiveness, but, if we are to make good use of them, we need to know what factors may influence student ratings. Some of these factors may be valid in the sense that students may learn more and rate teachers higher in certain situations; other variables may contribute to misinterpretation. In general, the results to be reported are encouraging in that most of the factors which might be expected to invalidate ratings have relatively small effects and those factors which affect ratings also affect learning. We shall examine the evidence with respect to characteristics of students, of courses, of teachers, and of the scales themselves.

Student Characteristics

A common misconception is that only more mature, more experienced students can be expected to rate instructors validly. As indicated in my 1969 article, and in more recent reviews, relatively few student characteristics have significant effects on student ratings. Age, sex, and level of student are among the variables that have been shown to have little effect upon student ratings of teaching.

Probably the single most important student variable affecting satisfaction is student expectations. Students who expect a course or teacher to be good generally find it to be so. As Leventhal, Abrami, Perry, and Breen have shown (1975), students may choose certain classes or sections of classes because of the reputation of the instructor. Thus a professor's current student rating may well be a function, in part, of the reactions of former students. Students who expect a teacher to be good may be more attentive, more highly motivated, and more likely to learn than those with poor expectations.

Some writers appear to believe that students should all evaluate teachers the same way; i.e., that a teacher is equally effective with all students. When they find that some kinds of student rate a teacher higher than others do, they assume that student ratings are invalid. However, since there is some evidence that teachers may be differentially effective for different students, within-class correlations between student characteristics and ratings are not necessarily indications of invalidity of ratings. Within-class correlations between student needs and course ratings may arise because teachers who met the relevant needs were indeed more effective for those students.

For example, some studies have found that particular types of students respond differently to different teaching styles. Domino (1971), for example, found that students scoring high on the Achievement via Conformance scale of the California Psychological Inventory achieved more and rated the teaching higher in psychology sections taught in a conforming manner; students high in Achievement via Independence did relatively better and rated the teaching as more effective in sections taught in a manner emphasizing independence.

Course and Class Characteristics

The size of a class, whether or not it is required, and the subject matter—these are all characteristics that may affect ratings. While some studies have shown these variables to make a difference, others have shown no effect, so that the amount of effect seems to be smaller than might be expected. Nevertheless, it seems wise not to lay heavy weight on comparisons of ratings in courses differing greatly in such characteristics. Centra (1979) reports that classes of fifteen and fewer are more effective in producing student learning and are also rated higher by students. Required courses tend to be rated lower than electives.

Many teachers recognize that some classes go well and others more poorly simply because of key individuals in a class or particular combinations of individuals. One student continually raising anxious questions about tests and grades can demoralize a whole class. Such characteristics of classes have not been assessed, but the possibility of such effects suggests that when student ratings are used in personnel decisions, ratings should be obtained from several classes.

Teacher Characteristics

What characteristics of instructors are related to student ratings of teaching effectiveness? For example, are certain personality characteristics related to effective teaching or to inflated student ratings? Do instructors who are easy graders get higher ratings?

Research shows relatively small effects of instructor characteristics. For example, sex of instructor makes little difference in the student ratings; conflicting results have been found with respect to faculty rank; and personality characteristics do not show consistent relationships to ratings of effectiveness. In one of our studies of student ratings at the University of Michigan, we did find that teaching assistants rated by their peers as high in general cultural attainment were rated as more effective by students.

Some other personality characteristics may be related to student ratings. For example, Hart and Driver (1978) found that teachers scoring high in extraversion, intuitiveness, and "feeling" on the Myers-Briggs Type Indicator tended to receive higher student ratings. Similarity of teacher and student personality and instructor personality did not affect ratings. Murray (1980) found that peer ratings of instructor extraversion, lack of anxiety, leadership, and objectivity correlated positively with mean student ratings of teaching effectiveness. Sherman and Blackburn (1975) found that highly rated teachers were perceived to be dynamic, amicable, and highly intellectual. However, we do not know whether these teachers were, or were not, effective in influencing student learning, nor can we explain the apparent contradiction between "intuitiveness" in the Hart and Driver findings and "objectivity" in the Murray results.

The research on grading practices has produced mixed results. A number of studies have found no overall effect of grading practices, although an instructor who is a hard grader is more likely to be rated low on the item, "Fairness in grading." Some studies have found a tendency for teachers giving higher grades to get higher ratings. However, one might argue that in courses in which students learn more the grades should be higher and the ratings should be higher so that a correlation between average grades and ratings is not necessarily a sign of invalidity. Palmer, Carliner, and Romer (1978) controlled for student achievement and found no effect of severity of grading on student ratings. My own conclusion is that one need not worry much about grading standards within the range of normal variability. If, however, grading standards seem unusually lenient, one might want to look more closely at the standards of achievement and the bases for grading in the course.

In general, it seems unwise to assume that certain characteristics denote good teaching and to use student judgments about these characteristics to evaluate teaching. There is ample research evidence that good teachers come in many styles. Most presumed essentials of good teaching, such as organization, warmth, or research ability, are not highly valid.

Other Factors

One would expect that the validity of ratings would be affected by the time when they are collected. This seems not to be a critical variable. Frey, Leonard, and Beatty (1975) found that ratings collected the last week of classes were not significantly different from those collected the first week of the following term.

It may make a difference, however, whether the ratings are to be used for improving the course or for evaluating the instructor for promotion. In the latter case ratings may be higher.

Reliability of Student Ratings

Questions are often raised about the reliability of student ratings, indicating that the questioner believes that a high degree of reliability is "good," but often with little understanding of why reliability is important or when it is important.

There are a number of ways of arriving at an index of a test's reliability. The use of any particular measure of reliability is, in at least a broad sense, also a measure of *construct validity*. By construct validity, we mean that a test does what it should do theoretically. We use a particular measure of reliability because we are making the theoretical assumption that the construct being measured should be stable or consistent under the conditions in which the reliability measure is obtained. Obtaining several different kinds of measures of reliability gives us some understanding of the factors influencing ratings. For example, one possible measure of the reliability of student evaluation of teaching would be the degree to which groups of students would rate teachers in the same way at two different points in time. For six classes we found that the correlation between mean student ratings of the teachers at the end of the course and mean ratings of the teachers by the same students fifteen months later was .94. The classic study in this respect is that of Drucker and Remmers (1951) who found correlations of about .6 between ratings at the end of the course by current students and ratings by alumni who had graduated at least ten years earlier. Overall and Marsh (1980) found that the ratings of individual students one year after graduation correlated .59 with those given at the end of a course. These correlations are in one sense measures of reliability; that is, they indicate that student ratings are not given randomly, but these results are also relevant to the problem of validity since one of the frequent criticisms directed at the validity of student ratings is that the true value of the faculty member can be apparent to students only some time after a course has been completed.

Conversely, a test-retest measure of reliability is obviously not what we want if our theory expects change between the two administrations of a student rating form. For example, a high test-retest correlation for administrations of a scale of teaching behavior in two different class periods may not be appropriate if we expect effective teachers to vary their behavior from class period to class period. Reliability in terms of student ratings on more general characteristics is reasonably high (.6 to .9) when students are asked to fill out the same scales with two weeks to four weeks intervening.

Some of the most common indices of reliability are computed from correlations between items. One would probably not want a high reliability coefficient on such a measure because this would indicate that we are measuring only one thing, and we usually design student rating forms to assess various characteristics of teaching rather than a single dimension. Despite this, such measures of reliability are usually high, indicating that on most student rating forms there is a strong evaluative dimension running through most of the items.

Another common confusion about reliability is the notion that students should agree on the ratings they assign an instructor. This is a reasonable expectation if the item asks students to report their observation of an instructor's behavior; e.g., "the instructor calls students by name." When, however, the item is evaluative, such as "rate the instructor's effectiveness," we can expect agreement only if we expect the instructor to be equally effective for all students, an assumption that research shows to be generally untrue. However, when one looks at *mean* ratings given by *groups* of students, the correlations between the mean ratings given by groups of students in the same class are very high, ranging from the mid-.80's for classes of ten to the .90's for classes of twenty.

Other measures of reliability might deal with the degree to which a teacher's ratings tend to be the same from semester to semester or from course to course. If one believes that classes have unique characteristics which make a difference in teaching, one should not expect correlations between ratings of a teacher by different classes to be high. In fact such correlations range from .34 to .67.

My point is that a reliability index is meaningful only in terms of 1) the goals for which one is administering a student ratings form; and 2) one's theoretical conception of what the constructs related to teaching effectiveness should be doing in the situations in which the measures are to be administered.

For the use of student ratings in personnel decisions, the measures of reliability one probably wants could be any of the following:

a. Would the same students rate the instructor as well if they had been given a different, but equivalent, rating form?
b. Would other students taking the same course have rated the instructor the same way?
c. Is the teacher's teaching rated the same in this course as in other courses?

Note that there are valid reasons why ratings on a different form, by different students, or in a different course might well differ. Thus we should not expect perfect correlations. Nevertheless all of these correlations tend to be quite high. Moreover, the reliability of classes of students rating teachers is substantially higher than that of colleague ratings. Reliability is not likely to be a concern for most uses of student ratings.

Despite these positive findings, it still seems wise in using ratings for personnel decisions to get ratings from more than one class and from more than one course and to have the ratings interpreted by individuals who know something about the difference between courses; for instance, the difference between a content course and a methodology course.

Choosing Scales or Items for Scales

Establishing the Purpose
of Collecting Student Opinion

Whether one plans to use one of the ready-made scales or construct one's own, a necessary prerequisite is to examine one's goals in gathering student impressions, for different goals imply different items. If the goal is to assist in personnel decisions, two to five general items may be sufficient; if the purpose is to improve instruction, a more detailed, behaviorally oriented set of items relevant to particular kinds of courses is probably more appropriate.

I shall discuss particular items useful for each of these purposes. But as an alternative to developing your own scales, you might wish to consider the use of a scale developed elsewhere, such as those developed at Educational Testing Service, Northwestern, Kansas State, or other universities included in the book by Genova, Madoff, Chin, and Thomas (1976).

In choosing items appropriate for different goals you may be helped by differentiating five types of items.

1. items in which students report classroom events or teacher behaviors
2. items reporting the student's perception of his or her achievement of course goals
3. items reporting the student's own evaluation of the effectiveness of different aspects of the course
4. items reporting the student's own behavior or thinking in the course
5. items reporting student satisfaction.

Different kinds of items are useful for each major purpose for which student ratings scales are used. Moreover, differing items are appropriate for differing types of instruction, such as lectures, seminars, laboratory, or tutorial instruction.

Choosing Student Rating Items
for Improving Instruction

As we saw earlier, the use of student ratings is likely to result in improvement when: a) the ratings provide new information; b) the teacher is motivated to improve; c) the teacher can use alternative methods of teaching effectively.

This has implications for choice of items. Items chosen by the instructor because he or she wants the information are more likely to be informative than items on scales written for more general purposes. Aside from an item or two to indicate general feelings of satisfaction, more specific items reporting perceptions or evaluations of teacher behaviors or specific aspects of the course are likely to be more helpful than very general items.

Moreover one would guess that items worded in an evaluative fashion would elicit more defensiveness then those that are worded descriptively. Thus one might prefer such an item as:

"The instructor writes key points on the blackboard,"

to an item such as:

"Lectures are well organized."

Factor analyses reveal the major dimensions students and faculty members use in thinking about teaching. In constructing a scale it seems reasonable to include one or two items from each of the major factors. Among the factors commonly identified are:

Skill—Enthusiasm
"The teacher was enthusiastic."

Structure
"The teacher defined the objectives of the discussion."

Rapport
"The teacher was friendly."

Work load—Difficulty
"The work load was heavy."

Group interaction
"The teacher encouraged class discussion."

Mazzuca and Feldhusen (1977) found in a survey of students that the first two factors above were particularly important to students.

To facilitate adaptation of student ratings to the needs of individual instructors, Purdue University developed the Purdue Cafeteria System. This system permits instructors to choose items from a catalogue of items that have been previously used. Other universities have now adopted or adapted the Cafeteria System to provide flexibility in obtaining student ratings likely to give the instructor useful information.

Choosing Student Rating Items for Personnel Decisions

The current press for teacher accountability is one of the factors leading to attempts to mandate the use of standard, uniform student rating scales for assessing teaching effectiveness. As we have already seen, student ratings of teaching *are* related to teacher effectiveness as measured by the achievement of the teacher's students. Nevertheless this does not mean that student ratings are sufficient evidence of teaching effectiveness. Ideally one would gather evidence from a number of sources, giving most weight to those sources most expert with respect to different aspects of teaching. For example, it is hard to conceive of anyone more expert than students themselves with respect to the degree to which the teacher has stimulated intellectual curiosity and interest in the subject-matter field— an important educational goal; on the other hand, one would expect peers to be most competent to judge the scholarly content of a course, assuming that they have examined syllabi, examination papers, instructor and student lecture notes, or other sources of evidence. Thus personnel decisions inevitably involve value judgments using data from several sources with respect to a teacher's effectiveness in achieving a number of different goals.

As suggested earlier, a uniform standard scale is not likely to be very helpful for improving teaching—nor is a lengthy standard scale likely to be helpful for personnel decisions since it is unlikely to be equally well suited for different disciplines or different courses within a discipline. Since comparisons between instructors in different courses can at best be only very general, one should probably not attempt much more than to determine whether students rate an instructor as excellent, adequate, or poor. An item or two of the degree to which a course stimulated interest or curiosity, and perhaps another item or two on general effectiveness, should be sufficient for most personnel purposes. In addition, it may be helpful to have marker items on some of the factors usually found to differentiate teachers. Some instructors achieve excellence through skillful presentations; others achieve excellence through stimulating high student involvement. It is all too easy for faculty committees to develop stereotypes of faculty teaching on the basis of hearsay, and having scores on somewhat differentiated dimensions of teaching should help break down the simple good-bad classification that we all too often fall into.

Certain items have proved to relate to teacher effectiveness as measured by mean student performance on an examination. Unfortunately such studies must be done in a multi-section course, and it is often difficult to know how much the results can be generalized to other courses. Frey, Leonard, and Beatty's (1975) validity studies included both calculus and psychology courses so that Frey's items are particularly worthy of consideration. Three likely candidates are:

> "Each class period was carefully planned in advance."
> "The instructor presented the material clearly."
> "This course has increased my knowledge and competence."

Other validated items include:

> "Does the professor make student feel free to ask questions, disagree, express their ideas, etc.?"
> "Does the professor use examples from his/her own research or experience?"

I like to use items which ask students about themselves rather than focusing on evaluation of the teacher. Examples of such items are:

> "I learned a great deal in this course."
> "I became more interested in this subject matter."
> "I tried to relate material in the course to my own experience."
> "I developed an overall framework for learning and understanding this topic."

One of the commonest misuses of student rating scales in personnel procedures is to sum ratings on a group of items and compute a mean. Such a procedure assumes that the items are all measuring the same thing—effective teaching. In fact most scales contain several types of items, each providing useful information. Their purposes are different and they cannot meaningfully be lumped together.

Choosing Student Rating Items to Assist Students in Choosing Courses

One of the first universities to collect student ratings was Harvard, where students began in the 1920s to publish a book reporting student opinion of courses and professors. Such books are now commonly found on college and university campuses. If this is to be the primary purpose of the scale, one would presumably want to include items that are likely to provide information that will make a difference for student decisions. So far as I know there are no data describing items that made a difference, but there have been a number of studies of qualities students believe to be related to superior teaching. Feldman's (1976) review of these studies lists the following qualities as being consistently reported:

➤ Stimulation of interest

➤ Clarity

➤ Fairness

➤ Preparation

➤ Enthusiasm

➤ Friendliness

➤ Helpfulness

➤ Openness to others' opinions

Items Designed to Be Educational for Students

One of the potential unfortunate outcomes of the use of student ratings is that students are influenced to focus upon the instructor as the person chiefly responsible for student learning. In fact, however, learning should be a joint responsibility of students and instructor. Before blaming the instructor for failure to achieve educational goals, students should consider whether they have done all they could to make the course a valuable experience.

On my own student rating form I include a section on student responsibility for learning. My purpose is to increase students' sense of responsibility for their own learning and to encourage them to think about their own educational goals. I include such items as:

➤ I attend class regularly.

➤ I have created learning experiences for myself in connection with the course.

➤ I have helped classmates learn.

General Comments About Procedures
for Student Ratings of Teaching

1. Allow space for comments. Faculty members uniformly report that these are helpful. Students need the chance to express feelings that do not quite fit the prestructured questionnaire format. Frequently comments give examples or incidents which clarify the meaning of ratings or indicate what changes need to be made.

2. Indicate in the instructions who will read the comments. Students will be more focused if they understand to whom they are writing.

3. I prefer items worded in terms of the individual student's perception or evaluation to more general statements. I think a faculty member is likely to resent global evaluations more than those worded in terms of the impression made on a particular student, and I think a student is generally better able to report how he or she felt than to make global judgments.

4. Faculty members should have the right to participate in the selection of items or forms to be used in evaluating teaching in order that the form may be appropriate for the goals of the particular classes in which the data are to be collected.

5. If ratings are to be used in personnel decisions, some control should be exercised over conditions of administration. Rumors circulate about instructors who roam up and down the aisles, lose poor evaluations, or introduce the ratings by announcing that the students will be determining not only the instructor's fate but that of spouse and children.

6. I believe teachers are likely to be more effective and are more likely to improve if they enjoy teaching. This implies that reports of student ratings should be in a format that encourages good feelings rather than discouragement. Thus a report emphasizing percentile ranks in relation to norms may be less helpful than a report emphasizing the distribution of student responses (since typical classes like their instructor). It probably is not very helpful to tell a teacher rated as "good" by his students that this is only "average."

7. If teaching ratings are to be published in a booklet for students and made available to colleagues, experience indicates that faculty mo-

tivation is enhanced if the booklet reports teacher strengths rather than weaknesses.

8. Effective teaching is a skill that can be learned and that develops over time. Teaching ratings can help development. Basing career decisions on ratings in a single course early in a teaching career is not wise or fair. Basing decisions on a single visit by a peer or superior is even more unwise.

9. If student ratings are used in personnel decisions, the instructor should have an opportunity to present his or her interpretation of the data as well as whatever additional evidence seems relevant.

10. Student ratings tend to focus on classroom teaching. Evidence with respect to out-of-class educational functions such as course planning, advising, etc., also is needed.

11. When student ratings are used in personnel decisions, they should be evaluated by peers who are familiar with the courses in which the ratings were gathered, who know the teaching methods used, and who can take into account the circumstances under which the course was taught.

Summary

Student ratings of teaching can be useful for several purposes, such as:

1. improving teaching
2. providing data relevant to judgment about teaching effectiveness
3. aiding student choice of course and instructor
4. stimulating students to think about their education.

Student ratings are not automatically valid and useful for any of these purposes. Thus we need to understand what student ratings can and cannot do before embarking upon large-scale institutional programs of student ratings.

We use ratings to improve the quality of education. No matter how technically sophisticated our questionnaire and our evaluation system, they are worthless if their use generates such conflict, anxiety, or confusion that education is affected adversely.

Student ratings should not be used as the single measure of teaching. Rather we should think of them as data valuable for problem solving.

Their impact upon the climate for teaching is more important than the technical excellence of the form to be used.

If students are to provide careful ratings and if faculty members are to make good use of the information, both need to have confidence in the methods used. Thus even a good form may need to be reexamined and revised frequently by student-faculty committees if new generations are to have a sense that the system is theirs rather than one imposed upon them.

In Appendix A I have suggested a form for collecting student opinion. Feel free to use any items from it which would be useful in your situation.

SUPPLEMENTARY READING

Kenneth O. Doyle, *Student evaluation of instruction* (Lexington, MA: D. C. Heath, 1975). Also, his *Evaluating teaching,* from the same publisher, 1983.

Herbert W. Marsh. Students' evaluations of university teaching: Dimensionality, reliability, validity, potential biases, and utility. *Journal of Educational Psychology,* 1984, 76, 707–754.

What should you do if your ratings on some items are lower than you'd like? Consult the manual by Barbara Gross Davis, Lynn Wood, and Robert C. Wilson, *ABCs of teaching with excellence* (Berkeley, CA: University of California, Berkeley, 1983). This book is a compendium of brief suggestions made by excellent teachers at the University of California, Berkeley. Many of these are directly related to items commonly included on student rating forms.

CHAPTER 31
Faculty Attitudes and Teaching Effectiveness

What can I say about the work of the teacher? Clearly it is not possible to detail in a few summary statements the "best" methods of teaching. Nevertheless, a conclusion that it doesn't make any difference which methods are used is clearly unjustified. Rather, research suggests that decisions about teaching methods do have important consequences in terms of differential achievement of the varying objectives of a course, differential effects upon various types of students, and probable differential effects depending upon other factors such as the instructor, the course content, and the overall "climate" of the institution. To analyze such complexities would obviously be a task for a giant computer. In the absence of the data necessary for such an analysis, educators must, as in other frontier areas, depend upon expert judgment. Most of the reports of research on teaching neglect to report the reactions of the faculty involved (except in the case of television where they are generally negative). Yet until we gain more confidence in our evaluation tools, we are almost forced to weigh faculty judgment heavily.

I would argue, however, that faculty judgments of teaching methods are extremely important even aside from their possible validity as expert judgments.

As I pointed out earlier, we seldom know how well a particular method was used in experimental studies of teaching methods, but it seems very likely that the effectiveness of a method depends upon the competence and enthusiasm of the teachers in the study. If the teachers are important, their enjoyment of the method becomes a critical variable. Thistlethwaite (1960) finds that National Merit Scholars report that one of the critical variables influencing their choice of a field is the instructor's enthusiasm. It seems probable that such enthusiasm is unlikely to be communicated if instructors find teaching distasteful. Thus, even though studies found that a particular method when ideally used is superior to other methods, I would be dubious about urging its widespread adoption if teachers using it become bored or dissatisfied.

What are the satisfactions in teaching? Certainly one is the pleasure of seeing a student develop. Another is the pleasure of intellectual interchange with young people possessing questioning minds and fresh ideas. Still another is the sense of satisfaction from pulling together ideas in a wide-ranging discussion, from asking the right question at the right time, and from finding the right example to clarify what was previously unclear. Perhaps a less laudable but nonetheless real satisfaction is that found in having disciples who respect and admire you. These satisfactions are difficult to secure without close sustained personal contact with students. If instructors are to know students well enough to see their progress, small classes are important, not only because they permit more individual interaction with students, but also because they permit instructors to use term papers, essay tests, and other evaluation methods that give them a greater understanding of what students are thinking. While objective tests might also be used to give a personalized understanding of each student's strengths and weaknesses, few teachers take the time to analyze the patterns of right and wrong answers that would be necessary for such understanding, and such an analysis becomes prohibitively time-consuming in a large class, whatever the testing methods used.

Moreover, if the satisfaction of observing student growth is important, opportunities for contacts between instructor and student over a period longer than a one-semester course need to be ensured. One of the advantages of the small college over the large university is that students in a small college not only are more likely to come into contact with their instructors outside of the classroom, but they are also more likely to elect later courses from the same professors. In a community where professors know most of the students, professors are more likely to discuss students with each other. In a large university a professor may teach a student one semester and never see that student again. Professors are very unlikely to discuss the student with other professors because they don't know which colleagues know the student.

Many professors conscientiously attend some social functions intended to promote contacts between students and faculty. In the small colleges it is likely that professors will meet at such functions some of the students they have taught and will have an opportunity to use this contact to gain greater understanding of the students and perhaps even to stimulate their thinking. But the larger the college the less the statistical chance that they will meet students they teach. This means that even professors who conscientiously devote a portion of their time to such "informal" contacts with students are unlikely to have significant encounters. Because they are nearly always dealing with strangers or near-strangers, the intellectual interchange is almost perforce limited to polite inquiry about the student's academic and vocational aspirations or conversation about the current film at the campus theater. In short, any satisfaction received from observing and contributing to a student's growth must ordinarily come during the semester (or at most two semesters) that the student is enrolled in your class. No matter how powerful your impact, it is asking a great deal to expect it to have noticeable effects in four months.

The size of an educational institution has a very similar relationship to the quality of education students receive from one another. The large institution with a student body of heterogeneous background offers students an opportunity to gain breadth, tolerance, and new perspectives from their contacts with one another. But large size is likely to reduce educational values by reducing intellectual interchange between students. There is certainly no reason why students at a large college could not discuss with other students an interesting problem raised by one of their mutual professors. But they are probably more likely to do so if they are living near another student who is also familiar with the problem and concerned about it. In a large college the statistical chances that another student in the same class will be in the same living group are smaller than in a small college. Students in a large college with many courses, and even many sections of the same course, have few common intellectual experiences. Consequently, it is difficult for them to communicate about intellectual problems outside of class, and the common concerns that become the basis of social communication are football, the student newspaper, and the dormitory food. With such barriers to inter-student education professors miss the good feeling that could be experienced if they found that their teaching had provided an intellectual stimulus reaching far beyond their classrooms.*

Of course there are also satisfactions in teaching a large class. You can gain a very satisfying sense of power from knowing that you are communicating your ideas to many students. The roar of laughter at a joke well told is music to a lecturer's ear. The satisfaction of carrying

---

* As a professor at a large university, let me note that I don't consider our case hopeless if we recognize what problems we need to solve.

through without interruption a well-planned lesson is satisfying to the "Master Teacher" whose performance is televised.

Although these are valid satisfactions, they seem less directly related to the goals of education than the satisfactions associated with observing student development. What would a college be like if its faculty were largely made up of teachers whose satisfactions were primarily those of a good performer?

As college budgets shrink, there is a natural tendency to routinize and automate educational processes in the interest of increased efficiency. In industry, assembly-line methods have long been effective. Yet, in recent years, industry has found that workers are even more efficient if, instead of performing one specific, repetitive task, their jobs are enlarged enough to provide variety and interest. While there is little likelihood that college administrators will intentionally insist upon uniform teaching methods, increasing class size indirectly limits the professors' choices of teaching methods, reducing their freedom to select the methods best suited for their objectives and reducing their satisfaction in teaching.

Although I have emphasized the case of the faculty against such pressures, let me also point out that resistance alone will probably not be enough. If teachers expect their administrations to preserve their freedom of choice, they incur a heavy responsibility for analyzing more carefully the manner in which they spend class time. Do teachers really teach differently in small classes than in large? Are they making optimal use of the flexibility in scheduling and the teaching aids that remain within their control? Can teachers honestly say that a change would be less effective or enjoyable without trying it? Let's not lose the enjoyment of teaching in a rut of convention.

Student Perceptions of Learning and Teaching

W. J. McKeachie
The University of Michigan*

The items on this questionnaire ask you to comment on various aspects of your course.

The questionnaire has eight brief parts. The first part is intended to assess your perception of your own learning; the second part is your perception of characteristics related to instructor effectiveness. Other parts are not evaluative, but are intended to assess aspects of teacher style. They ask for a description, not an evaluation. For example, either a high or low degree of structure may be effective.

Thank you for taking the time to fill this form out thoughtfully. Your answers and comments will help your teacher improve the course.

Date: _____ Your Class Standing (Circle):

Course: _____ FR SOPH JR SR GRAD

Instructor: _____

Your GPA in all courses at this college:

3.5–4.0 _____ 2.0–2.4 _____ Sex: Male Female

3.0–3.4 _____ 0–1.9 _____

2.5–2.9 _____

Use the following scale:

1–almost never or almost nothing   4–often or much
2–seldom or little   5–very often
3–occasionally or moderate   6–almost always, a great deal
                                        If not applicable, leave blank

---

* Teachers are welcome to use this form or items from it without requesting permission from the author.

Impact on Students

1. My intellectual curiosity has been stimulated by this course.
   Comments:

2. I am learning how to think more clearly about the area of this course.
   Comments:

Student Information Processing

3. My mind wandered a good deal during class.
   Comments:

4. The instructor introduced new concepts so fast that I could not grasp them.
   Comments:

5. I tried to relate the course material to other things I know.
   Comments:

6. The course is increasing my interest in learning more about this area.
   Comments:

Instructor Effectiveness

7. The instructor is enthusiastic.
   Comments:

8. The instructor gives good examples of the concepts.
   Comments:

9. The instructor goes into too much detail.
   Comments:

10. The instructor is helpful when students are confused.
    Comments:

11. The instructor seems knowledgeable in many areas.
    Comments:

Rapport

12. The instructor knows students' names.
    Comments:

13. The instructor is friendly.
    Comments:

Group Interaction

14. Students volunteer their own opinions.
    Comments:

15. Students discuss one another's ideas.
    Comments:

16. Students feel free to disagree with the instructor.
    Comments:

Difficulty

17. The instructor makes difficult assignments.
    Comments:

18. The instructor asks for a great deal of work.
    Comments:

Structure

19. The instructor plans class activities in detail.
    Comments:

20. The instructor follows an outline closely.
    Comments:

Feedback

21. The instructor keeps students informed of their progress.
    Comments:

22. The instructor tells students when they have done a particularly good job.
   Comments:

23. Tests and papers are graded and returned promptly.
   Comments:

Notice!!! This Scale Is Different!!!

Student Responsibility

1–definitely false	4–more true than false
2–more false than true	5–definitely true
3–in between	If not applicable, leave blank

24. I had a strong desire to take this course.
   Comments:

25. I actively participate in class discussions.
   Comments:

26. I try to make a tie-in between what I am learning through the course and my own experience.
   Comments:

27. I attend class regularly.
   Comments:

28. I utilize all the learning opportunities provided in the course.
Comments:

29. I have created learning experiences for myself in connection with the course.
Comments:

30. I have helped classmates learn.
Comments:

Overall Evaluation

Indicate your evaluation of characteristics below, using numbers based on the following scale:

1. Poor   2. Fair   3. Good   4. Very Good   5. Excellent

31. Rate the instructor's general teaching effectiveness for you.
Comments:

32. Rate the value of the course as a whole to you.
Comments:

Added Comments Below

Comments

APPENDIX B
Checklist of Teaching Techniques

Technique	Goals Potentially Achieved
Books	Knowledge Critical thinking
Lecture	Knowledge Inspiration, motivation (a "cutting edge" lecture) Identification with a scholar Critical thinking (by example)
Discussion	Critical thinking Relating knowledge to student experiences Application Attitude change
PSI	Knowledge. Can achieve application and higher level objectives depending on tests and tutors.
Student panel, student reports	Interest and motivation (at least for participants)
Guest lecturer or resource person	Added interest and information
Films	Make materials more concrete Facilitate learning materials involving motion or visual detail Interest
TV	Interest (greater involvement than film) Motion, visual details
Slides	Permit visual materials to be greatly enlarged and held in view while explained
Audio-tutorial	Knowledge. Skill. Problem solving

Bulletin boards, mock-up	Provide opportunity for learning at student's
	    own pace
	May help student relate learning in classrooms to
	    materials presented in mass media
	Provide concrete examples

Technique	Goals Potentially Achieved
Recordings	Provide concrete auditory experience Taped recordings can be made cheaply by instructor to bring situations outside the classroom to the class
Field trips	First-hand knowledge Interest
Laboratory	First-hand experience Scientific method
Role playing	Real-life experience Develops human relations skills Interest
Buzz groups	Create awareness of problems Practice in problem solving Increased involvement
Study guides, workbooks	Aid organization and learning of materials Promote application of knowledge
Periodicals	Bridge gap between classroom and other experiences of students
Teaching machines and programmed texts	Knowledge and skills, particularly those requiring repetition and immediate feedback
Computer-aided instruction	Potentially can achieve any of these goals when combined with other materials, but currently limited by availability of college-level programs. Can be highly motivating

References

Adams, J. C.; Carter, C. R.; and Smith, D. R., eds. *College teaching by television*. Washington, D.C.: American Council on Education, 1959.

Aleamoni, L. M. *The usefulness of student evaluations improving college teaching*. Urbana: University of Illinois Office of Instructional Resources, Measurement and Research Division, 1974.

Aleamoni, L. M. Student ratings of instruction. In J. Millman, ed., *Handbook of teacher evaluation,* pp. 110–145. Beverly Hills, CA: Sage, 1981.

Allen, W. H. Audio-visual communication. In C. W. Harris, ed. *Encyclopedia of educational research,* 3rd. ed. New York: Macmillan, 1960.

Anandam, K. Camelot is here and now. *TIES* (Technological Innovations in Educational Settings), 1984, No. 10, 1–2.

Anderson, C. A., and Jennings, D. L. When experiences of failure promote expectations of success: The impact of attributing failure to ineffective strategies. *Journal of Personality,* 1980, *48,* 393–407.

Anderson, R. C. Learning in discussion: A resume of the authoritarian-democratic studies. *Harvard Educational Review,* 1959, *29,* 201–267.

Anderson, R. P., and Kelly, B. L. Student attitudes about participation in classroom groups. *Journal of Educational Research,* 1954, *48,* 255–267.

Annis, L. F. Effect of preference for assigned lecture notes on student achievement. *Journal of Educational Research,* 1981, *74,* 179–181.

———. The processes and effects of peer tutoring. *Human Learning,* 1983, *2,* 39–47.

——— ——. *Study techniques.* Dubuque: Wm. C. Brown, 1983.

Antioch College. Experiment in French language instruction. *Antioch College Reports.* Yellow Springs, OH: Office of Educational Research, Antioch College, October 1960.

Arbes, B., and Kitchener, K. G. Faculty consultation: a study in support of education through student interaction. *Journal of Counseling Psychology*, 1974, *21*, 121–126.

Argyris, C. Some limitations of the case method. *Academy of Management Review*, 1980, *5*, 291–298.

Arons, A. B. Computer-based instructional dialogs. *Science*, 1984, *224*, 1051–1056.

Asch, M. J. Non-directive teaching in psychology: an experimental study. *Psychological Monographs*, 1951, *65*, no. 4.

Ashmus, M., and Haigh, G. *Some factors which may be associated with student choice between directive and non-directive classes.* Springfield, MA: Springfield College, 1952.

Atkinson, J. E., and Litwin, G. H. Achievement motive and test anxiety conceived as motive to approach success and motive to avoid failure. *Journal of Abnormal and Social Psychology*, 1960, *60*, 52–63.

Atkinson, J. W., and O'Connor, P. A. *Effects of ability grouping in schools related to individual differences in achievement-related motivation.* Final Report, Office of Education, Cooperative Research Project 1238, 1963.

Atkinson, R. C. Ingredients for a theory of instruction. *American Psychologist*, 1972, *27*, 921–931.

Attiyeh, R., and Lumsden, K. G. Some modern myths in teaching economics: the U.K. experience. *American Economics Review*, 1972, *62*, 429–433.

Axelrod, J. Group dynamics, nondirective therapy, and college teaching. *Journal of Higher Education*, 1955, *26*, 200–207.

Bainter, M. E. A study of the outcomes of two types of laboratory techniques used in a course in general college physics for students planning to be teachers in the elementary grades. *Dissertation Abstracts*, 1955, *15*, 2485–2486.

Balcziak, L. W. The role of the laboratory and demonstration in college physical science in achieving the objectives of general education. Ph.D. diss., University of Minnesota. *Dissertation Abstracts*, 1954, *14*, 502–503.

Banathy, B. H., and Jordan, B. A classroom laboratory instructional system (CLIS). *Foreign Language Annals*, 1969, *2*, 466–473.

Bandura, A. Self-efficacy: toward a unifying theory of behavioral change. *Psychological Review,* March 1977, *84*(2), 191–215.

Bane, C. L. The lecture vs. the class-discussion method of college teaching. *School and Society,* 1925, *21,* 300–302.

Bargh, J. A., and Schul, Y. On the cognitive benefits of teaching. *Journal of Educational Psychology,* 1980, *72*(5), 593–604.

Barnard, J. D. The lecture demonstration vs. the problem-solving method of teaching a college science course. *Science Education,* 1942, *26,* 121–132.

Barnard, W. H. Note on the comparative efficacy of lecture and socialized recitation method vs. group study method. *Journal of Educational Psychology,* 1936, *27,* 388–390.

Bauer, R. The obstinate audience: the influence of process from the point of view of social communication. *American Psychologist,* 1964, *19,* 319–328.

Beach, L. R. Sociability and academic achievement in various types of learning situations. *Journal of Educational Psychology,* 1960, *51,* 208–212.

———. *Student interaction and learning in small self-directed college groups.* Final Report. Washington, D.C.: Department of Health, Education and Welfare, June 1968.

Beach, R., and Bridwell, L. Learning through writing. A rationale for writing across the curriculum. In A. Pellegrini and T. Yawkey, eds., *The development of oral and written language in social contexts.* Norwood, NJ: Abbey, 1984.

Beard, R. M. *Teaching and learning in higher education.* Middlesex, England: Penguin Books, 1972.

Beardslee, D.; Birney, R.; and McKeachie, W. J. Summary of conference on research in classroom processes. Mimeo, Department of Psychology, University of Michigan, 1951.

Becker, S. K.; Murray, J. N.; and Bechtoldt, H. P. *Teaching by the discussion method.* Iowa City: State University of Iowa, 1958.

Bendig, A. W. Ability and personality characteristics of introductory psychology instructors rated competent and empathic by their students. *Journal of Educational Research,* 1955, *48,* 705–709.

Berlyne, D. E. A theory of human curiosity. *British Journal of Psychology,* 1954a, *45,* 180–181.

———. An experimental study of human curiosity. *British Journal of Psychology,* 1954b, *45,* 256–265.

———. *Conflict, arousal, and curiosity.* New York: McGraw-Hill, 1960.

Berman, A. I. *Balanced learning.* New York: Harper & Row, 1973.

———. Media-activated seminar. *Educational Technology,* March 1974, 43–45.

Bills, R. E. Investigation of student centered teaching. *Journal of Educational Research,* 1952, *46,* 313–319.

Bligh, D. A. A pilot experiment to test the relative effectiveness of three kinds of teaching methods. *Research in Librarianship,* 1970, *3,* 88–93.

———; Ebrahims, G. J., Jacques, D.; and Piper, D. W. *Teaching students.* Devon, England: Exeter University Teaching Service, 1975.

Bligh, D., et al. *Methods and techniques of teaching in post-secondary education.* Paris: UNESCO, 1980.

Bloom, B. S. Thought processes in lectures and discussions. *Journal of General Education,* 1953, *7,* 160–169.

———, ed. *Taxonomy of educational objectives, handbook I: cognitive domain.* New York: Longmans, Green, 1956.

Borgida, E., and Nisbett, R. E. The differential impact of abstract vs. concrete information on decisions. *Journal of Applied Social Psychology,* 1977, *7,* 258–271.

Boris, E. Z. Classroom minutes: A valuable teaching device. *Improving college and university teaching,* 1983, *31*(2), 70–73.

Bork, A. *The physics computer development project.* Irvine, CA: Department of Physics, University of California, 1975.

———. *Learning with computers.* Bedford, MA: Digital Press, 1981.

Bouton, C., and Garth, R. *Learning in Groups.* New Directions for Teaching and Learning, 14. San Francisco: Jossey-Bass, 1983.

Bovard, E. W., Jr. Group structure and perception. *Journal of Abnormal and Social Psychology,* 1951a, *46,* 398–405.

———. The experimental production of interpersonal affect. *Journal of Abnormal Psychology,* 1951b, *46,* 521–528.

Bradley, R. L. Lecture demonstration vs. individual laboratory work in a natural science course at Michigan State University. *Dissertation Abstracts,* 1963, *23,* 4568.

Bransford, J. D. *Human cognition: Learning, understanding, and remembering.* Belmont, CA: Wadsworth, 1979.

————, and Stein, B. S. *The Ideal Problem Solver.* New York: W. H. Freeman, 1984.

Braunstein, D. N.; Klein, G. A.; and Pachla, M. Feedback, expectancy and shifts in student ratings of college faculty. *Journal of Applied Psychology,* 1973, *58,* 254–258.

Bronfenbrenner, U. A Cornell study relating to grading conditions. *Center for Improvement of Undergraduate Education Notes,* 1972, *3,* 2–4.

Brown, G. *Lecturing and explaining.* London: Methuen, 1980.

Burke, H. R. An experimental study of teaching methods in college freshman orientation course. Ph.D. diss., Boston University. *Dissertation Abstracts,* 1956, *16,* 77–78.

Cahn, M. M. Teaching through student models. In P. Runkel et al., eds., *The changing college classroom.* San Francisco: Jossey-Bass, 1972.

Calvin, A. D.; Hoffman, F. K.; and Harden, E. L. The effect of intelligence and social atmosphere on group problem solving behavior. *Journal of Social Psychology,* 1957, *45,* 61–74.

Calvin, A. D.; McGuigan, F. J.; and Sullivan, M. W. A further investigation of the relationship between anxiety and classroom examination performance. *Journal of Educational Psychology,* 1957, *48,* 240–244.

Carpenter, C. R. The Penn State pyramid plan: interdependent student work study grouping for increasing motivation for academic development. Paper read at 14th National Conference on Higher Education, Chicago, March 1959.

————, and Greenhill, L. P. *An investigation of closed-circuit television for teaching university courses.* Instructional Television Research Project No. 1. University Park: Pennsylvania State University, 1955.

————. *An investigation of closed-circuit television for teaching university courses.* Instructional Television Research Project No. 2. University Park: Pennsylvania State University, 1958.

Carrier, N. A. The relationship of certain personality measures to examination performance under stress. *Journal of Educational Psychology,* 1957, *48,* 510–520.

Carroll, J. B. Research on teaching foreign languages. In N. L. Gage, ed., *Handbook of research on teaching,* pp. 1060–1100. Chicago: Rand McNally & Company, 1963.

Casey, J. E., and Weaver, B. F. An evaluation of lecture method and small-group method of teaching in terms of knowledge of content, teacher attitude, and social status. *Journal of Colorado-Wyoming Academy of Science,* 1956, 7, 54.

Centra, J. A. The effectiveness of student feedback in modifying college instruction. *Journal of Educational Psychology,* 1973, 65, 395–401.

————. The relationship between student and alumni ratings of teachers. *Educational and Psychological Measurement,* 1974, 34(2), 321–326.

————. Student ratings of instruction and their relationship to student learning. *American Educational Research Journal,* 1977, 14, 17–24.

————. *Determining faculty effectiveness.* San Francisco: Jossey-Bass, 1979.

Chance, C. W. Experimentation in the adaptation of the overhead projector utilizing 200 transparencies and 800 overlays in teaching engineering descriptive geometry curricula. *Audio-Visual Communications Review,* 1961, 9, A17–A18.

Chang, T. M.; Crombag, H. F.; van der Drift, K. D. J. M.; and Moonen, J. M. *Distance learning: On the design of an open university.* Boston: Kluwer-Nijhoff, 1983.

Cheydleur, F. D. Criteria of effective teaching in basic French courses. *Bulletin of the University of Wisconsin,* August 1945.

Churchill, R. *Preliminary report on reading course study.* (Mimeo) Yellow Springs, OH: Antioch College, 1957.

Churchill, R., and Baskin, S. *Experiment on independent study.* (Mimeo) Yellow Springs, OH: Antioch College, 1958.

Churchill, R., and John, P. Conservation of teaching time through the use of lecture classes and student assistants. *Journal of Educational Psychology,* 1958, 49, 324–327.

Clark, R. E. Reconsidering research on learning from media. *Review of Educational Research,* 1983, 53, 445–459.

Cohen, P. A. Student ratings of instruction and student achievement: A meta-analysis of multisection validity studies. *Review of Educational Research,* 1981, *51,* 281–309.

Cole, M.; Cay, J.; Glick, J.; and Sharp, D. W. *The cultural context of learning and thinking.* New York: Basic Books, 1971.

Coleman, J., and McKeachie, W. Effects of instructor/course evaluations on student course selection. *Journal of Educational Psychology,* 1981, *73,* 224–226.

Coleman, W. Role-playing as an instructional aid. *Journal of Educational Psychology,* 1948, *39,* 427–435.

Collins, A. M., and Quillian, M. R. How to make a language user. In E. Tulving and W. Donaldson, eds. *Organization of memory.* New York: Academic Press, 1972.

Coombs, P. H. *The world educational crisis: A systems analysis* (Swedish ed.). Stockholm, Sweden: Bonniers, 1971.

Costin, F. Three-choice versus four-choice items: Implications for reliability and validity of objective achievement tests. *Educational and Psychological Measurement,* 1972, *32,* 1035–1038.

Craik, F. I. M., and Lockhart, R. S. Levels of processing: A framework for memory research. *Journal of Verbal Learning and Verbal Behavior,* 1972, *11,* 671–684.

Creager, J. G., and Murray, D. L., eds. *The use of modules in college biology teaching.* Washington, D.C.: Commission on Undergraduate Education in the Biological Sciences, 1971.

Cronbach, L. J., and Snow, R. E. *Aptitudes and instructional methods: a handbook for research on interaction.* New York: Irvington, 1977.

Cross, D. An investigation of the relationships between students' expressions of satisfaction with certain aspects of the college classroom situation and their achievement on final examinations. Honors thesis, University of Michigan, 1958.

Cutler, R. L.; McKeachie, W. J.; and McNeil, E. B. Teaching psychology by telephone. *American Psychologist,* 1958, *13,* 551–552.

Dahlgren, L. O., and Marton, F. Investigations into the learning and teaching of economics. *Reports from The Institute of Education, University of Göteborg,* September 1976, No. 54.

Davage, R. H. *The pyramid plan for the systematic involvement of university students in teaching-learning functions.* Division of Academic Research and Services, Pennsylvania State University, 1958.

————. *Recent data on the pyramid project in psychology.* Division of Academic Research and Services, Pennsylvania State University, 1959.

Davis, B. G.; Wood, L.; and Wilson, R. C. *ABCs of teaching with excellence.* Berkeley, CA: University of California, 1983.

Davis, J. R. *Teaching strategies for the college classroom.* Boulder, CO: Westview Press, 1976.

Dawson, M. D. Lectures vs. problem-solving in teaching elementary soil section. *Science Education,* 1956, *40,* 395–404.

Day, R. S. Teaching from notes: Some cognitive consequences. In McKeachie, W. J., ed. *Learning, cognition, and college teaching.* New Directions for Teaching and Learning, 2. San Francisco: Jossey-Bass, 1980.

Dearden, D. M. An evaluation of the laboratory in a college general biology course. *Journal of Experimental Education,* March 1960, *26*(3), 241–247.

De Cecco, J. P. Class size and coordinated instruction. *British Journal of Educational Psychology,* 1964, *34,* 65–74.

Deese, J., and Deese, E. K. *How to study,* 3rd ed. New York: McGraw-Hill, 1979.

Deignan, F. J. A comparison of the effectiveness of two group discussion methods. Ph.D. diss., Boston University. *Dissertation Abstracts,* 1956, *16,* 1110–1111.

Dekkers, J., and Donatti, S. The integration of research studies on the use of simulation as an instructional strategy. *Journal of Educational Research,* 1981, *74*(6).

Della-Piana, G. M. Two experimental feedback procedures: A comparison of their effects on the learning of concepts. Ph.D. diss., University of Illinois. *Dissertation Abstracts,* 1956, *16,* 910–911.

Deutsch, M. An experimental study of the effects of cooperation and competition upon group processes. *Human Relations,* 1949, *2,* 199–232.

Diamond, M. J. Improving the undergraduate lecture class by use of student-led discussion groups. _American Psychologist,_ 1972, _27,_ 978–981.

Dillon, J. T. The effect of questions in education and other enterprises. _Journal of Curriculum Studies,_ 1982, _14,_ 127–152.

———. Using questions to foil discussion. Address at School of Education, University of California, Riverside, 1983.

———. _Teaching and the art of questioning._ Bloomington, IN: Phi Delta Kappa Educational Foundation, 1983.

Di Vesta, F. J. Instructor-centered and student-centered approaches in teaching a human relations course. _Journal of Applied Psychology,_ 1954, _38,_ 329–335.

Domino, G. Differential prediction of academic achievement in conforming and independent sections. _Journal of Educational Psychology,_ 1968, _59,_ 256–260.

———. Interactive effects of achievement orientation and teaching style on academic achievement. _Journal of Educational Psychology,_ 1971, _62,_ 427–431.

———. Aptitude by treatment interaction effects in college instruction. Paper presented at the meeting of the American Psychological Association, New Orleans, 1974.

Donald, J., and Sullivan, A., eds. _Using research to improve university teaching._ San Francisco: Jossey-Bass, forthcoming.

Dowaliby, F. J., and Schumer, H. Teacher-centered vs. student-centered mode of college classroom instruction as related to manifest anxiety. _Journal of Educational Psychology,_ 1973, _64,_ 125–132.

Downing, R. E. Methods in science teaching. _Journal of Higher Education,_ 1913, _2,_ 316–320.

Doyle, K. O., Jr. _Student evaluation of instruction._ Lexington, MA: Lexington Books, 1975.

Dressel, P. L., and Marcus, D. _On teaching and learning in college._ San Francisco: Jossey-Bass, 1982.

Drucker, A. J., and Remmers, H. H. Do alumni and students differ in their attitudes toward instructors? _Journal of Educational Psychology,_ 1951, _42,_ 129–143.

Duchastel, P. C., and Merrill, P. F. The effects of behavioral objectives on learning: a review of empirical studies. *Review of Educational Research,* 1973, *43,* 53–69.

D'Ydewalle, G.; Swerts, A.; and de Corte, E. Study time and test performance as a function of test expectations. *Contemporary Educational Psychology,* 1983, *8*(1), 55–67.

Dzich, B. W., and Winer, L. *The Lecherous Professor.* Boston: Beacon Press, 1984.

Eble, K. E. *The craft of teaching.* San Francisco: Jossey-Bass, 1976.

————. *The aims of college teaching.* San Francisco: Jossey-Bass, 1983.

Edmondson, J. B., and Mulder, F. J. Size of class as a factor in university instruction. *Journal of Educational Research,* 1924, *9,* 1–12.

Egan, D. E., and Greeno, J. G. Acquiring cognitive structure by discovery and rule learning. *Journal of Educational Psychology,* 1973, *64*(1), 85–97.

Elliot, D. N. Characteristics and relationships of various criteria of teaching. Ph.D. thesis. Purdue University, 1949.

Ellner, C. L., and Barnes, C. P. *Studies of college teaching.* Lexington, MA: D. C. Heath, 1983.

Entwistle, N. *Personality, learning and teaching.* London: Wiley, forthcoming.

Ericksen, S. C. *Motivation for learning. A guide for the teacher of the young adult.* Ann Arbor: University of Michigan Press, 1974.

————. *The essence of good teaching.* San Francisco: Jossey-Bass, 1984.

Faw, V. A. A psychotherapeutic method of teaching psychology. *American Psychologist,* 1949, *4,* 104–109.

Feldhusen, J. R. The effects of small- and large-group instruction on learning of subject matter, attitudes, and interests. *Journal of Psychology,* 1963, *55,* 357–362.

Feldman, K. A. The superior college teacher from the students' view. *Research in Higher Education,* 1976, *5,* 243–288.

Feurzeig, W.; Munter, P. K.; Swets, J. A.; and Breen, M. N. Computer-aided teaching in medical diagnosis. *Journal of Medical Education,* August 1964, *39*(8).

Frey, P. W.; Leonard, D. W.; and Beatty, W. W. Students' ratings of instruction: Validation research. _American Educational Research Journal,_ 1975, _12,_ 327–336.

Friedman, C. P.; Hirschi, S.; Parlett, M.; and Taylor, E. F. The rise and fall of PSI in physics at MIT. _American Journal of Physics,_ 1976, _3,_ 204–211.

Fuhrmann, B., and Grasha, A. _A practical handbook for college teachers._ Boston: Little, Brown, 1983.

Gamson, W. A. _SIMSOC: a manual for participants._ Ann Arbor: Campus Publishers, 1966.

Gates, A. I. Recitation as a factor in memorizing. _Archives of Psychology,_ 1917, _6,_ No. 40.

Genova, W. J.; Madoff, M. K.; Chin, R.; and Thomas, G. B. _Mutual benefit evaluation of faculty and administrators in higher education._ Cambridge, MA: Ballinger, 1976.

Gerberich, J. R., and Warner, K. O. Relative instructional efficiencies of the lecture and discussion methods in a university course in American national government. _Journal of Educational Research,_ 1936, _29,_ 574–579.

Gerlach, V., and Ely, D. _Teaching and media: A systematic approach,_ 2nd ed. Englewood Cliffs, NJ: Prentice-Hall, 1980.

Gibb, C. A. Classroom behavior of the college teacher. _Educational and Psychological Measurement,_ 1955, _15,_ 254–263.

Glasnapp, D. R.; Poggio, J. P.; and Ory, J. C. End-of-course, and long term retention outcomes for mastery and nonmastery, learning paradigms. _Psychology in the Schools,_ 1978, _15_(4), 595–603.

Gibb, J. R. The effects of group size and of threat reduction upon creativity in a problem-solving situation. _American Psychologist,_ 1951, _6,_ 324 (Abstract).

Gibb, L. M., and Gibb, J. R. The effects of the use of "participative action" groups in a course in general psychology. _American Psychologist,_ 1952, _7,_ 247 (Abstract).

Goldschmid, B., and Goldschmid, M. L. Peer teaching in higher education: a review, _Higher Education,_ 1976, _5,_ 9–33.

Goldschmid, C. A., and Wilson, E. K. *Passing on Sociology: The teaching of a discipline*. Belmont, CA: Wadsworth, 1980.

Goldschmid, M. L. Instructional options: adapting the large university course to individual differences. *Learning and Development,* 1970, *1*(5), 1–2.

————. The learning cell: an instructional innovation. *Learning and Development,* 1971, *2*(5), 1–6.

————. When students teach students. Paper presented at the International Conference on Improving University Teaching, Heidelberg, Germany, May 1975.

Goldschmid, M. L., and Shore, B. M. The learning cell: a field test of an educational innovation. In W. A. Verreck, ed., *Methodological problems in research and development in higher education,* pp. 218–236. Amsterdam: Swets and Zeitlinger, 1974.

Goldstein, A. A controlled comparison of the project method with standard laboratory teaching in pharmacology. *Journal of Medical Education,* 1956, *31,* 365–375.

Greene, E. B. Relative effectiveness of lecture and individual readings as methods of college teaching. *Genetic Psychology Monographs,* 1928, *4,* 457–563.

Greenhill, L. P. New direction for communication research. *Audio-Visual Communications Review,* 1959, *7,* 245–253.

Greeno, J. G. Process of understanding in studying from text. Paper prepared for the Symposium, "Information Processing Analyses of Instruction," presented at AERA, San Francisco, April 1976.

Gregg, L. W., and Steinberg, E. R., eds. *Cognitive processes in writing.* Hillsdale, NJ: Lawrence Erlbaum, 1980.

Gronlund, N. E. *Constructing achievement tests,* 3rd ed. Englewood Cliffs, NJ: Prentice-Hall, 1982.

Gruber, H. E., and Weitman, M. Cognitive processes in higher education: curiosity and critical thinking. Paper read at Western Psychological Association, San Jose, CA, April 1960.

————. *Self-directed study: experiments in higher education,* Report No. 19. Boulder: University of Colorado, Behavior Research Laboratory, April 1962.

Guetzkow, H. S. *Simulation in social sciences:* Readings. Englewood Cliffs, NJ: Prentice-Hall, 1962.

————, Kelly, E. L.; and McKeachie, W. J. An experimental comparison of recitation, discussion, and tutorial methods in college teaching. *Journal of Educational Psychology*, 1954, *45*, 193–209.

Gullette, M. M. ed. *The art and craft of teaching*. Cambridge, MA: Harvard-Danforth Center for Teaching and Learning, 1982.

Haigh, G. V., and Schmidt, W. The learning of subject matter in teacher-centered and group-centered classes. *Journal of Educational Psychology*, 1956, *47*, 295–301.

Haines, D. B., and McKeachie, W. J. Cooperative vs. competitive discussion methods in teaching introductory psychology. *Journal of Educational Psychology*, 1967, *58*, 386–390.

Hansen, W. L.; Kelley, A. C.; and Weisbrod, B. A. Economic efficiency and the distribution of benefits from college instruction. *American Economic Review*, May 1970, *60*(2), 364–369.

Hart, J., and Driver, J. Teacher evaluation as a function of student and instructor personality. *Teaching of Psychology*, 1978, *5*, 198–200.

Harter, S. Effective motivation reconsidered: Toward a developmental model. *Human Development*, 1978, *21*, 34–64.

Hartley, J., and Davies, I. K. Note-taking: A critical review. *Programmed Learning and Educational Technology*, 1978, *15*, 207–224.

Hartman, F. R. Recognition learning under multiple channel presentation and testing conditions. *Audio-Visual Communication Review*, 1961, *9*, 24–43.

Haythorn, W.; Couch, A.; Haefner, D.; Langham, P.; and Carter, L. The effects of varying combinations of authoritarian and equalitarian leaders and followers. *Journal of Abnormal Psychology*, 1956, *53*, 210–219.

Heckhausen, H. How to improve poor motivation in students. Paper presented at the 18th International Congress of Applied Psychology, Montreal, August 1974.

Henderson, W. T., and Wen, S. Effects of immediate positive reinforcement on undergraduates' course achievement. *Psychological Reports*, 1976, *39*, 568–570.

Hill, R. J. *A comparative study of lecture and discussion methods*. New York: Fund for Adult Education, 1960.

Hill, W. F. *Learning through discussion*. Beverly Hills, CA: Sage, 1977.

Hirsch, R. S., and Moncreiff, B. A simulated chemistry lab. Paper presented at the 56th National meeting of the American Institute of Chemical Engineers, San Francisco, CA, May 1965.

Hirschman, C. S. An investigation of the small groups discussion classroom method on criteria of understanding, pleasantness, and self-confidence induced. Master's thesis, University of Pittsburgh, 1952.

Hoban, C. F. The dilemma of adult ITV college courses. *Educational Broadcasting Review,* June 1968, 31–36.

Hockenberry-Boeding, C., and Vattano, F. J. Undergraduates as teaching assistants: a comparison of two discussion methods. Manuscript, 1975.

Horwitz, M. The verticality of liking and disliking. In R. Taguiri and L. Petrullo, eds. *Person perception and interpersonal behavior.* Stanford: Stanford University Press, 1958.

Houston, J. P. Alternate test forms as a means of reducing multiple-choice answer copying in the classroom. *Journal of Educational Psychology,* 1983, 75(4), 572–575.

Hovland, C. I., ed. *The order of presentation in persuasion.* New Haven: Yale University Press, 1957.

Hovland, C. I.; Lumsdaine, A. A.; and Sheffield, F. D. *Experiments in mass communication.* Princeton: Princeton University Press, 1949.

Hudelson, E. *Class size at the college level.* Minneapolis: University of Minnesota Press, 1928.

Hunt, P. The case method of instruction. *Harvard Educational Review,* 1951, 3, 1–19.

Hurd, A. W. *Problems of science teaching at the college level.* Minneapolis: University of Minnesota Press, 1929.

Husband, R. W. A statistical comparison of the efficacy of large lecture vs. smaller recitation sections upon achievement in general psychology. *Journal of Psychology,* 1951, 31, 297–300.

Jackson, C. M. Experiment in methods of teaching gross human anatomy. In E. Hudelson, ed. *Problems of college education,* pp. 444–449. Minneapolis: University of Minnesota Press, 1929.

Jenkins, R. L. The relative effectiveness of two methods of teaching written and spoken English. Ph.D. diss., Michigan State University. *Dissertation Abstracts,* 1952, 12, 258.

Johnson, D. M. Increasing originality on essay examinations in psychology. *Teaching of Psychology,* 1975, *2,* 99–102.

Johnson, D. M., and Smith, H. C. Democratic leadership in the college classroom. *Psychological Monographs,* 1953, *67,* no. 2 (Whole No. 361).

Johnson, R. B., and Johnson, S. R. *Assuring learning with self-instructional packages or, up the up staircase, a how-to-do workbook.* Chapel Hill, NC: Self-instructional Packages, Inc., 1971.

Johnston, R. E., Jr. *Magnetic recordings and visual displays as aids in teaching introductory psychology to college students.* OE Grant No. 73056, Drexel Institute of Technology, Philadelphia, May 1969.

Judd, W. A. Learner-controlled computer-assisted instruction. In K. Zinn; M. Refice; and A. Romano, eds. *Computers in the instructional process: report of an instructional school.* Amsterdam: Elsevier, 1973.

Katona, G. *Organizing and memorizing.* New York: Columbia University Press, 1940.

Katz, D. *Gestalt psychology.* New York: Ronald Press, 1950.

Keller, F. S. Goodbye teacher, . . . *Journal of Applied Behavior Analysis,* 1968, *10,* 165–167.

————, and Sherman, J. G., eds. *The Keller Plan handbook.* Menlo Park, CA: W. A. Benjamin, Inc., 1974.

Kelley, A. C. An experiment with TIPS: a computer-aided instructional system for undergraduate education. *American Economic Review,* May 1968, *2,* 446–457.

————. The economics of teaching: The role of TIPS. In K. G. Lumsden, ed. *Recent research in economics education,* pp. 44–66. Englewood Cliffs, NJ: Prentice-Hall, 1970.

Kemp, J. F. *Planning and producing audiovisual materials,* 4th ed. New York: Harper & Row, 1980.

Kirk, T. G., ed. *Increasing the teaching role of academic libraries.* New directions for teaching and learning, 18. San Francisco: Jossey-Bass, 1984.

Kitchener, K. G., and Hurst, J. C. Education through student interaction manual. Manuscript, Colorado State University, 1972.

————. Faculty consultation: changing role for the counseling psychologist. *Journal of Counseling Psychology,* 1974.

Klapper, H. L. *Closed-circuit television as a medium of instruction of N.Y. University.* New York: N.Y. University, 1958.

Koenig, K., and McKeachie, W. J. Personality and independent study. *Journal of Educational Psychology,* 1959, *50,* 132–134.

Kozma, R. B.; Belle, L. W.; and Williams, G. W. *Instructional techniques in higher education.* Englewood Cliffs, NJ: Educational Technology Publications, 1978.

Krathwohl, D.; Bloom, B. S.; and Masia, B., eds. *Taxonomy of educational objectives: affective domain.* New York: David McKay, 1964.

Krauskopf, C. J. The use of written responses in the stimulated recall method. Ph.D. diss., Ohio State University. *Dissertation Abstracts,* 1960, *21,* 1953.

Kruglak, H. Experimental outcomes of laboratory instruction in elementary college physics. *American Journal of Physics,* 1952, *20,* 136–141.

Krumboltz, J. D. The nature and importance of the required response in programmed instruction. *American Educational Research Journal,* 1964, *1,* 203–209.

—————, and Farquhar, W. W. The effect of three teaching methods on achievement and motivational outcomes in a how-to-study course. *Psychological Monographs,* 1957, *71,* no. 14 (Whole No. 443).

Kulik, J. A.; Cohen, P. A.; and Ebeling, B. J. Effectiveness of programmed instruction in higher education: A meta-analysis of findings. *Educational Evaluation and Policy Analysis,* 1980, *2,* 51–64.

Kulik, J. A. Individualized systems of instruction. In H. E. Mitzel, ed. *The encyclopedia of educational research,* 5th ed. New York: Macmillan Co., 1982.

Kulik, J. A., and Jaksa, P. *A review of research on PSI and other educational technologies in college teaching.* Report No. 10, Center for Research on Learning and Teaching, Ann Arbor, MI, May 1977.

Kulik, J. A.; Kulik, C.; and Cohen, P. Instructional technology and college teaching, *Teaching of Psychology,* 1980a, *7,* 199–205.

—————. Effectiveness of computer-based college teaching: A meta-analysis of findings. *Review of Educational Research,* 1980b, *50*(4), 525–544.

Kulik, J. A.; Kulik, C.; and Smith, B. B. Research on the personalized system of instruction. *Programmed Learning and Educational Technology,* February 1976, *13,* 23–30.

Lahti, A. M. The inductive-deductive method and the physical science laboratory. _Journal of Experimental Education_, 1956, _24_, 149–163.

Lancaster, O. E.; Manning, K. V.; White, M. W. et al. The relative merits of lectures and recitation in teaching college physics. _Journal of Engineering Education_, 1961, _51_, 425–433.

Landsman, T. An experimental study of a student-centered learning method. Ph.D. diss., Syracuse University, 1950.

Lange, P. C. _Today's education_. National Education Association, 1972, _61_, 59.

Larkin, J. H.; Heller, J. I.; and Greeno, J. G. Instructional implications of research on problem solving. In McKeachie, W. J., ed., _Learning, cognition, and college teaching_. New directions for teaching and learning, 2. San Francisco: Jossey-Bass, 1980.

LaPree, G. Establishing criteria for grading student papers: Moving beyond mysticism. _Teaching and Learning_ (Indiana University), 1977, _3_, (1).

Lee, C. B. T., ed. _Improving college teaching_. Washington, D.C.: American Council on Education, 1967.

Leith, G. O. M. Conflict and interference: Studies of the facilitating effects of reviews in learning sequences. _Programmed Learning and Educational Technology_, 1971, _8_, 41–50.

———. Individual differences in learning: interactions of personality and teaching methods. In Association of Educational Psychologists, _Personality and Academic Progress_, London, 1974a.

———. Goals, methods and materials for a small-group, modular-instruction approach to teaching social psychology. Paper presented for the Institute of Social Psychology, University of Utrecht, 1974b.

———. Implications of cognitive psychology for the improvement of teaching and learning in universities. In B. Massey, ed. _Proceedings of the Third International Conference, Improving University Teaching_, pp. 111–138, College Park, MD: University of Maryland, 1977.

———. The influence of personality on learning to teach: Effects and delayed effects of microteaching. _Educational Review_, 1982, _34_(3), 195–204.

Lempert, R. Law school grading: an experiment with pass-fail. _Journal of Legal Education_, 1972, _24_, 251–308.

Lepper, M. R., and Malone, T. W. Intrinsic motivation and instructional effectiveness in computer-based education. In R. E. Snow and M. J. Farr, eds., *Aptitude, learning and instruction: III. Conative and affective process analyses.* Hillsdale, NJ: Erlbaum, 1985.

Leventhal, L.; Abrami, P. C.; Perry, R. P.; and Breen, L. J. Section selection in multi-section courses: Implications for the validation and use of student rating forms. *Educational and Psychological Measurements,* 1975, *35,* 885–895.

Lewin, K. Group decision and social change. In G. E. Swanson; T. M. Newcomb; and E. L. Hartley, eds. *Readings in social psychology,* 2nd ed., pp. 330–344. New York: Holt, 1952.

Lewin, K.; Lippitt, R.; and White, R. K. Patterns of aggressive behavior in experimentally created social climates. *Journal of Social Psychology,* 1939, *10,* 271–299.

Lewis, D. R.; Dalgaard, B. R.; and Boyer, C. M. Is CAI economical in economics? Paper presented at AERA meeting, April 1984.

Lifson, N.; Rempel, P.; and Johnson, J. A. A comparison between lecture and conference methods of teaching psychology. *Journal of Medical Education,* 1956, *31,* 376–382.

Lumsdaine, A. A. Instruments and media of instruction. In N. L. Gage, ed. *Handbook of research on teaching,* pp. 583–682. Chicago: Rand McNally, 1963.

Lumsden, E. A. Use of student feedback cards for diagnostic purposes during classroom lectures. *Improving College and University Teaching Yearbook 1976* (Oregon State University Press, 1976), 39.

Lyle, E. An exploration in the teaching of critical thinking in general psychology. *Journal of Educational Research,* 1958, *52,* 129–133.

McClelland, D. C. *Human Motivation.* Glenville, IL: Scott, Foresman, 1985.

Macomber, F. G., and Siegel, L. Experimental study in instructional procedures. *Progress Report No. 1.* Oxford, OH: Miami University, 1956.

———. A study of large-group teaching procedures. *Educational Research,* 1957a, *38,* 220–229.

———. Experimental study in instructional procedures. *Progress Report No. 2.* Oxford, OH: Miami University, 1957b.

————. Experimental study in instructional procedures. _Final Report._ Oxford, OH: Miami University, 1960.

Mager, R. F. _Preparing instructional objectives._ Palo Alto: Fearon Publishers, 1962.

Maier, N. R. F. _Principles of human relations._ New York: Wiley, 1952.

————. _Problem-solving discussions and conferences._ New York: McGraw-Hill, 1963.

————. Innovation in education. _American Psychologist,_ 1971, 26(8), 722–725.

————, and Maier, L. A. An experimental test of the effects of "developmental" vs. "free" discussion on the quality of group decisions. _Journal of Applied Psychology,_ 1957, 41, 320–323.

Maier, N. R. F., and Solem, A. R. The contribution of a discussion leader to the quality of group thinking. _Human Relations,_ 1952, 5, 277–288.

Maier, N. R. F., and Zerfoss, L. F. MRP: A technique for training large groups of supervisors and its potential use in social research. _Human Relations,_ 1952, 5, 177–186.

Maimon, E. P., et al. _Writing in the arts and sciences._ Cambridge, MA: Winthrop, 1981.

Malone, T. W., and Lepper, M. R. Making learning fun: A taxonomy of intrinsic motivations for learning. In R. E. Snow and M. J. Farr, eds. _Aptitude, learning, and instruction: III. Conative and affective process analysis._ Hillsdale, NJ: Erlbaum, 1985.

Maloney, R. M. Group learning through group discussion: a group discussion implementation analysis. _Journal of Social Psychology,_ 1956, 43, 3–9.

Mann, R. D. et al. _The college classroom._ New York: Wiley, 1970.

Mann, W. R. Changes in the level of attitude sophistication of college students as a measure of teacher effectiveness. Ph.D. diss., University of Michigan, 1968.

Marsh, H. W. Students' evaluations of university teaching: Dimensionality, reliability, potential biases, and utility. _Journal of Educational Psychology,_ 1984, 76, 707–754.

Marton, F.; Hounsell, D.; and Entwistle, N., eds. _The experience of learning._ Edinburgh: Scottish Academic Press, 1984.

Marton, F., and Säljö, R. On qualitative differences in learning: I—outcome and process. *British Journal of Educational Psychology*, 1976a, 46, 4–11.

―――. On qualitative differences in learning: II—outcome as a function of the learner's conception of the task. *British Journal of Educational Psychology*, 1976b, 46, 115–127.

Mayer, R. E. *Thinking and problem solving: An introduction to human cognition and learning.* Glenview, IL: Scott Foresman, 1974.

Mayer, R. E.; Stiehl, C. C.; and Greeno, J. G. Acquisition of understanding and skill in relation to subjects' preparation and meaningfulness of instruction. *Journal of Educational Psychology*, 1975, 67(3), 331–350.

Mazzuca, S. A., and Feldhusen, J. F. Effective college instruction: How students see it. Paper presented at the annual meeting of the American Psychological Association, San Francisco, August 29, 1977.

McClusky, H. Y. An experimental comparison of two methods of correcting the outcomes of examination. *School and Society*, 1934, 40, 566–568.

McCollough, C., and Van Atta, E. L. Experimental evaluation of teaching programs utilizing a block of independent work. Paper read at Symposium, "Experimental Studies in Learning Independently," American Psychological Association, Washington, D.C., September 1958.

McKeachie, W. J. Anxiety in the college classroom. *Journal of Educational Research*, 1951, 45, 153–160.

―――. Individual conformity to attitudes of classroom groups. *Journal of Abnormal and Social Psychology*, 1954, 49, 282–289.

―――. Improving your teaching. *Adult Leadership*, 1955, 3, 14–16.

―――. Students, groups, and teaching methods. *American Psychologist*, 1958, 13, 580–584.

―――. Appraising teaching effectiveness. In W. J. McKeachie, ed. *The appraisal of teaching in large universities*, pp. 32–36. Ann Arbor: University of Michigan Extension Services, 1959.

―――. College grades: A rationale and mild defense. *AAUP Bulletin*, 1976, 62, 320–322.

―――. Student ratings of faculty: A reprise. *Academe*, 1979, 65, 384–397.

————. ed. *Learning, cognition, and college teaching.* New Directions for Teaching and Learning, 2. San Francisco: Jossey-Bass, 1980.

————. Faculty as a renewable resource. In R. G. Baldwin and R. T. Blackburn (eds.) *College faculty: Versatile human resources in a period of restraint,* pp. 57–66. New Directions for Institutional Research. San Francisco: Jossey-Bass, 1983.

McKeachie, W. J.; Forrin, B.; Lin, Y-G.; and Teevan, R. Individualized teaching in elementary psychology. *Journal of Educational Psychology,* 1960, *51,* 285–291.

McKeachie, W. J.; and Kulik, J. A. Effective college teaching. In F. N. Kerlinger, ed. *Review of research in education,* vol. 3. Itasca, IL: Peacock, 1975.

McKeachie, W. J.; Lin, Y-G.; Daugherty, M.; Moffett, M.; Neigler, C.; Nork, J.; Walz, M.; and Baldwin, R. Using student ratings and consultation to improve instruction. *British Journal of Educational Psychology,* 1980, *50,* 168–174.

McKeachie, W. J.; Lin, Y-G.; Milholland, J.; and Isaacson, R. Student affiliation motives, teacher warmth, and academic achievement. *Journal of Personality and Social Psychology,* 1966, *4,* 457–461.

McKeachie, W. J.; Lin, Y-G.; Moffett, M.; and Daugherty, M. Effective teaching and facilitative vs. directive style. *Teaching of Psychology,* 1978, *5,* 193–194.

McKeachie, W. J.; Pollie, D.; and Speisman, J. Relieving anxiety in classroom examinations. *Journal of Abnormal Psychology,* 1955, *50,* 93–98.

McKeachie, W. J.; and Solomon, D. Student ratings of instructors: a validity study. *Journal of Educational Research,* 1958, *51,* 379–382.

McMichael, J. S., and Corey, J. R. Contingency management in an intro ductory psychology course produces better learning. *Journal of Applied Behavior Analysis,* 1969, *2,* 79–83.

McNair, M., ed., *The case method at Harvard Business School.* New York: McGraw-Hill, 1954.

McTavish, C. L. *Effect of repetitive film showings on learning.* Instructional Film Research Report, SDC 269-7-12, Special Devices Center, Office of Naval Research, November 1949.

Means, G., and Means, R. Achievement as a function of the presence of prior information concerning aptitudes. *Journal of Educational Psychology*, 1971, *62*, 185–187.

Mehrens, W. A., and Lehmann, I. J. *Measurement and evaluation in education and psychology*. New York: Holt, Rinehart & Winston, 1973.

Meier, R. S., and Feldhusen, J. F. Another look at Dr. Fox: Effect of stated purpose for evaluation, lecturer expressiveness, and density of lecture content on student ratings. *Journal of Educational Psychology*, 1979, *71*(3), 339–345.

Melton, A. W.; Feldman, N. G.; and Mason, C. N. *Experimental studies of the education of children in a museum of schools*. Washington, D.C.: Publications of the American Association of Museums, 1936, *15*, 1–106.

Messick, S., et al. *Individuality in learning*. San Francisco: Jossey-Bass, 1976.

Metzger, R. L.; Boschee, P. F.; Haugen, T.; and Schnobrich, B. L. The classroom as learning context: Changing rooms affects performance. *Journal of Educational Psychology*, 1979, *71*(4), 440–442.

Michael, D. N., and Maccoby, N. Factors influencing the effects of student participation on verbal learning from films: motivation vs. practice effects, feedback, and overt vs. covert responding. In A. A. Lumsdaine, ed., *Student response in programmed instruction: a symposium*. Washington, D.C.: NAS-NRC (National Academy of Sciences-National Research Council) 1953, *943*, 18.

Michaelsen, L. K. *Team learning in large classes*. New directions for teaching and learning, 14. San Francisco: Jossey-Bass, 1958.

Michaelsen, L. K.; Watson, W. E.; Cragin, J. P.; Fink, L. D. Team learning: A potential solution to the problems of large classes. *Exchange: The Organizational Behavior Teaching Journal*, 1982, *7*(1).

Miller, N. M. Scientific principles for maximum learning from motion pictures. *Audio-Visual Communication Review*, 1957, *5*, 61–113.

Miller, R. I. *Developing programs for faculty evaluation*. San Francisco: Jossey-Bass, 1974.

Milton, O. *Alternatives to the traditional*. San Francisco: Jossey-Bass, 1972.

Monaco, G. E. *Inferences as a function of test-expectancy in the classroom.* Kansas State University Psychology Series, KSU-HIPI Report 73-3, 1977.

Moore, J. W.; Smith, W. I.; and Teevan, R. *Motivational variables in programmed learning: The role of need achievement, fear of failure, and student estimate of achievement.* Final Report U.S.O.E., Title 7, Grant No. 7-48-0070-149, Lewisburg, PA: Bucknell University Press, 1965.

Moore, M. R., and Popham, W. J. The role of extra-class student interviews in promoting student achievement. Paper read at joint session of American Association for the Advancement of Science and American Educational Research Association, Chicago, December 1959.

Morris C. J., and Kimbrell, G. McA. Performance and attitudinal effects of the Keller method in an introductory psychology course. *Psychological Record,* 1972, *22,* 523–530.

Mueller, A. D. Class size as a factor in normal school instruction. *Education,* 1924, *45,* 203–227.

Mueller, D. J., and Wasser, V. Implications of changing answers on objective test items. *Journal of Educational Measurement,* 1977, *14*(1), 9–13.

Murray, H. G. *Evaluating university teaching: A review of research.* Toronto, Canada: Ontario Confederation of University Faculty Associations, 1980.

Nachman, M., and Opochinsky, S. The effects of different teaching methods: a methodological study. *Journal of Educational Psychology,* 1958, *49,* 245–249.

Naftulin, D. H.; Ware, J. E.; and Donnelly, F. A. The Doctor Fox lecture: A paradigm of educational seduction. *Journal of Medical Education,* 1973, *48,* 630–635.

Nash, A. N.; Muczyk, J. P.; and Vettori, F. L. The relative practical effectiveness of programmed instruction. *Personnel Psychology,* 1971, *24,* 397–418.

Nelson, T. Teaching and learning at Kalamazoo College. Manuscript, Kalamazoo College, Kalamazoo, MI, 1970.

Noll, V. H. The optimum laboratory emphasis in college chemistry. *School and Society,* 1930, *32,* 300–303.

Norman, D. *Teaching learning strategies.* Mimeo, University of Calif., San Diego, April 11, 1977.

Novak, J. D. An experimental comparison of a conventional and a project centered method of teaching a college general botany course. *Journal of Experimental Education,* 1958, *26,* 217–230.

Olson, D. Toward a theory of instructional means. *Educational Psychologist,* 1976, *12,* 14–35.

Overall, J. U., and Marsh, H. W. Students' evaluations of instruction: A longitudinal study of their stability. *Journal of Educational Psychology,* 1980, *72,* 321–325.

———. Midterm feedback from students: Its relationship to instructional improvement and students' cognitive and affective outcomes. *Journal of Educational Psychology,* 1979, *71,* 856–865.

Palmer, J.; Carliner, G.; and Romer, T. Leniency, learning and evaluations. *Journal of Educational Psychology,* 1978, *70*(5), 855–863.

Pambookian, H. S. The effect of feedback from students to college instructors on their teaching behavior. Ph.D. diss., University of Michigan, 1972.

Parman, Susan. The film essay as an educational device. *Innovation Abstracts,* 1984, *6*(26).

Parsons, T. S. A comparison of instruction by kinescope, correspondence study, and customary classroom procedures. *Journal of Educational Psychology,* 1957, *48,* 27–40.

———; Ketcham, W. A.; and Beach, L. R. Effects of varying degrees of student interaction and student-teacher contact in college courses. Paper read at American Sociological Society, Seattle, Washington, August 1958.

Pask, G. Conversational techniques in the study and practice of education. *British Journal of Educational Psychology,* 1976, *46,* 12–25.

———, and Scott, B. C. E. CASTE: a system for exhibiting learning strategies and regulating uncertainties. *International Journal of Man-Machine Studies,* 1973, *5.*

Patton, J. A. A study of the effects of student acceptance of responsibility and motivation on course behavior. Ph.D. diss., University of Michigan, 1955.

Paul, J. B. The length of class periods. *Educational Research,* 1932, *13,* 58–75.

Paul, J., and Ogilvie, J. C. Mass media and retention. *Explorations,* 1955, *4,* 120–123.

Peper, R. J., and Mayer, R. E. Note taking as a generative activity. *Journal of Educational Psychology,* 1978, *70*(4), 514–522.

Perkins, H. V. The effects of climate and curriculum on group learning. *Journal of Educational Research,* 1950, *44,* 269–286.

Perry, R. P.; Abrami, P. C.; and Leventhal, L. Educational seduction: The effect of instructor expressiveness and lecture content on student ratings and achievement. *Journal of Educational Psychology,* 1979, *71*(1), 107–116.

Perry, W. G., Jr. Cognitive and ethical growth: The making of meaning. In A. W. Chickering, ed. *The modern American college,* pp. 76–116. San Francisco: Jossey-Bass, 1981.

Peterson, P. L. Interactive effects of student anxiety, achievement orientation, and teacher behavior on student achievement and attitude. Ph.D. diss., Stanford University, 1976.

Powers, S. M. Teaching the basic research paper: Use of a portfolio method. Paper presented at the 91st Annual Convention of the American Psychological Association, Anaheim, CA, August 1983.

Postlethwait, S. N.; Novak, J.; and Murray, H. T., Jr. *The audio-tutorial approach to learning: through independent study and integrated experiences,* 2nd ed. Minneapolis: Burgess, 1969.

Potter, S. *One-upmanship.* New York: Henry Holt, 1955.

Pressey, S. L. A simple apparatus which gives tests and scores—and teaches. *School and Society,* 1926, *23,* 373–376.

Rasmussen, G. R. Evaluation of a student-centered and instructor-centered method of conducting a graduate course in education. *Journal of Educational Psychology,* 1956, *47,* 449–461.

Reder, L. M., and Anderson, J. R. Effects of spacing and embellishment on memory for the main points of a text. *Memory and Cognition,* 1982, *10*(2), 97–102.

Remmers, H. H. Learning, effort, and attitudes as affected by three methods of instruction in elementary psychology. *Purdue University Studies in Higher Education,* 1933, *21.*

Romig, J. L. An evaluation of instruction by student-led discussion in the college classroom. *Dissertation Abstracts International,* 1972, *32,* 6816.

Rosen, E. F.; Frincke, G. L.; and Stolurow, L. M. Principles of programming: II, Champaign community unit school district number 4 high schools, *Comparative studies of principles for programming mathematics in automated instruction,* Technical Report No. 15. University of Illinois, September, 1964.

Ross, I. C. Role specialization in supervision. Ph.D. diss., Columbia University. *Dissertation Abstracts,* 1957, *17,* 2701–2702.

Rothkopf, E. Z. Variable adjunct question schedules, interpersonal interaction, and incidental learning from written material. *Journal of Educational Psychology,* 1972, *63,* 87–92.

Roueche, S. D., ed. *Camelot: An individualized information system. Innovation Abstracts,* VI(14), 1984.

———, ed. *The film as an educational device. Innovation Abstracts,* 1984, VI(26).

Royer, P. N. Effects of specificity and position of written instructional objectives on learning from a lecture. *Journal of Educational Psychology,* 1977, *69,* 40–45.

Ruja, H. Outcomes of lecture and discussion procedures in three college courses. *Journal of Experimental Education,* 1954, *22,* 385–394.

Scheidemann, N. V. An experiment in teaching psychology. *Journal of Applied Psychology,* 1929, *13,* 188–191.

Schirmerhorn, S.; Goldschmid, M. L.; and Shore, B. S. Learning basic principles of probability in student dyads: a cross-age comparison. *Journal of Educational Psychology,* 1975, *67*(4), 551–557.

Schramm, W. L. *The research on programmed instruction.* Washington, D.C.: U.S. Government Printing Office, 1964.

Seashore, C. E. Elementary psychology: an outline of a course by the project method. *Aims and Progress Research,* No. 153. Iowa City: University of Iowa Studies, 1928.

Seashore, S. E. *Group cohesiveness in the industrial group.* University of Michigan Survey Research Center, Publication No. 14, 1954.

Shaycroft, M. F. *Handbook of criterion-referenced testing.* New York: Garland. STPM Press, 1979.

Sherman, B. R., and Blackburn, R. T. Personal characteristics and teaching effectiveness of college faculty. *Journal of Educational Psychology,* 1975, *67,* 124–131.

Shulman, L. S., and Tamir, P. Research on teaching in the natural sciences. In R. N. W. Travers, ed. *Second Handbook of Research on Teaching,* pp. 1098–1148. Chicago: Rand McNally, 1973.

Siegel, L.; Adams, J. F.; and Macomber, F. G. Retention of subject matter as a function of large-group instructional procedures. *Journal of Educational Psychology,* 1960, *51,* 9–13.

Siegel, L., and Siegel, L. C. The instructional gestalt: a conceptual framework and design for educational research. *Audio-Visual Communication Review,* 1964, *12,* 16–45.

Simpson, B. Heading for the ha-ha. *British Journal of Educational Technology,* 1983, *14,* 19–26.

Slomowitz, M. A comparison of personality changes and content achievement gains occurring in two modes of instruction. Ph.D. diss., N.Y. University. *Dissertation Abstracts,* 1955, *15,* 1790.

Smith, D. E. P. Application transfer and inhibition. *Journal of Educational Psychology,* 1954, *45,* 169–174.

————— et al. Reading improvement as a function of student personality and teaching methods. *Journal of Educational Psychology,* 1956, *47,* 47–58.

Smith, H. C. Team work in the college class. *Journal of Educational Psychology,* 1955, *46,* 274–286.

Smith, N. H. The teaching of elementary statistics by the conventional classroom method vs. the method of programmed instruction. *Journal of Educational Research,* 1962, *55,* 417–420.

Smith, W. F., and Rockett, F. C. Test performance as a function of anxiety, instructor and instructions. *Journal of Educational Research,* 1958, *52,* 138–141.

Snow, R. E. *Research on aptitudes: a progress report.* Technical Report No. 1, Aptitude Research Project, School of Education, Stanford University, September 1976.

—————, and Peterson, P. L. Recognizing differences in student attitudes. In W. J. McKeachie, ed., *Learning, cognition, and college teaching.* New Directions for Teaching and Learning, 2. San Francisco: Jossey-Bass, 1980.

Solomon, D.; Rosenberg, L.; and Bezdek, W. E. Teacher behavior and student learning. *Journal of Educational Psychology,* 1964, *55,* 23–30.

Spence, R. B. Lecture and class discussion in teaching educational psychology. *Journal of Educational Psychology,* 1928, *19,* 454–462.

Stasheff, E., et al. *The television program: Its direction and production,* 5th ed. New York: Hill and Wang, 1976.

Stinard, T. A., and Dolphin, W. D. Which students benefit from self-mastery instruction and why. *Journal of Educational Psychology,* 1981, 73(5), 754–763.

Stolurow, L. M., et al. Pilot studies of principles of programming, *Comparative studies of principles for programming mathematics in automated instruction,* Technical Report No. 9 (University of Illinois, July 1964).

Stuit, D. B., and Wilson, J. T. The effect of an increasingly well-defined criterion on the prediction of success at Naval Training School (Tactical Radar). *Journal of Applied Psychology,* 1946, *30,* 614–623.

Sturgis, H. W. The relationship of the teacher's knowledge of the student's background to the effectiveness of teaching: a study of the extent to which the effectiveness of teaching is related to the teacher's knowledge of the student's background. Ph.D. diss., New York University. *Dissertation Abstracts,* 1959, *19,* No. 11.

Sullivan, A. M.; Andrews, E. A.; Hollinghurst, F.; Maddigan, R.; and Noseworthy, C. M. The relative effectiveness of instructional television. *Interchange,* 1976, 7(1), 46–51.

Sullivan, A. M., and Skanes, G. R. Validity of student evaluation of teaching and the characteristics of successful instructors. *Journal of Educational Psychology,* 1974, *66,* 584–590.

Svensson, L. *Study skill and learning.* Göteborg, Sweden: Acta Universitates Gothoburgensis, 1976.

Thistlethwaite, D. L. College environments and the development of talent. *Science,* 1959, *130,* 71–76.

————. *College press and changes in study plans of talented students.* Evanston, IL: National Merit Scholarship Corporation, 1960.

Thomas, E. J., and Fink, C. F. The effects of group size. *Psychological Bulletin,* 1963, *60,* 371–385.

Travers, R. M. W. Appraisal of the teaching of the college faculty. *Journal of Higher Education,* 1950, *21,* 41–42.

————. *How to make achievement tests:* New York: Odyssey Press, 1950.

Trotter, V. Y. A comparison of the laboratory and the lecture demonstration methods of teaching survey of food preparation for freshman home economics at the University of Vermont. Unpublished paper, Ohio State University, 1960.

Trowbridge, N. An approach to teaching a large undergraduate class. Manuscript, Drake University, Des Moines, IA, 1969.

Vandermeer, A. W. *Relative effectiveness of instruction by films exclusively, films plus study guides, and standard lecture methods.* Instructional Film Research Report SDC 269-7-12, Special Devices Center, Office of Naval Research, July 1950.

Vattano, E. J.; Hockenberry, C.; Grider, W.; Jacobson, L.; and Hamilton, S. Employing undergraduate students in the teaching of psychology. *Teaching of Psychology Newsletter,* March 1973, 9–12.

Wakely, J. H.; Marr, J. N.; Plath, D. W.; and Wilkins, D. M. Lecturing and test performance in introductory psychology. Paper read at Michigan Academy, Ann Arbor, Michigan, March 1960.

Wales, C. E., and Nardi, A. *Teaching decisionmaking with guided design.* Idea paper no. 9. Kansas State University, Center for Faculty Evaluation and Development, November 1982.

Wales, C. E., and Stager, R. A. *Guided design.* Morgantown, WV: Center for Guided Design, West Virginia University, 1977.

Walter, T., and Seibert, A. *Student success,* 3rd ed. New York: Holt, Rinehart & Winston, 1984.

Ward, J. Group-study vs. lecture-demonstration method in physical science instruction for general education college students. *Journal of Experimental Education,* 1956, *24,* 197–210.

Warren, R. A comparison of two plans of study in engineering physics. Ph.D. diss., Purdue University. *Dissertation Abstracts,* 1954, *14,* 1648–1649.

Waterhouse, I. L., and Child, I. L. Frustration and the quality of performance. *Journal of Personality,* 1953, *21,* 298–311.

Watson, C. E. The case-study method and learning effectiveness. *College Student Journal,* 1975, *9*(2), 109–116.

Webb, N. J. Student preparation and tape recording of course lectures as a method of instruction. *Psychological Reports,* 1965, *16,* 67–72.

————, and Grib, T. F. *Teaching process as a learning experience: the experimental use of student-led groups.* Final Report, HE-000-882. Washington, D.C.: Department of Health, Education and Welfare, October 1967.

Weiland, A., and Kingsbury, S. J. Immediate and delayed recall of lecture material as a function of note taking. *Journal of Educational Research,* 1979, 72(4), 228–230.

White, J. R. A comparison of the group-laboratory and the lecture-demonstration methods in engineering instruction. *Journal of Engineering Education,* 1945, 36, 50–54.

Wieder, G. S. Group procedures modifying attitudes of prejudice in the college classroom. *Journal of Educational Psychology,* 1954, 45, 332–334.

Wilhite, S. C. Prepassage questions: The influence of structural importance. *Journal of Educational Psychology,* 1983, 75(2), 234–244.

Wilson, R. C.; Gaff, J. G.; Diensky, E. R.; Wood, L.; and Bavry, J. L. *College professors and their impact on students.* New York: Wiley, 1975.

Wine, J. Test anxiety and direction of attention. *Psychological Bulletin,* 1971, 76(2), 92–104.

Wispe, L. G. Evaluative section teaching methods in the introductory course. *Journal of Educational Research,* 1951, 45, 161–168.

Witters, D. R., and Kent, G. W. Teaching without lecturing: evidence in the case for individualized instruction. *Psychological Record,* 1972, 22, 169–175.

Wittich, W. A., and Schuller, C. F. *Instructional technology: Its nature and use,* 6th ed. New York: Harper & Row, 1979.

Wolfle, D. The relative efficacy of constant and varied stimulation during learning. *Journal of Comparative Psychology,* 1935, 19, 5–27.

Wood, L. E. An "intelligent" program to teach logical thinking skills. *Behavior research methods and instrumentation,* 1980, 12(2), 256–258.

Wortman, C. B., and Hillis, J. W. Undergraduate-taught "minicourses" in conjunction with an introductory lecture course. *Teaching of Psychology,* 1976, 3(2), 69–72.

Wrigley, C. Undergraduate students as teachers: apprenticeship in the university classroom. *Teaching of Psychology Newsletter,* March 1973, 5–7.

Zeleny, L. D. Experimental appraisal of a group learning plan. *Journal of Educational Research,* 1940, *34,* 37–42.

Zimbardo, P. G., and Newton, J. W. *Instructor's Resource Book to Accompany Psychology and Life* (Glenview, IL: Scott, Foresman, 1975).

3, 1, 2 4, app A, 4, 5
Chapters for
test

Index